Ancestry and Descendants

OF

SIR RICHARD SALTONSTALL

FIRST ASSOCIATE OF THE
MASSACHUSETTS BAY COLONY AND
PATENTEE OF CONNECTICUT

Printed at The Riverside Press
FOR PRIVATE DISTRIBUTION
M DCCC XCVII

Notice

In many older books, foxing (or discoloration) occurs and, in some instances, print lightens with wear and age. Reprinted books, such as this, often duplicate these flaws, notwithstanding efforts to reduce or eliminate them. The pages of this reprint have been digitally enhanced and, where possible, the flaws eliminated in order to provide clarity of content and a pleasant reading experience.

Ancestry and Descendants of Sir Richard Saltonstall: First Associate of the Massachusetts Bay Colony and Patentee of Connecticut

Author: Leverett Saltonstall

Copyright © 1897, by Richard M. Saltonstall

Originally published:
Cambridge, Massachusetts
1897

Reprinted by

Janaway Publishing, Inc.
732 Kelsey Ct.
Santa Maria, California 93454
(805) 925-1038
www.janawaygenealogy.com

2016

ISBN: 978-1-59641-300-9

Made in the United States of America

PREFACE

THE pedigree of the family of Saltonstall in England and America has long been known in a general way to genealogists, but its history in a connected form has never been fully presented.

The deep interest which I feel in the preservation of its record, and the care I have taken to obtain information, induced me to attempt the compilation of the work herewith presented. Long-continued illness has prevented more exhaustive research, but I trust that what is here shown will prove satisfactory and instructive to those who value descent from so long a line of worthy ancestors.

For information concerning the earlier generations of the family of Saltonstall I have taken the accounts given in the following works: "History and Antiquities of the Parish of Halifax in Yorkshire," by Rev. John Watson, 1775; Whitaker's Thoresby's "History of Leeds;" Morant's "History of Essex;" Lipscomb's "History of Buckinghamshire;" Baker's "History of Northamptonshire;" Clutterbuck's "History of Hertfordshire;" Heralds' Visitations of Yorkshire, 1612, of Hertfordshire, of Essex, and of Suffolk; Harleian and Lansdowne MSS.; Ayscough's MSS.; Hopkinson's MSS.; Davy's MSS. of Suffolk pedigrees; and investigations made for me in 1853 by H. G. Somerby in the Prerogative Courts of York and Canterbury, and in the Parish Records of Halifax, York, and many other places.

The history of the New England families has been drawn from colonial records, private manuscripts, local histories, Massachusetts Historical Society's Collections, New England

Historic Genealogical Society's Collections, Bond's "Genealogies and History of Watertown," and other sources.

The book consists of two parts: Part I. records the Genealogy; Part II. brings down the descent through female lines,
and contains, in addition to several ancestral pedigrees,
memoirs and matters of interest, with which I did not wish
to incumber the Genealogy.

The following order has been pursued in the Genealogy:
The English family has been traced direct from Thomas de
Saltonstall (No. 1) to Frederick, 2d Earl of Guilford and 8th
Baron North (83), and to Lucy his sister (84). It includes
Sir Richard Saltonstall (13) of Huntwicke (of New England,
1630), and Richard his son (39), whose children (85–89) are
then taken up, and the Massachusetts line is given the numbers from 85 to 148. The Connecticut branch of the family
follows, and is numbered from 149 (Governor Gurdon Saltonstall) to 217. This was found to be a far better and
clearer mode of classification than to number the generations
of the three families together.

The arrangement of the numbers is very simple: each
member of the family is numbered successively, the first time
the number appears being against the name, as one of his
father's children, as, for example, Richard Saltonstall (39), one
of the children of Sir Richard (13), bears the number 39 in
the list of Sir Richard's children as given under the number
13; while the numbers against Richard, when his name is
reached in the Genealogy, are 39, 13, Richard (39) son of Sir
Richard (13).

The roman numerals show the number of their generation from Gilbert Saltonstall (9) of the Rookes, grandfather of
Sir Richard.

For though I might with perfect propriety have begun with
Richard (4), five generations earlier, or even with Thomas
(1), seven generations earlier, yet I preferred beginning the
generations with Gilbert (9), whose will, as well as that of his
son Samuel (10), father of Sir Richard (13), are found in Part
II., it not being absolutely certain that the Gilbert of Shelf,

Halifax, who died in 1518, and whose curious will is copied in Part II. 6, was Gilbert (6), ancestor of Gilbert (9) of Rookes.

Should those interested in the subject discover errors or omissions, I hope that they may be excused by reason of my illness during almost the entire period of my labors.

I desire to acknowledge my indebtedness to F. G. Saltonstall, Esq., of New York, descendant of Governor Gurdon Saltonstall of Connecticut, for his constant and zealous co-operation, the extension of the descendants of Governor Gurdon Saltonstall, known as the Connecticut branch of the family, being done by him ; also to my cousin, the late Henry Saltonstall, for his kind encouragement and generous assistance in carrying out this work.

In conclusion, I take pleasure in presenting the book to the descendants of that excellent man our ancestor, Sir Richard Saltonstall.

LEVERETT SALTONSTALL.

Chestnut Hill, March, 1895.

Note. — The Author of this work, Hon. Leverett Saltonstall, died at Chestnut Hill, Massachusetts, on April 15, 1895, within a few days after the completion of his labors upon the manuscript. It had been his earnest desire personally to superintend the publishing of the book, for which he left careful instructions in writing, in case the work should be done by others than himself. I have endeavored in every respect to carry out these instructions.

Richard M. Saltonstall.

CONTENTS

PART I

PART II

CONTENTS

LIST OF ILLUSTRATIONS

THE FAMILY OF SALTONSTALL

PART I

GENEALOGY

THE ancestors of SIR RICHARD SALTONSTALL resided for centuries in the parish or vicarage of Halifax, in the West Riding of Yorkshire, England. (Part II. p. 47.) The name is derived from Saltonstall, a village or hamlet in the township of Warley, in that parish.

The earliest date at which we find this name recorded is in " Rotuli Hundredorum," 4th Edward I., or 1276; but the following extract from Allen's " History of Yorkshire " goes to prove that the place is far more ancient: " In the ninth year of Edward 1st (1281) John de Warren, Earl of Surry, was summoned to answer by what warrant he appropriated to himself as a forest the Divisions of Halifax, Overdon, Saltonstall, Heptenstall and others; to which the Earl answered that he claimed no forest in said lands, but that ' he and his Ancestors had free chase in said lands from time immemorial,' and he produced a charter from Henry 3rd dated 37th year of his reign (1253), of free warren in all his Demesne lands which he then had or should acquire." The hamlet was divided into Nether and Over Saltonstall.

" The first grants made by copy of Court Roll of Saltonstall, which was in the latter end of Edward II., were made upon division of the whole into six equal parts, and every part was called a Sextondole of Saltonstall."

" In 17th Edward III. (1343) John de Brownhirste surrendered in Court two parts of a sixth part of Saltonstall, with

Nether Saltonstall.

the reversion of a third part of said sixth part, which Isabel, mother of said John, held as the dower, the moiety of which was granted to John, son of Thomas de Saltonstall, another moiety to Richard, son of Thomas de Saltonstall, and William de Saltonstall and his heirs." "At Halifax in 1376 John Cape surrendered a sixth part of Saltonstall to the use of Richard Saltonstall and heirs."[1]

After this, as will be seen, the lands of Saltonstall were held by the family for eight generations, till they were inherited by Samuel, the father of Sir Richard Saltonstall of New England. The old manor house has been neglected, and only its picturesque remains can be seen at the present day. The place is described as being most attractive in the character of its scenery, and evidently was more valued for the wealth of its forests and the various kinds of game which frequented them than for purposes of husbandry. Though in the neighborhood of one of the busiest manufacturing districts in England, — the fine stream flowing through it supplying Halifax with water and furnishing power to the mills along its banks, — yet it is a wild and picturesque region. As one writer says, "quite like the Highlands of Scotland." Tradition says that very many years ago all its inhabitants were swept away by the plague, and that since that sad event but few people have lived there, chiefly small farmers and workers in the mills near by.

Another says Saltonstall is familiar to him from childhood. "There is a great moor of that name well known to sportsmen." A friend writes, "A few years ago I visited Saltonstall, England, with my family. It was six miles from Halifax, a beautiful place, but too hilly for pleasant travel. The family mansion was gone, but the church, modernized, is in excellent order. The graveyard and monuments have been much neglected."

[1] Watson's *History and Antiquities of the Parish of Halifax in Yorkshire,* 1775.

1. THOMAS DE SALTONSTALL of the West Riding of Yorkshire. This is the first of the name of whom any record is preserved.[1]

2. and 3. 1. JOHN SALTONSTALL and RICHARD SALTONSTALL, sons of Thomas de Saltonstall, with William de Saltonstall, were granted moieties of two parts of a sixth part of Saltonstall (17 Edward III., 1343), with reversion of dower held by Isabel, mother of John de Brownhirste.[2]

4. 3. RICHARD SALTONSTALL at Halifax in 1376 received from John Cape a sixth part or sextondole of Saltonstall. 6 Henry IV. (1404), Richard Saltonstall surrendered two sixth parts of Saltonstall, and half a sixth part, lying between Blakebrook, Depeclough, the water of Liddingden, and Hoore Stones, in Sowerby, to the use of Richard Saltonstall and heirs.

5. 4. RICHARD SALTONSTALL. This Richard, 15 Edward IV. (1475), surrendered the same lands to his son Gilbert.

6. 5. GILBERT SALTONSTALL, who in the 23d year of Henry VII. (1507) surrendered the same lands to Richard his son. Gilbert Saltonstall of Shelf, Halifax, died in 1518, leaving a brother Edward, and sons Richard, Edward, and William. Will dated 28 March, 1517; proved 28 April, 1518. (Part II. 6.)

7. 6. RICHARD SALTONSTALL, son of Gilbert (6), held the same lands till his death, when they passed to his son.

8. 7. RICHARD SALTONSTALL, son and heir of Richard (7), made fine of heriot, 30 Henry VIII. (1538), for the said lands. He had issue Gilbert, from whom the same estate descended to his son Samuel.

9. 8. (I.) GILBERT SALTONSTALL of Halifax had a seat at Rookes Hall in Hipperholme, which he purchased of an ancient family of that name, in the 8th year of Elizabeth (1565), with other lands. He m. Isabel ——, named in the will of her husband; died in 1598 and was buried at Halifax 29 Dec. Will dated at Rookes 23 Nov., 1598.

[1] Watson's *History*.   [2] *Ibid.*

He gave to the poor at Hipperholme and Halifax a stipend
at Christmas for ten years from his house at the Rookes.
He also gave for repairs of the church at Halifax; to the
chapel at Hipperholme; to the Halifax Grammar School in
money and rent. (Part II. 9.)

A Gilbert Saltonstall subscribed £25 towards repelling
the Spanish invasion in 1588.[1]

Children: —

    10. Samuel.
    11. Mary.
    12. Richard.

" The Saltonstalls had been seated at an estate called
Rookes in Hipperholme adjoining North Ouram since the
year 1565, when it was purchased by Gilbert Saltonstall of
Halifax. His son, Samuel of Rookes, was the father of Sir
Richard, who with Governor Winthrop and others got up the
well-known expedition to New England in 1630. The inhabitants of North Ouram, Shelf, and Hipperholme were under
the ministry of Coley Chapel, which was built by their joint
contributions about the year 1500." [2]

10. 9. (II.) SAMUEL SALTONSTALL, son and heir of Gilbert
(9), owned Rookes and Huntwicke. In the 40th Elizabeth
(1597), he made fine of heriot for the ancient lands in Saltonstall. In 1599 Winter-Edge Hall at Hipperholme was
held of the Crown in fee by him, also Rogerthorpe in Badsworth. He d. 8 Jan., 16$\frac{12}{13}$, buried in Holy Trinity Church
in Hull. Will dated 31 Dec., 1612, proved 22 July, 1613,
wherein he calls himself of Kingston-upon-Hull. (Part
II. 10.) Watson in his " History of Halifax" calls him " Sir
Samuel," and thinks he was knighted. He was three times
married. His first wife was Anne, dau. of John Ramsden of
Longley, Esquire (grandfather of Sir John Ramsden).

" Ramsden of Longley near Hothersfield, in the Wapentake of Agbrigg and Morley, bears, Argent, on a chevron,

[1] Watson's *History*, and Thoresby's *History of Leeds* (Whitaker, 1816).
[2] *Hist. and Gen. Register*, vol. xvii. p. 110.

sable, three rams' heads couped, of the first, between as many fleurs-de-lis of the second.

" Robert Ramsden of Longley near Hothersfield married and had issue John; Ellen, married to Mr. Henry Saville. John married and had issue William ; John of Lassell Hall; Elizabeth, married to Edward Beaumont of Whitley Hall, Esquire; Anne, to Mr. Samuel Saltonstall" (father of Sir Richard Saltonstall of New England).[1] His second wife was Elizabeth, dau. of Mr. Thomas Ogden. His third wife was Elizabeth Armine, widow of Hugh Armine, Mayor of Hull, who d. 1606.

Children by first wife, Anne : —

13. Richard.
14. Gilbert.

Children by second wife, Elizabeth : —

15. Samuel.
16. John.
17. Thomas.
18. Anne.
19. Elizabeth.
20. George.
21. Mary.
22. Margaret.
23. Barbara.

All the above children are mentioned in his will.[2]

11. 9. (II.) MARY SALTONSTALL, dau. of Gilbert Saltonstall (9), m. Francis Saville, son of Henry Saville of Lupsett, Esquire, High Sheriff of Yorkshire 1567, 2d brother of Sir George Saville of Thornhill, Knight and Baronet. The pedigree of Francis Saville, her husband, for thirteen generations back to Sir John Saville of Saville Hall, Barnsley, is found in the Visitation of Yorkshire, 1612, and Harleian MSS. 4630.

---

[1] Pedigrees of Yorkshire families, Harleian MSS. 4630. Visitation of Yorkshire, 1612. A long letter of Samuel Saltonstall is in Ayscough's MSS. vol. iii. No. 4111, fol. 29.
[2] See Part II. 10, for extracts from this will.

12. 9. (II.) Sir Richard Saltonstall, b. 1521 ; knighted by Queen Elizabeth 1598 ; member of Merchant Adventurers and Furriers' Hall ; Sheriff of London 1588 ; Lord Mayor 1597–8 ; Member of Parliament for City of London. He was lord of the Manor of Moorhall in Yardley and Barkway, Co. Northampton, and of a moiety of Groves in South Okenden, Co. Herts, and of Chipping Warden, Co. Essex ; d. 17 March, 160$\frac{9}{1}$, buried in South Okenden church 7 April following, with epitaph.[1] By will, dated 1597, he left £100 to be distributed in money or bread annually to the poor of Halifax. From him were descended the Saltonstalls of London and Co. Herts. (Part II. 12.) The signature of the Lord Mayor is in the Lansdowne MSS. No. 145, p. 25, Library of the British Museum.

The Arms of Sir Richard are shown on the title-page of this book, a sketch in colors and description of them having been furnished the author by the Heralds' College, London. Arms: Or, a bend between two eaglets displayed sable. Crest, on a wreath, an eaglet's head and neck couped azure, issuing out of a ducal coronet or. The Records of the Heralds' College contain an elaborate entry as to the pedigree and funeral of Sir Richard Saltonstall, with paintings of his official standard, shield, sword, helmet and crest, surcoat and quarterings blazoned in colors, which are also here reproduced.

Sir Richard m. Susanna, dau. of Thomas Poyntz of North Okenden, Esquire, and sister of Sir Gabriel Poyntz, — a very ancient family recorded in Visitation of Essex, often knighted. She was wife of Sir Richard fifty years, and she had five sons and ten daughters.[2] Her will, dated 16 Nov., 1612, proved 23 Feb., 16$\frac{12}{13}$, contains legacies to poor of Barkway in Co. Herts, and St. Dunstan in the East, London. Sundry MS. letters of hers and her children relating to the settlement of Sir Richard's estate are preserved in the Lansdowne Col-

---

[1] For account of Manor of Groves, South Okenden, see Morant's *History of Essex.*

[2] For pedigree of the Poyntz family, see Part II. 12.

Points

The Righte worshipfull Sr Richard Saltonstall, Knighte, maior of London Anno 1597 Departed this life the XVIIth of marche at his howse in Essex the yeare of Our Lord 1600 he maried Susanna the daughter of Thomas Pointz, gent : by whom he had yssue fower sonnes & nine daughters, vidzt Richard Salton- stall, esquier, eldest son & heyre married Iane daughter to ffrancis Bernard in ye Countie of Northampton, gent : & by her hathe yssue Richard & Bernard, Iohn & Sussanna — Samuel Saltonstall 2^d sonne vnmarried, Peter Saltonstall, gent : 3^d son maried Anne daughter to Thomas Waller in the Countie of Buckingham, gent : Edward Saltonstall 4th son vnmarried, Anne eldiste daughter wyfe to Iohn Harby of London, gent : by whom she hathe yssue Richard, Susanna 2^d daughter wyffe to Wm Browne, gent : by whom she hathe yssue Thomas, Samuel & Sara, Hester 3^d daughter Wyffe to Thomas Midelton of London, gent, by whom she hath yssue Richard & Thomas, Elizabeth 4th daũr wyfe to Richard Wiche of London, gent by whome she hathe yssue, Richard Thomas, George, Samuel, Peter, Ieames, Edward, Susanna, Elizabeth & Anne — Sara fiveth daughter Wyffe to Thomas wheler of London, gent:, Marie sixte daughter wyfe to Richard Sunderland of Yorkshire gent, by whome she hathe yssue, Abraham, Robert, Samuel, Sussanna & Marie — Iudithe seaventh daughter wyfe to Edward Riche of Hovenden in the Countie of Essex, esquier by whome she hathe yssue Edward & Richard — Martha eyghte daughter a maide — Abigaell ninthe daughter maried Henry Baker of Bowers-gyfford in the Countie of Essex, esquier by whom she had yssue Richard & Susanna but they are dead, his funeralle weare right worshipfully solemnized accordinge to his Degree at Southockenden in Essex vppon tewsday the seaventh of April 1601. The Standarte borne by Richard Wiche. The penon of his Armes by Iohn Harby the penon of London by Thomas Mydelton. The penon of the Skyners by Tho: Wheler, the penon of the marchant venturers by Henry Baker, the penon of the Company of Muscovia by William Browne. Mr Deiwood the Preacher the principall morner Mr Richard Saltonstall the Assistantes his brether- erin Mr Samuel Saltonstall, Mr Peter Saltonstall, Mr Edward Saltonstall, Mr Gabriell Poyntz — William Camden Clarentiulx Kinge of Armes & Ieames Thomas a^ts Chester Attendinge at the saide funerall.

Subcribed by { Sufanna Saltonstall, wydow
             { S^d Saltonftall

I hereby certify the above written certificate and the Arms depicted in the margin thereof to be faithfully extracted from the official records of the College of Arms, London and examined therewith by me this Twenty seventh day of August 1896.   G. Ambrose Lee
Bluemantle

Pursuivant of Arms.

lection in the British Museum. Part of the ancient manor
house, the residence of the Saltonstall family, was remaining
in 1855, on the south side of the churchyard.
Children : —

24. Gilbert.
25. Richard.
26. Eleanor.
27. Peter.
28. Edward.
29. Samuel.
30. Anne.
31. Susanna.
32. Hester.
33. Elizabeth.
34. Sarah.
35. Mary.
36. Judith.
37. Abigail.
38. Martha.

13. 10. (III.) SIR RICHARD SALTONSTALL of Huntwicke,
b. 1586, bap. at Halifax 4 April, 1586, son of Samuel (10)
of Rookes and Huntwicke, by his first wife, Anne, dau. of
John Ramsden; lord of the Manor of Ledsham, near Leeds,
which he purchased of the Harebreds, and afterwards sold to
the Earl of Strafford; Justice of the Peace, and Treasurer
for Lame Soldiers, 1st year of Charles I. (1605). After the
death of his first wife he sold his lands and removed with his
children to New England. First Associate, Massachusetts
Bay Company; and was appointed First Assistant. He commenced the settlement of Watertown 1630; returned to England 1631. He was an original patentee of Connecticut
with Lord Say and Seal, Lord Brook, and others, and ever
maintained a strong interest in the New England colonies.
He died about 1658, and left a legacy to Harvard College,
his will bearing that date.
He married 1st, Grace, dau. of Robert Kaye, of Wood-

some, Esquire, and aunt to Sir John Kaye,—a very ancient
family of Yorkshire.[1]　(Part II. 13.)

　　Children by first wife, Grace : —

　　　39. Richard.

　　　40. { Rosamond.
　　　　　 { Grace.

　　　41. Robert.
　　　42. Samuel.
　　　43. Henry.
　　　44. Peter?

Sir Richard m. 2d, Elizabeth, dau. of Sir Thomas West
(Lord Delaware 1602); m. 3d, Martha Wilfred.　No children
by second and third marriages.

　　14. 10. (III.)　Gilbert Saltonstall, son of Samuel (10),
d. young.　Not living at time of father's death, 1612.

　　15. 10. (III.)　Samuel Saltonstall of Rogerthorpe, first
son of Samuel (10) by second wife, Elizabeth Ogden, m.
Barbara, dau. of Walter Rudston of Hayton, Esquire.　" The
head of a very ancient house." [2]

　　Children : —

　　　45. Samuel.

　　　46. { Walter.
　　　　　 { Thomas.
　　　　　 { Richard.

　　　47. Frances.

　　16. 10. (III.)　John Saltonstall, second son of Samuel
(10) by second wife, Elizabeth Ogden, in his minority in 1612,
by will of father had an annuity of £80.

　　17. 10. (III.)　Thomas Saltonstall, son of Samuel (10)

---

[1] See Thoresby's *History of Leeds* (Whitaker, 1816), for fuller account of Sir
Richard and pedigree of Kaye.

　For account of Saltonstall of Huntwicke in the wapentake of Osgolderosse, see
pedigrees of Yorkshire families, West Riding, Harleian MSS. No. 4630.

　Matthew Kaye of Eastcome in the Parish of East Greenwich, Kent, gentleman,
by his will dated 14 Nov., 1610, proved 5 Oct., 1612, gives " To my well beloved
brother Robert Kaye of Woodsome in the County of York, Esq. a gold ring of
three pounds price.　To my cousin, Grace Saltonstall, my said brother's daughter,
a like ring of goulde of like price."

[2] Visitation of Yorkshire, 1610, and Harleian MSS. No. 4630.

FAMILY OF SIR THOMAS WEST

FROM EDMONSON'S COLLECTIONS IN THE HERALDS' COLLEGE

Sir Thomas West, only son and heir, succeeded as Baron de la Warre 1595; and was restored to the place and precedence of his ancestors 1597; d. 1602.

Sir Thomas West = Cicely, dau. of Sir Thomas Shirley of Wissen in Sussex, Knt.

Walsingham West ob. s. p.

Nathan West m. Dorothy Grevile.

Robert West m. Elizabeth, dau. of Sir Henry Cook, Knt.

Lettice m. Henry Lud-low of Ted-ley, Co. Southamp-ton, Esq.

Penelope m. Herbert Pel-ham, the elder, of Michalen, Co. Sussex, Esq.

Katherine d. unmarried.

Helena m. Wm. Savage of Winchester, Esq.

Elizabeth m. Sir Richard Saltonstall.

Anne m. John Pellet.

Sir Thomas West, first son, succeeded as Baron de la Warre 1602; Capt. General of all the Colonies in Virginia 1609; d. 1618.

Anne, dau. of Sir Francis Knowles, Knight of the Garter.

by second wife, Elizabeth Ogden, had by his father's will, 1612, a quarter of Grainge Hall, called Hassle, in York, purchased of Sir Jarvis Clifton.

18. 10. (III.) ANNE SALTONSTALL, dau. of Samuel (10) by second wife, Elizabeth Ogden, living in 1612, had a legacy from her father of £400.

19. 10. (III.) ELIZABETH SALTONSTALL, dau. of Samuel (10) by second wife, Elizabeth Ogden, m. at Doncaster, 1623, Mr. Henry Bunny, younger son of Richard Bunny and nephew of Edward and Francis, both divines. Francis m. dau. of Henry Priestly, mentioned in her father's will.[1]

20. 10. (III.) GEORGE SALTONSTALL, son of Samuel (10), by his father's will, 1612, had his messuage in High Street, Kingston-upon-Hull.

21. 10. (III.) MARY SALTONSTALL, dau. of Samuel (10), d. in 1622, said to have married John Bateman. Her will, dated 18 March, 1622, proved 9 May, 1622, gives everything to her brother, Sir Richard Saltonstall (13), Knt.

22. 10. (III.) MARGARET SALTONSTALL, dau. of Samuel (10), m. Henry Gamble.

23. 10. (III.) BARBARA SALTONSTALL, dau. of Samuel (10), m. Christopher Rasby of an ancient family of Smeaton, Co. York.[2]

24. 12. (III.) GILBERT SALTONSTALL, son of Sir Richard (12), Lord Mayor of London 1597–8, m. Anne, dau. of Sir John Harleston; d. 17 Nov., 1585. Bur. in church at South Okenden with epitaph.[3] Held half of the Manor of Groves in South Okenden, Essex. No issue.

[1] Pedigree of Henry Bunny five generations from Richard Bunny, of Bunny Hall, near Wakefield, in Yorkshire. See Visitation of Yorkshire, 1612.
[2] See Harleian MSS. 4630, for pedigree of Christopher Rasby, ten generations to John Rasby of Rasby.
[3] Morant's *History of Essex*. In the *London Standard* of 10 Sep., 1889, a writer who had visited many old churches and churchyards, complaining of the removal of old brasses and other monuments from old churches as a sacrilegious robbery, wrote the following: "Gilbert Saltonstall (Co. Essex, South Okenden) A. D. 1585. Inscription and Shield of Arms formerly on the Sanctuary pavement, now removed." It would appear from this that there had been restorations (so called!) in the church at South Okenden, where, as stated above, he was buried in 1585 "with epitaph."

25. 12. (III.) SIR RICHARD SALTONSTALL, Knt., son of Sir Richard (12), lord of the Manor of Groves in Chipping Warden, Co. Northampton, and of South Okenden in Essex; knighted in 1619. He d. 11 Dec., 1619. Will dated 30 Nov., 1618. (Part II. 25.) First wife, Anne, dau. of Thomas Waller, son of Robert of Bucks. No issue. Second wife, Jane, dau. of Francis Bernard, Co. Northampton. Her will dated 21 May, 1619.

Children by second wife, Jane: —
    49. Richard.
    50. Bernard.
    51. John, prob. Sir John.
    52. Susanna.

26. 12. (III.) ELEANOR SALTONSTALL, daughter of Sir Richard (12), m. 1st, Robert Hervey of London; m. 2d, Robert Middleton of London, merchant.

27. 12. (III.) SIR PETER SALTONSTALL, son of Sir Richard (12), knighted by King James 1605; of Barkway, Co. Herts, owner of the Rectory of Barkway, etc. He was buried at Barkway 27 Sep., 1651. Will dated 12 July, 1651, proved 1659. His first wife was Anne Waller, dau. of Robert Waller and wife, Anne Hampden. She was the sister of Edmund Waller, the statesman and poet, and cousin to both John Hampden and Oliver Cromwell. She was buried 3 May, 1604.[1] No issue. His second wife was Christian, dau. of Sir John Pettus, Knt.,[2] of Rackheath, Norfolk, m. about 1607. She was his wife thirty-nine years; d. 21 June, 1646, aged 60; bur. at Barkway church with epitaph. (Part II. 27.)

Children by second wife, Christian: —
    53. James.
    54. Peter.
    55. John.
    56. Susannah.

[1] See Lipscomb's *History of Buckinghamshire* and Berry's *County Genealogies of Buckinghamshire* for the Waller pedigree.

[2] Sir John Pettus of Norwich, Knight, 10 Jan., 1613, in his will proved 13 May, 1614, made bequests to his grandchildren Susan (56), Bridget (57), and Christian (58) Saltonstall, children of Sir Peter Saltonstall (27), one hundred pounds each.

57. Bridget.
58. Christian.
59. Anne.
60. Elizabeth.

He appears to have had a third wife, Mary (perhaps Parker), who survived him. Her will was proved 21 May, 1662.

28. 12. (III.) EDWARD SALTONSTALL, son of Sir Richard (12); of Cockenhatch, Herts, Gent. Will dated 22 Dec., 1663; proved 23 March, 166¾; bur. in chancel of church at Barkway; vicar of the church his executor.

29. 12. (III.) SIR SAMUEL SALTONSTALL, Knt., son of Sir Richard (12), held a moiety of Groves, Co. Essex, with his brothers. His MS. letter, dated 21 May, 1593, and others are preserved in Ayscough's MSS. 3411. He m. Elizabeth, dau. and heir of William Wye. He d. 30 June, 1640. His son Wye wrote an elegy to his memory. He was named executor under the will of John Smith, who was concerned in the settlement of Virginia.[1] In the third charter of King James to the Treasurer and Company of Virginia his name appears. (Part II. 29.)

Children : —

61. Wye.
62. Samuel (no further record).
63. Henry (no further record).
64. Elizabeth.
65. Sarah (no further record).
66. Charles.

30. 12. (III.) ANNE SALTONSTALL, dau. of Sir Richard (12), m. Joseph Harbye of London, citizen merchant of Muscovy, Spain, and the Indies.

31. 12. (III.) SUSANNA SALTONSTALL, dau. of Sir Richard (12), m. William Brown, Gent., London.[2]

32. 12. (III.) HESTER SALTONSTALL, dau. of Sir Richard (12), m. Sir Thomas Middleton, Knt., Lord Mayor of London.

---

[1] See extract from the will of John Smith, Part II. 29.
[2] Thoresby (*History of Leeds*) says Susanna married Richard Sunderland, Esq.

33. 12. (III.) ELIZABETH SALTONSTALL, dau. of Sir Richard (12), m. Richard Wyche, Gent., of London.

34. 12. (III.) SARAH SALTONSTALL, dau. of Sir Richard (12), m. Thomas Wheeler or Whaler, Gent., of London.

35. 12. (III.) MARY SALTONSTALL, dau. of Sir Richard (12), m. Richard Sunderland of Colay Hall near Halifax, Esquire,[1] Treasurer Lame Soldiers 1619; Justice of the Peace 1620.

36. 12. (III.) JUDITH SALTONSTALL, dau. of Sir Richard (12), m. 1st, Edw. Riche of Heredon, Co. Essex, Esquire; m. 2d, Sir Arthur Forest of Co. Huntingdon.

37. 12. (III.) ABIGAIL SALTONSTALL, dau. of Sir Richard (12), m. Henry Baker, Esq., of Bowers Gifford, Co. Essex.

38. 12. (III.) MARTHA SALTONSTALL, dau. of Sir Richard (12), m. —— Bonner of Buckinghamshire.

39. 13. (IV.) RICHARD SALTONSTALL of Massachusetts, son of Sir Richard of Huntwicke, Knt. (13), was born at Woodsome, seat of the Kaye family, Yorkshire, 1610; matriculated as " Mr. Fellow Commoner" in Emmanuel College, Cambridge, 14 Dec., 1627.   He came with his father to New England in 1630, before taking a degree. Was admitted freeman 18 May, 1631. He returned to England in 1631, where he remained about four years and a half, and married there in June, 1633, Muriel Gurdon, daughter of Brampton Gurdon of Assington, Suffolk, Esquire,[2] and wife, Muriel Sedley. He embarked at London, 1635, in the Susan and Ellen, with his wife Muriel, aged 22, and daughter Muriel,

---

[1] Pedigree of Sunderland, Harleian MSS. 4830. Thoresby (*History of Leeds*) says Susanna (not Mary) married Richard Sunderland.

[2] Brampton Gurdon, Esq., of Assington, Co. Suffolk, was M. P. for Sudbury 1620; High Sheriff 1629. See Burke, and Suffolk Pedigrees, for his descent from Sir Adam Gurdon, time of Henry III. (1272).

"This ancient family was seated at Assington Hall. John Gurdon, Esq., was one on the Council of State in the time of the Long Parliament. Sir Adam Gurdon was an inhabitant of Selborne, and a man of the first rank and property in the parish. He was that leading and accomplished malcontent in the Montfort faction who distinguished himself by his daring conduct in the reign of Henry III." (See Part II. 39.)

I thanck you for yr letter, for yr expressing
of so many good purposes in wch since I graunt
those, about ye mayor of Sudbury on fryday
at ye hyre in grafton, he tolde me it yt &c.
I never tooke it very unkindly at his hand yt
he learned not to thob you although there
by yt he say it &c neuer made his mynd
so knowne to him, & yo waldgreve &c met
there to byyge burges, otherwise by prest
too manye keepeng an occasion g in suer
on speak in mighty to learne yt came it to ye
yworld. it amay be aught if it wear good if ye
parlamunt would reforme yt by arryge of
yor Burges, &c &c. neuer I heare is agayn
too to by to moror night at brentwood
I pray for &c then Corbet bosbn you com
away y you send me to hm I will writte
hm at mon lay sturi. w: but my sister ba
ron on thursday at morsten there had a very
yearfule missing I pray to god for all his
mercyes. & then sunder goe to moror
to york, g intend to stay there for y com
pany till thursday or fryday. if you have
any opportunyte I pray tarke order for ye
marifest. it was sayd on fryday morning
by a servant it was sayd on fryday morning
could not thin line on sermon but I came
send nothing since. g thus with my best lone
us a comfortable missing I pray god grom
meeting & so grost

oyster Apr 19 hour

yr very louing frend
Brampton under

aged 9 months,[1] and settled at Ipswich, Mass. He was a Deputy to the General Court in 1635-7, and an Assistant from 1637 to 1649, in 1664, and from 1680 to 1683. He visited England several times, the last time in 1683, and died at Hulme, Lancaster, the seat of his son-in-law, Sir Edward Moseley, 29 April, 1694.[2]

Children : —
85. Muriel.
86. Richard.
87. Nathaniel.
88. Abigail.
89. Elizabeth.

40. 13. (IV.) Rosamond Saltonstall and Grace Saltonstall, daughters of Sir Richard (13), came to New England with their father in 1630, and returned with him in 1631.[3] In 1642-4 Rosamond resided with Lord Warwick, and Grace with Lady Manchester; both are mentioned in their brother Robert's will in 1650. (Part ii. 41.)

While at Warwick House Rosamond wrote to her brother a very interesting letter, which is copied and heliotyped in Part ii. 40.

41. 13. (IV.) Robert Saltonstall, son of Sir Richard

---

[1] Savage, in his "Gleanings," *Mass. Hist. Coll.* 3d series, vol. viii. p. 258, gives a list of the passengers who embarked for New England in April, 1635, among whom are named, Richard Saltonstall aged 23 (on his return to New England); Meriall Saltonstall, aged 22; Meriall Saltonstall, aged 9 months. A mistake was made either in the original entry in the MS. volume or in copying Richard's age, as he was then 25.

[2] In an old letter from Muriel, wife of Richard Saltonstall (39), to her brother, Brampton Gurdon, dated "20, 17, 3½," sent the author by Sir William Brampton Gurdon, she refers to *her son Gurdon* thus, "that letter gave you the good tidings of my daughter Horsey's safe delivery of a son, and this acquaints you with the sad tidings of *my son Gurdon's* weakly condition. I have small hope of his recovery. This is the 9th day, Dr. Gurdon speaks as if there were some hope. He is in the hands of a merciful God, who I trust will deal well with him." The letter is signed, "Your reall loving sister, Muriall Saltonstall." Addressed, "To my Dear Brother, Brampton Gurdon." This shows conclusively that Richard (39) had another son, who has never been included in the pedigrees of the family in this country. An old pedigree sent the author by Sir William Brampton Gurdon records this son as dying without issue.

[3] Winthrop's *Journal*, i. 49; Prince's "Annals," *Mass. Hist. Coll.* 2d series, vol. vii.

(13), came to New England in 1630; resided at Watertown, was afterwards of Boston; member of Artillery Company 1638; unmarried; d. in summer of 1650. Will in Hist. and Gen. Reg. vii. 334. (Part II. 41.)

42. 13. (IV.) SAMUEL SALTONSTALL, son of Sir Richard (13), resided many years in Watertown; had sundry lots of land granted him there; d. 21 Jan., 1696, unm. (Part II. 42.)

43. 13. (IV.) HENRY SALTONSTALL, son of Sir Richard (13), member of Artillery Company 1639; had farm of 300 acres and 88 acres of meadow in Watertown; graduated in the first class Harv. Coll. (1642); returned to England; visited Holland with his father 1644, where the portrait of Sir Richard was painted by Rembrandt; at University of Padua, Italy, 1649, at Oxford 1652, and was a Fellow of New College in that University. He received the degree of M. D. (Part II. 43.)

44. 13. PETER SALTONSTALL, member of Artillery Company 1644, has been conjectured a son of Sir Richard (13), but it is nearly certain that he was not. (See Peter (54), son of Sir Peter.)

45. 15. (IV.) SAMUEL SALTONSTALL of Rogerthorpe, son of Samuel (15) by his second wife, Barbara, dau. and co-heir of Mr. John Flower of Methley, living in 1666. Her second husband, George Abbot of Preston Jackling near Pontefract. Her 3d husband, Robert Nunnes of Methley, living in 1666.

Child : —

48. Samuel.

46. 15. (IV.) WALTER, THOMAS, and RICHARD. These three sons of Samuel (15) died young.

47. 15. (IV.) FRANCES SALTONSTALL, daughter of Samuel (15), m. Mr. Ross, citizen of London.

48. 45. (V.) SAMUEL SALTONSTALL of Rogerthorpe, son of Samuel (45), m. 1st, Mary, dau. of Mr. John Shann of Methley; m. 2d, Mary, dau. of Richard Elmhurst. By first wife he had 3 sons and 1 dau. d. young; by second wife, Richard, William (of Leeds), Thomas, Elizabeth, Ann.

49. 25. (IV.) SIR RICHARD SALTONSTALL, Knt., b. 1596, succeeded his father, Sir Richard (25), in his estates. Will dated 16 Feb., 1649, proved 6 March, 16$\frac{49}{50}$. He m. Elizabeth Bas, the niece of Samuel Clarkson of London. (Part II. 49.)
Children : —
   67. Richard.
   68. Philip.
   69. Anne.

50. 25. (IV.) BERNARD SALTONSTALL, son of Sir Richard (25), mentioned in his father's will. By his will dated 20 Sep., 1630, proved March, 1632, he makes his brother John executor, and his brother Sir Richard (49) overseer.

51. 25. (IV.) JOHN SALTONSTALL, son of Sir Richard (25), probably the Sir John, nephew of Sir Peter (27), mentioned in his will in 1651.

52. 25. (IV.) SUSANNA SALTONSTALL, dau. of Sir Richard (25), m. Wm. Paulen of Co. Wilts, Esquire.

53. 27. (IV.) JAMES SALTONSTALL, son of Sir Peter (27), bap. at Barkway 27 Oct., 1616 ; d. 1649 ; bur. 19 April, *s. p.*

54. 27. (IV.) PETER SALTONSTALL, son of Sir Peter (27), bap. at Barkway 12 Sep., 1624. Perhaps came to New England. Member Artillery Company 1644.

55. 27. (IV.) JOHN SALTONSTALL, son of Sir Peter (27), named in the will of his father, dated 12 July, 1651, as was also Sir Peter's nephew, Sir John Saltonstall.

56. 27. (IV.) SUSANNAH SALTONSTALL, dau. of Sir Peter (27), m. Robert Castel of E. Harley, Co. Cambridge, 13 Feb., 1631. Had a son Robert. She d. 21 June, 1633; bur. at Barkway church with epitaph. (Part II. 56.)

57. 27. (IV.) BRIDGET SALTONSTALL, dau. of Sir Peter (27), b. 1614; unmarried; d. Feb., 1639, aged 25. Buried in chancel of Barkway church with epitaph. (Part II. 57.)

58. 27. (IV.) CHRISTIAN SALTONSTALL, dau. of Sir Peter (27), unmarried; d. 23 Dec., 1639. Buried in chancel of Barkway church with epitaph. (Part II. 58.)

59. 27. (IV.) ANNE SALTONSTALL, dau. and heir of Sir Peter (27), bap. 29 Oct., 1618; m. Sir Edward Chester of Cockenhatch, of Royston in Herts, Knight.   She d. 14 Jan., 1647, aged 30; bur. 17 Jan. at Barkway with epitaph.   Had son Edward, Sheriff of Herts 1666.   Sir Edward m. 2d, Katharine, dau. of —— Johnstone of London.   She was living in 1642.   Sir Edward d. 1664.   (Part II. 59.)

60. 27. (IV.) ELIZABETH SALTONSTALL, dau. of Sir Peter (27), bap. 2 Aug., 1621; ob. cel. 18 May, 1639, aged 17; bur. at Barkway with epitaph.

61. 29. (IV.) WYE SALTONSTALL, son of Sir Samuel (29); educated at Oxford; an author and poet of good repute. (Part II. 61.)

64. 29. (IV.) ELIZABETH SALTONSTALL, dau. of Sir Samuel (29), m. 1st, George Sewster, Gent.; m. 2d, George Parkins.   In her will, dated 4 Sep., 1644, proved 14 June, 1653, she mentions her sons Samuel and Charles Sewster, also "Wye Saltonstall and Henry Saltonstall my brothers.   My brother Charles Saltonstall, gentleman."

66. 29. (IV.) CHARLES SALTONSTALL, son of Sir Samuel (29), b. about 1613.   Called Captain Charles; author of the "Navigator, or Theoret. and Pract. Prompter of the Art of Navigation," London, 1642, 4th ed., with his likeness.   In 1647, "Surveyor of Est. Bishoprick, England and Wales." Was living in 1651.

67. 49. (V.) RICHARD SALTONSTALL of Chipping Warden, Esquire, son of Sir Richard (49), grandson of Sir Richard, Lord Mayor, was bur. 31 Aug., 1688.   He m. Margaret ——. (Part II. 67.)

Children : —
  70. William.
  71. Richard.
  72. Elizabeth.
There were other children who died young.

68. 49. (V.) PHILIP SALTONSTALL, son of Sir Richard (49), lord of the Manor of Groves in South Okenden, Essex,

Richard Saltonstall of Chipping Warden, Northamptonshire (1688).
(From a portrait in the possession of the Author.)

Esquire. He d. by a fall from his horse 14 Sep., 1688, aged 33.
A patron of the church. He m. Alice, dau. of —— Graham.
Children : —

   73. Philip.
   74. Miserecord (no further record).
   75. Anne (no further record).
   76. Richard (no further record).
   77. James (no further record).
   78. Mary (no further record).

   69. 49. (V.) ANNE SALTONSTALL, dau. of Sir Richard (49),
m. George Chamberlayne of Wardington, Co. Oxon, Esquire,
youngest brother of Sir Thomas Chamberlayne, Bart.

   70. 67. (VI.) WILLIAM SALTONSTALL, son of Richard (67),
d. 1679, aged 19 ; bur. 19 June.

   71. 67. (VI.) RICHARD SALTONSTALL [1] of Chipping Warden in Northamptonshire, son of Richard (67), m. in 1688,
Silence, dau. of John Parkhurst of Catesby, Esquire. He d.
in London 29 Dec., 1688; bur. at Chipping Warden 2 Jan.,
168⅞. She d. 26 April, 1698, and was buried at Walston, Co.
Warwick. (Part II. 71.)
Child : —
   80. Ricarda Posthuma.

   72. 67. (VI.) ELIZABETH SALTONSTALL, dau. of Richard
(67), m. 18 June, 1689, William Peyton of Chesterton, Co.
Warwick, Esquire.

   73. 68. (VI.) PHILIP SALTONSTALL, son of Philip (68), of
Groves, Co. Essex, Esquire ; m. Sarah, dau. of Sir Capel
Luckyn of Messing Hall, Essex, Baronet, b. 1668.
Child : —
   79. Phillippa.

   79. 73. (VII.) PHILLIPPA SALTONSTALL, dau. and heir of

---

[1] Two fine portraits of Richard Saltonstall (71) and of Silence his wife, for
some time owned by Lord North, his descendant, were recently presented by him
to Hon. Theodore Roosevelt of New York. They are at present in the possession of
the author at his house at Chestnut Hill, Mass. They are thought to have been
painted by Sir Peter Lely. They are here reproduced in heliotype.

Philip (73), m. John Goodere, Esq., of Claybury, and brought him Groves in South Okenden. Her second husband was Dacres Barrett of Bellehouse, in Averly, Co. Essex, Esquire.

80. 71. (VII.) RICARDA POSTHUMA SALTONSTALL, dau. of Richard (71), m. Hon. George Montague, afterwards 2d Earl of Halifax, K. B. (Part II. 71.) She d. 1711; bur. 5 April. He d. 9 May, 1739; bur. at Horton 15 May. His second wife was Mary, dau. of Richard, 1st Earl of Scarborough. She d. 10 Sep., 1726; bur. at Horton 17 Sep.

Children:—

81. Ricarda Maria, b. 14 Jan., 17$\frac{10}{11}$; d. in infancy.

82. (VIII.) Lucy, heir of her mother, m. at Bushey, Co. Middlesex, 16 June, 1728, Francis, 3d Baron Guilford, b. 13 April, 1704; M. P. for Branbury 1727–9; Baron North of Kirtling on decease of William, 6th Baron, in 1734; Earl of Guilford, patent dated 8 April, 1752; Lord Lieut. of Co. Somerset; d. in London 4 Aug., 1790; bur. 18 Aug., 1790. Succeeded by his son Frederick. She d. in London 7 May, 1734; bur. 15 May, aged 25 years. Children:

83. (IX.) Frederick, 2d Earl of Guilford and 8th Baron North of Kirtling, b. 13 April, 1732; bap. in London. Lord North was Prime Minister during the Revolutionary War.

84. Lucy, b. 26 April, 1734; d. in infancy.

With the marriage of Ricarda Posthuma Saltonstall and Hon. George Montague, afterwards Earl of Halifax, the extension of the pedigree in England ends; but it is known that one Elizabeth Saltonstall married a Dawbarn (of Wisbech, Camb. probably), and that Cardinal Wiseman and Sir William Saltonstall Wiseman, admiral in the English Navy, with other noted families, trace their descent from the family of Saltonstall.[1]

[1] Baker's *History of Northamptonshire;* Visitation of Hertfordshire, 1634.

Silence, Wife of Richard Saltonstall (1688).
(From a portrait in the possession of the Author.)

85. 39. (V.) MURIEL SALTONSTALL, eldest child of Richard (39) and wife, Muriel Gurdon, b. in England 1634. In pedigree of Moseley called Jane Muriel; m. Sir Edward Moseley of Hulme, Co. Lancaster, Knight. Had Anne, only dau. and heir, who m. Sir John Bland of Kippax Park, Halifax, Baronet, 1712. Sir Edward d. in 1695, aged 77, and was buried at Didsbury.

Baine's "History of Lancashire" gives an account of the ancestry of Sir Edward Moseley, with a pedigree from the time of King John.

86. 39. (V.) RICHARD SALTONSTALL, son of Richard (39), citizen of London, d. about 1666, *s. p.* Will dated 25 Aug., 1665, proved 16 Oct., 1666. It mentions his father, Richard Saltonstall, Esq., and his mother, Mrs. Merial Saltonstall; sister Merial, wife of Edward Mosely, Esq.; sister Abigail, wife of Thomas Harby; sister Elizabeth, wife of Hercules Horsey; cousin Philip Gurdon, M. D.; cousin Mr. Roger Hill; cousin Anne, daughter of Uncle John Gurdon, Esq.; partner Mr. Edward Turgis; brother Nathaniel Saltonstall, and his wife Elizabeth, principal legatees.

87. 39. (V.) NATHANIEL SALTONSTALL, son of Richard (39), b. at Ipswich, Mass., about 1639; grad. Harv. Coll. 1659; m. 28 Dec., 1663, Elizabeth Ward, b. 9 April, 1647, dau. of Rev. John and Alice (Edmunds) Ward [1] of Haverhill, where he settled, when his father made a settlement upon him of 800 acres of land at Ipswich, and other lands.[2] He took the oath of freeman 1665; was chosen Representative 1666; from 1669 to 1671 was Town Clerk of Haverhill (Part II. 87 B); from 1679 to 1686, Colonel of Essex Regiment; Assistant, 1679 to 1686, and again in 1689 to 1692 (from 1680 to 1683 he and his father were both Assistants); Member of the Council; Judge Oyer and Terminer Court 1692, refused to serve in

---

[1] Rev. John Ward settled at Ipswich, took a prominent part in the settlement of the town, and was greatly beloved and respected. He was son of Rev. Nathaniel Ward of Ipswich, the author of the *Simple Cobbler of Agawam*, and a grandson of Rev. John Ward, a minister of Haverhill, England. (See Part II. 87 A.)

[2] Essex Deeds, ii. 208.

witchcraft trials. He d. 21 May, 1707, and his widow Elizabeth d. 29 April, 1741. (Part II. 87.)

Children : —

90. Gurdon.
91. Elizabeth.
92. Richard.
93. Nathaniel.
94. John.

His will, dated 19 May, 1707, made a bequest to his niece
Meriell Horsey ; mentions his sister, Elizabeth Horsey, and
his rents in Killingly, England.

88. 39. (V.) ABIGAIL SALTONSTALL, dau. of Richard (39),
b. at Woodsome 1610 ; m. Thomas Harley of Hinsham
Court, Co. Hereford, younger son of Sir Robert Harley,
whose elder son, Sir Edward, was father of Robert, Earl of
Oxford.

89. 39. (V.) ELIZABETH SALTONSTALL, dau. of Richard
(39), m. Hercules Horsey, Esq.; had a dau. Muriel, who had
a bequest in her uncle Nathaniel's will, 1707.

90. 87. (VI.) GURDON SALTONSTALL, eldest son of Nathaniel (87), b. at Haverhill, Mass., at the Saltonstall seat,
27 March, 1666 ; grad. Harv. Coll. 1684 ; d. 20 Sep., 1724 ;
minister, settled at New London, Conn., 19 Nov., 1691. He
was Governor of Connecticut from 1708 till his death in 1724.

Governor Gurdon Saltonstall was the founder of the Connecticut branch of the family of Saltonstall ; and as such his
proper place is at the head of that part of the family record.
(See No. 149, at page 31.)

91. 87. (VI.) ELIZABETH SALTONSTALL, dau. of Nathaniel
(87), b. 17 Sep., 1668 ; m. 1st, Rev. John Denison, Harv.
Coll. 1684, d. 1689 ; had one child, John, who m. Mary Leverett, dau. of John Leverett, President Harv. Coll. She m.
2d, Rev. Roland Cotton of Sandwich, son of John Cotton,
Jr., of Plymouth, and had five sons and five daughters. She
d. 8 July, 1726, aged 58. (See Part II. 91, for her numerous
descendants.)

Rich. Saltonstall
(BOSTON)

92. 87. (VI.) RICHARD SALTONSTALL, son of Nathaniel (87), b. 25 April, 1672; grad. Harv. Coll. 1695; m. 25 March, 1702, Mehitabel, dau. of Captain Simon and Sarah Wainwright of Haverhill, and granddaughter of Francis Wainwright of Ipswich; Representative from Haverhill 1699; Major 1704; afterwards Colonel of regiment; d. 22 April, 1714. Administration was granted to his nephew, John Denison, 28 June, 1714, and the same day Rev. Roland Cotton was appointed guardian of his children.

Children: —
    95. Richard.
    96. Ward.
    97. Nathaniel.
    98. Elizabeth.

93. 87. (VI.) NATHANIEL SALTONSTALL, son of Nathaniel (87), b. 5 Sep., 1674; grad. Harv. Coll. 1695; Tutor and Librarian 1697–1701; m. Dorothy, widow of John Frizel, merchant of Boston. She d. 1733 and left a legacy of £300 to Harvard College. He d. at Woburn 1739, aged 65. (Part II. 93.) No children.

94. 87. (VI.) JOHN SALTONSTALL, son of Nathaniel (87), b. 14 Aug., 1678; d. 2 Oct., 1681.

95. 92. (VII.) RICHARD SALTONSTALL, son of Richard (92), b. at Haverhill, Mass., 24 June, 1703; grad. Harv. Coll. 1722; in 1726 commissioned as Colonel at the age of 23; Judge of Superior Court, 1736, at the age of 33, until his death, which occurred 20 Oct., 1756; Representative from Haverhill 1728, and often afterwards.[1] In June, 1726, he m. 1st, Abigail Waldron, b. 1702, descendant of Richard Waldron, who came to New England 1635. She d. 16 March, 1735. He m. 2d, Mary Jekyll, dau. of John Jekyll, Esq., Collector of Customs at Boston. She d. at Boston 4 March, 1740, *s. p.* He m. 3d, Mary Cooke, dau. of Elisha

[1] Some of the original commissions to Richard Saltonstall are in the author's possession: By Governor Belcher in 1732, commissioned a Colonel. By Governor Belcher in 1736, appointed Judge of the Superior Court. By Governor Pownall in 1738, appointed Justice of the Peace.

Cooke, Jr., by wife Jane, granddaughter of Richard Middle-cott, Esq., of Boston (Part II. 95 C), who m. in 1672 a niece of Governor Edward Winslow. Mary Cooke was a grand-daughter of Elisha Cooke, Sr., Esq. (Part II. 95 B), who married Elizabeth, dau. of Governor Leverett (Part II. 95 A). He d. 20 Oct., 1756.

Children by first wife, Abigail : —
    99. Abigail.
    100. Elizabeth.
    101. Richard.
    102. William.
    103. William.

Children by third wife, Mary : —
    105. Nathaniel.
    106. Mary.
    107. Middlecott Cooke.
    108. Leverett.

96. 92. (VII.) WARD SALTONSTALL, son of Richard (92), b. 21 May, 1705; d. 5 Aug., 1706.

97. 92. (VII.) NATHANIEL SALTONSTALL, son of Richard (92), b. 3 June, 1706; bap. at Haverhill 9 June; grad. Harv. Coll. 1727; was a merchant.

98. 92. (VII.) ELIZABETH SALTONSTALL, dau. of Richard (92), b. 25 June, 1707 ; bap. at Haverhill 29 June; d. young.

99. 95. (VIII.) ABIGAIL SALTONSTALL, dau. of Richard (95), by first wife, b. 5 Oct., 1728 ; m. Colonel George Watson of Plymouth. (Part II. 99.)

100. 95. (VIII.) ELIZABETH SALTONSTALL, dau. of Richard (95), b. 5 June, 1730 ; d. 19 Oct., 1737.

101. 95. (VIII.) RICHARD SALTONSTALL, son of Richard (95), b. 5 April, 1732; grad. Harv. Coll. 1751, with high rank; Representative from Haverhill 1761 to 1769. Colonel of Essex Regiment 1754, and in service to end of the French War, 1760; High Sheriff of Essex; a loyalist; unmarried; d. at Kensington, England, 6 Oct., 1785, and has a monument to his memory there. (Part II. 101.)

102. 95. (VIII.) WILLIAM SALTONSTALL, son of Richard (95), b. 2 Nov., 1733; d. 15 Nov.

103. 95. (VIII.) WILLIAM SALTONSTALL, son of Richard (95), b. 17 Oct., 1734; d. 25 Oct., 1737.

105. 95. (VIII.) NATHANIEL SALTONSTALL, son of Richard (95) by his third wife; b. 10 Feb., 1746; grad. Harv. Coll. 1766; physician; lived in Haverhill, Mass.; avoided public life, and devoted himself to his profession; was supporter of the patriot cause, and through life enjoyed the esteem of his fellow-citizens. He d. 15 May, 1815, aged 69. (Part II. 105.) He m. 21 Oct., 1780, Anna, dau. of Samuel and Sarah White of Haverhill, b. 12 April, 1752; d. 21 Oct., 1841, aged 89. She was a descendant of William White of Ipswich 1635, one of the first settlers of Haverhill 1640. (Part II. 105 A.)

Children : —

109. Mary Cooke.
110. Leverett.
111. Nathaniel.
112. Anna.
113. Sarah.
114. Richard
115. Matilda.

106. 95. (VIII.) MARY SALTONSTALL, dau. of Richard (95), b. 4 Sep., 1749; m. Rev. Moses Badger, grad. Harv. Coll. 1761, an Episcopal minister, and a loyalist, removed to Halifax 1776, and d. at Providence, R. I., in 1792. She d. 24 Dec., 1791.

107. 95. (VIII.) MIDDLECOTT COOKE SALTONSTALL, son of Richard (95), b. 24 Jan., 1752; d. 10 March.

108. 95. (VIII.) LEVERETT SALTONSTALL, son of Richard (95), b. 25 Dec., 1754; commenced mercantile education in Boston; loyalist; Captain in English Army; d. at New York 20 Dec., 1782, aged 28. (Part II. 108.)

109. 105. (IX.) MARY COOKE SALTONSTALL, dau. of Nathaniel (105), b. 20 Sep., 1781; m. 9 Oct., 1806, Hon. John Varnum, grad. Harv. Coll. 1798, lawyer of Haverhill, Representative in Congress, d. 23 July, 1836. She d. 7 Aug., 1817.

Children : —

1. Nathaniel, b. 1812.
2. John Jay, b. 5 Dec., 1814 ; d. 6 Nov., 1889.
3. Richard Saltonstall, b. 12 April, 1817; d. 26 Dec., 1880. He m. 1st, 1844, Sarah Potter at Jonesville, Mich., who d. 7 Aug., 1845 ; m. 2d, 29 June, 1854, Harriet Champlain, and had three sons : —
    1a. Grover Champlain, b. 28 Aug., 1857 ; m. 25 May, 1881, Ida M. Benner. They had one child, Hattie Champlain, b. 17 Dec., 1883.
    2a. Freeland Gardner, b. 6 Oct., 1859 ; m. 27 Oct., 1883, Sarah Kelsey.
    3a. Edward Champlain, b. 15 April, 1862 ; m. 25 Oct., 1885, Mary Carr.

110. 105. (IX.) LEVERETT SALTONSTALL, son of Nathaniel (105), b. 13 June, 1783 ; grad. Harv. Coll. 1802 ; studied law with Hon. William Prescott (then of Salem), was eminent as an advocate ; Speaker of Massachusetts House of Representatives ; President of the Senate ; first Mayor of Salem ; Representative in Congress ; President of the Bible Society ; President of the Essex Bar ; President Essex Agricultural Society ; Fellow American Academy ; Member of Massachusetts Historical Society ; LL. D., Harv. Univ. 1838, and member Board of Overseers, Harv. Univ. He d. 8 May, 1845. (Part II. 110.) He m. 7 March, 1811, Mary Elizabeth, dau. of Thomas Sanders, Esq., merchant of Salem (Part II. 110 A), b. 29 Feb., 1788; d. 11 Jan., 1858.

Children : —

116. Anne Elizabeth, b. 16 Feb., 1812 ; unmarried ; d. 10 July, 1881. (Part II. 116.)
117. Caroline, b. 2 Sep., 1815 ; unmarried ; d. 23 Feb., 1883. (Part II. 117.)
118. Richard Gurdon, b. 29 June, 1820 ; d. 22 Feb., 1821.
119. Lucy Sanders.
120. Leverett.

111. 105. (IX.) NATHANIEL SALTONSTALL, son of Nathaniel (105), b. 1 Oct., 1784; merchant at Baltimore, afterwards of Salem; m. at Salem 30 Nov., 1820, Caroline, youngest dau. of Thomas Sanders, Esq., b. 2 Jan., 1793, d. 1 March, 1882. He d. 19 Oct., 1838. (Part II. 111.)
Children : —
   121. Gurdon, b. 14 Aug., 1821 ; d. 20 Aug., 1821.
   122. Catherine Pickman.
   123. Elizabeth Sanders.
   124. Henry.
   125. William Gurdon.

112. 105. (IX.) ANNA SALTONSTALL, dau. of Nathaniel (105), b. 3 Nov., 1787; m. 28 Nov., 1820, Hon. James Cushing Merrill, son of Rev. Gyles Merrill, grad. Harv. Coll. 1807; a lawyer and Judge Police Court, Boston. He d. 4 Oct., 1853. She d. 17 Oct., 1865.
Children : —
   1. James Cushing, b. 9 Aug., 1822; grad. Harv. Coll. 1842; m. 3 Oct., 1850, Jane Hyslop, dau. of Daniel and Sarah Stoddard Hammond of Boston, b. 26 March, 1827. He d. 7 March, 1869. Child: —
     James Cushing, b. 26 March, 1853.
   2. Samuel Gyles, b. 15 April, 1824; d. 28 April, 1830.
   3. Anna Saltonstall, b. 19 June, 1828; m. 23 April, 1862, Henry V. Ward of Baltimore. Children: —
     1a. Anna Saltonstall, b. 13 Feb., 1863.
     2a. Henry De Courcy, b. 16 Sep., 1864; d. 13 July, 1865.
     3a. Marion De Courcy, b. 25 Dec., 1865.
     4a. Robert De Courcy, b. 29 Nov., 1867.
     5a. Elsa, b. 10 Jan., 1870; d. 25 March, 1871.
   4. Matilda Elizabeth, b. 22 June, 1832; m. 16 Oct., 1860, Edward F. Adams of Boston.

113. 105. (IX.) SARAH SALTONSTALL, dau. of Nathaniel (105), b. 5 Nov., 1790; m. 16 June, 1816, Isaac R. Howe, lawyer, of Haverhill, grad. Harv. Coll. 1810, d. 15 Jan., 1860. She d. 25 July, 1870.

Children: —

1. Nathaniel Saltonstall, b. 24 April, 1817; grad. Yale Coll. 1835; Judge Probate Essex Co., Mass.; m. 1st, Sophia Murphy; m. 2d, Anna Maria Murphy; m. 3d, Sarah Ann Bradley, 26 May, 1846. He d. 20 Feb., 1885. Children: —

   1a. Susan Bradley, b. 25 June, 1847; m. 6 June, 1866, Thomas Sanders of Salem, afterwards of Haverhill (grandson of Thomas Sanders, the father of Mrs. Leverett and Mrs. Nathaniel Saltonstall). Children: —

      1b. George Thomas, b. 5 March, 1867; m. 10 Dec., 1891, Lucy Swett. Child: Dorothy Bell, b. 27 Jan., 1893.
      2b. Mary Williams, b. 5 Feb., 1869.
      3b. Nathaniel Saltonstall Howe, b. 13 Feb., 1871; m. 27 Oct., 1894, Mary Kemble Webb.
      4b. Charles Bradley, b. 24 Sep., 1878.
      5b. Anne Elizabeth, b. 23 April, 1880.
      6b. Janet Rand, b. 26 Jan., 1884.
      7b. Muriel Gurdon, b. 13 Nov., 1886.
      8b. Helen Bradley, b. 2 Aug., 1890; d. 18 Dec., 1891.

   2a. Henry Saltonstall, 2d child of Hon. Nathaniel Saltonstall Howe, b. 12 Aug., 1848; grad. Harv. Coll. 1869; m. 2 Oct., 1874, Katherine Dexter Wainwright, dau. of Henry Wainwright, Esq., of Boston. Children: —

      1b. Henry Wainwright, b. 20 Sep., 1875.
      2b. James Carleton, b. 1 Aug., 1877.
      3b. Susan Bradley, b. 28 July, 1879.
      4b. Dudley Rogers, b. 22 Feb., 1881.
      5b. Parkman Dexter, b. 20 Sep., 1889.

2. Mary Cooke (named for her great-grandmother, dau. of Elisha Cooke, Jr.), sister of Hon. Nathaniel Saltonstall Howe, b. 25 March, 1819; m. 30 Sep., 1851, James H. Carleton of Haverhill, who d. 27 March, 1893. She d. 2 Sep., 1882. He purchased the birth-

To Henry Saltonstall Howe:

To ready faith at my hands,
    my schoolmate's son has claim,
Who bears beside our Merrimack
    Its best and noblest name.
God bless and give thee grace to keep
    Still green the ancient tree,
The brave old stock of Saltonstall
    Must nothing lose in thee.

John G. Whittier,

Amesbury 26th 4th mo
        1862.

place and homestead of Whittier, the poet, and gave
it to the city of Haverhill.
3. Caroline Matilda, b. 27 Sep., 1821 ; d. 9 Aug., 1844.
4. Anne Elizabeth, b. 18 Nov., 1823 ; d. 7 July, 1845.
5. William Garland, b. 28 June, 1826 ; d. 26 Aug.,1826.
6. Frances, b. 8 Oct., 1827; d. 5 Sep., 1828.
7. William Garland, b. 1 Aug., 1829; m. 30 July, 1862,
   Mary McK. Kinsman, b. 10 March, 1839, d. 2 Nov.,
   1867. Children : —
   1a. Sarah Saltonstall, b. 8 July, 1863; d. 25 Oct.,
   1868.
   2a. Henry Kinsman, b. 15 Aug., 1865; d. 15 Nov.,
   1868.
   3a. Gurdon Saltonstall, b. 30 Nov., 1866 ; grad. Harv.
   Coll. 1889; lawyer.
8. Francis Saltonstall, b. 8 Nov., 1831 ; grad. Harv.
   Coll. 1852; m. 1866, Frances Jane Fogg of Chicago;
   a lawyer in Chicago; d. 1878. Children : —
   1a. Mary Ware, b. 2 May, 1867.
   2a. Caroline, b. 6 Dec., 1868.
114. 105. (IX.) RICHARD SALTONSTALL, son of Nathaniel
(105), b. 16 June, 1794 ; grad. Harv. Coll. 1813; merchant at
Baltimore; m. 24 Oct., 1822, Margaret Ann Savage of Virginia. He was lost at sea 1834. She d. 1 Nov., 1834.
Children : —
   1. 126. Richard, b. 28 Aug., 1823, m. 1 Feb., 1848, Mrs.
   Maria J. Daniel, who d. 28 Feb., 1866. He lived in
   New York; d. 10 Feb., 1875. Children : —
   1a. 139. Margaret Ann, b. 19 Feb., 1851.
   2a. Julia, b. 26 Aug., 1852 ; d. 15 Sep., 1852.
   3a. 140. Leverett, b. 11 Aug., 1853.
   4a. 141. Nathaniel, b. 10 Dec., 1855.
   5a. Fanny, b. 26 Oct., 1857; d. 14 Aug., 1858.
   6a. 142. Laura, b. 31 March, 1860; m. William G. A.
   Pattee of Quincy. Children : —
   1b. Richard Saltonstall.
   2b. Elizabeth Greenleaf.

2. Sarah Smith, b. 7 July, 1825; d. 4 June, 1826.
3. 127. Anna White, b. 19 Oct., 1827; d. 29 Oct., 1884.
She lived at Haverhill, and was much esteemed for
her Christian character and benevolent disposition.
4. Mary Elizabeth, b. 20 Sep., 1830; d. 12 Oct., 1830.

115. 105. (IX.) MATILDA SALTONSTALL, dau. of Nathaniel
(105), b. 9 Dec., 1796; m. 16 June, 1825, Fisher Howe, Esq.,
of New York, merchant. She d. 21 May, 1831. He was b.
3 Sep., 1798; d. 7 Nov., 1871.
Children: —

1. Henry Fisher, b. 30 March, 1826; d. 8 July, 1827.
2. Matilda Saltonstall, b. 15 May, 1828; m. 19 April,
1848, William R. Gould, b. 12 July, 1816. Children:
1a. William Saltonstall, b. 7 Feb., 1849; m. 26 April,
1886, Jane Lowndes Bache, b. 17 May, 1855.
2a. Edward Peters, b. 6 March, 1850.
3a. Frederick, b. 20 Nov., 1851.
4a. Edward Peters, b. 10 April, 1853.
5a. Matilda G., b. 6 May, 1855.
6a. Charles, b. 20 Oct., 1861.

(Fisher Howe m. 2d, 1 Oct., 1832, Elizabeth Leavitt, dau.
of David and Maria Clarissa Leavitt of Brooklyn, N. Y.
Children: Fisher, b. 13 Aug., 1833; d. 21 Dec., 1837.
Leavitt, b. 1 June, 1835; d. 6 Sep., 1836. Leavitt, b. 24
Nov., 1836. Edward, b. 8 March, 1839. Elizabeth Leavitt,
b. 26 Feb., 1841. Charles Albert, b. 1 June, 1843; d. 7 Dec.,
1844. Anna, b. 12 July, 1845. Fisher, b. 19 April, 1851.)

119. 110. (X.) LUCY SANDERS SALTONSTALL, dau. of
Leverett (110), b. 10 Feb., 1822; m. 30 June, 1847, John
Francis Tuckerman, grad. Harv. Coll. 1837, M. D. 1841,
Surgeon U. S. Navy, d. 27 June, 1885. She d. 24 Dec.,
1890. (Part II. 119.) Children: —

1. Leverett Saltonstall, b. 19 April, 1848; grad. Harv.
Coll. 1868; A. M., LL. B.
2. Francis, b. 11 June, 1849; m. 18 June, 1885, Alice
Dearborn Leavitt of Salem.

3. Charles Sanders, b. 31 Jan., 1852; grad. Harv. Coll.
1874; m. 15 April, 1880, Ruth, eldest dau. of Daniel
F. Appleton of New York. Children: —
  1a. Muriel, b. 6 March, 1881.
  2a. John Appleton, b. 26 Nov., 1883.
  3a. Julia Appleton, b. 17 May, 1888.
  4a. Leverett Saltonstall, b. 2 Dec., 1892.
4. Mary Saltonstall, b. 12 July, 1856; m. 13 Jan., 1887,
William P. Parker, b. 29 June, 1855. Children:
  1a. Francis Tuckerman, b. 17 Feb., 1889.
  2a. William Bradstreet, b. 24 July, 1890.

120. 110. (X.) LEVERETT SALTONSTALL, only surviving
son and 5th child of Leverett (110) and Mary E. (Sanders)
Saltonstall, b. 16 March, 1825, in Salem; grad. Harv. Coll.
1844; A. M., LL. B. 1847; Overseer Harv. University
for three terms, 18 years; member Massachusetts Historical
Society (Part II. 120); m. 19 Oct., 1854, Rose S. Lee, dau.
of John Clarke and Harriet (Rose) Lee of Salem (Part II.
120 A), b. 24 Jan., 1835.
Children: —
  128. (XI.) Leverett, b. 3 Nov., 1855; d. 14 Feb., 1863.
    (Part II. 128.)
  129. (XI.) Richard Middlecott, b. 28 Oct., 1859; grad.
    Harv. Coll. 1880; member Suffolk bar; m. 17 Oct.,
    1891, Eleanor Brooks, b. 18 Sep., 1867, dau. of Peter
    C. Brooks of West Medford, a descendant of Eliza-
    beth (91), dau. of Nathaniel Saltonstall (87), by second
    husband, Roland Cotton. (Part II. 91.) Children:
  .143. (XII.) Leverett, b. 1 Sep., 1892.
  144. (XII.) Eleanor, b. 19 Oct., 1894.
  145. (XII.) Muriel Gurdon, b. 26 March, 1896.
  130. (XI.) Rose Lee, b. 17 June, 1861, m. 6 Nov.,
    1884, George Webb West, b. 17 May, 1850, grad.
    Harv. Coll. 1872, M. D. 1880. She d. 28 Feb.,
    1891. Children: —
  1. Alice Lee, b. 26 Oct., 1885.
  2. George Saltonstall, b. 26 June, 1887.

131. (XI.) Mary Elizabeth, b. 17 Oct., 1862; m. 30 June, 1884, Louis Agassiz Shaw, son of Quincy A. and Pauline Shaw, dau. of Professor Louis Agassiz, b. 18 Sep., 1861, grad. Harv. Coll. 1884. He d. 3 July, 1891. Children: —
  1. Quincy Adams, b. 21 May, 1885.
  2. Louis Agassiz, b. 25 Sep., 1886.
132. (XI.) Philip Leverett, b. 4 May, 1867; grad. Harv. Coll. 1889; m. 18 June, 1890, Frances Anna Fitch Sherwood. Children: —
  146. Katharine, b. 10 April, 1891.
  147. Rose Lee, b. 27 May, 1892.
  148. Frances Sherwood, b. 11 Oct., 1893.
133. (XI.) Endicott Peabody, b. 25 Dec., 1872; grad. Harv. Coll. 1894.

"There is no family but the Saltonstall which has sent seven successive generations, all in the male line, to Harvard University. They are Nathaniel, H. U. 1659; Richard, H. U. 1695; Richard, H. U. 1722; Nathaniel, H. U. 1766; Leverett, H. U. 1802; Leverett, H. U. 1844; and Richard Middlecott, H. U. 1880. Henry Saltonstall, H. U. 1642, son of Sir Richard Saltonstall, and uncle of Nathaniel, H. U. 1659, makes *eight generations.*" (Sibley's "Harvard Graduates," vol. ii. p. 8.)

  122. 111. (X.) Catherine Pickman Saltonstall, dau. of Nathaniel (111), b. 18 May, 1823; m. 28 April, 1846, Edward Brooks Peirson of Salem, grad. Harv. Coll. 1840, M. D. 1844; d. 25 June, 1852, *s. p.* He m. 2d, Ellen Elizabeth Perry of Keene, N. H., and d. 19 Nov., 1874, leaving children: Katharine, m. William H. Ramsey; Margaret, m. Maurice H. Richardson; Ellen Perry, m. Frank W. Benson; Edward Lawrence; and Horatio Perry.

  123. 111. (X.) Elizabeth Sanders Saltonstall, dau. of Nathaniel (111), b. 26 May, 1825; m. 16 Dec., 1852, George Z. Silsbee of Salem, merchant; d. 9 Aug., 1887. Children: —
  1. George Saltonstall, b. 21 Aug., 1854, grad. Harv.

SALTONSTALL FAMILY

MALE LINE

Copy of an exhibit made by Harvard University in the Department of Education at the Columbian Exhibition at Chicago, 1893. The Graduates of Harvard College are indicated by the Year of Graduation prefixed to the Names

GENERATIONS OF GRADUATES

1	2	3	4	5	6	7	8
Sir Richard of Yorkshire, England, settled in Watertown, Mass., July, 1630. Court of Assistants.	1642. Henry, M.D. Padua, 1649. Fellow of Oxford, 1652.						
	Richard ; . . . Emmanuel College, Cambridge, England. Court of Assistants.	1684. Gurdon ; Minister of New London. Governor of Connecticut.	1720. Rosewell.				
			1720. Gurdon ; A. B. Yale College, 1725.	1770. Gilbert.			
	1659. Nathaniel . . . Court of Assistants. Council. Colonel.	1695. Richard ; . . . Colonel.	1722. Richard ; . . . Judge of Superior Court. Colonel.	1751. Richard, Colonel.	1802. Leverett, LL.D. Overseer of Harvard College. Speaker and President of Senate, Mass. Member of Congress.	1844. Leverett ; . . . Overseer of Harvard College.	1880. Richard Middicott.
							1889. Philip Leverett.
							1894. Endicott Peabody.
				1766. Nathaniel ; Physician.	1813. Richard.		
		1695. Nathaniel, Librarian of Harvard College and Tutor.	1727. Nathaniel,		Nathaniel . . .	1848. Henry.	
						William Gurdon .	
						Robert.	

Coll. 1874; Treasurer of Pacific Mills; m. Sarah
Frances Gray, b. 20 March, 1865. Children: —

1a. George Saltonstall, b. 2 Nov., 1890.

2a. Elizabeth, b. 18 Oct., 1893.

2. Catherine Elizabeth, b. 14 Sep., 1856.

3. Francis Boardman, b. 28 May, 1867.

124. III. (X.) HENRY SALTONSTALL, son of Nathaniel
(111), b. 2 March, 1828; grad. Harv. Coll. 1848; m. 12 Sep.,
1855, Mrs. Georgiana C. Appleton, dau. of Hon. Nathaniel
(Part II. 124 A.) and Mary (Crowninshield) Silsbee of Salem,
and widow of Francis Appleton of Boston. He d. 4 Dec.,
1894. (Part II. 124.) Child: —

134. (XI.) Gurdon, b. 15 Aug., 1856; d. 22 May, 1878.

125. III. (X.) WILLIAM GURDON SALTONSTALL, son of
Nathaniel (111), b. 22 Dec., 1831; m. 18 Dec., 1867, Josephine Rose Lee (Part II. 120 A), b. 21 Dec., 1843, dau. of John
Clarke Lee and sister of Rose S., wife of Leverett Saltonstall
(120). He d. 21 July, 1889. (Part II. 125.) She d. 14 Jan.,
1889.

Children: —

135. (XI.) Robert, b. 3 Jan., 1870; grad. Harv. Coll.
1893.

136. (XI.) Lucy Sanders, b. 19 March, 1871; m. 24
June, 1893, Neal Rantoul of Salem, b. 17 Sep., 1870,
grad. Harv. Coll. 1892. Child: Josephine Lee, b.
12 Aug., 1894.

137. (XI.) John Lee, b. 23 May, 1878.

138. (XI.) Rosamond, b. 3 March, 1881.

CONNECTICUT BRANCH

149. 87. (VI.) GURDON SALTONSTALL (90, 87), Governor of
Connecticut, b. 27 March, 1666; grad. Harv. Coll. 1684; d.
20 Sep., 1724; minister, settled at New London 19 Nov.,
1691; Governor of Connecticut 1708 to his death, 1724.
Founder of the Connecticut branch of the family of Salton-

stall; held the Manor of Killingly near Pontefract in Yorkshire, England; built a mansion at Lake Saltonstall near
Branford, five miles from New Haven, Conn. He m. 1st,
Jerusha, dau. of James Richards of Hartford. She d. at Boston 25 July, 1697.

Children : —
    150. Elizabeth.
    151. Mary.
    152. Sarah.
    153. Jerusha.
    154. Gurdon.

He m. 2d, Elizabeth, dau. and sole heir of William Rosewell of Branford, Esquire, and Catherine his wife, dau. of
Hon. Richard Russell of Charlestown. She d. at New London 12 Sep., 1710.

Children : —
    155. Rosewell.
    156. Katherine.
    157. Nathaniel.
    158. Gurdon.
    159. Richard.

He m. 3d, Mary Clarke, dau. of William and Mary (Lawrence) Whittingham and relict of William Clarke of Boston.
She d. in Boston 23 Jan., 1730, *s. p.* A liberal benefactress
of Harvard and Yale colleges. She was great-granddaughter of Rev. William Whittingham[1] and his wife, sister of
John Calvin. (Part II. 149.)

150. 149. (VII.) ELIZABETH SALTONSTALL, dau. of Governor Gurdon Saltonstall by first wife, Jerusha Richards, was
born 11 May, 1690, m. 1st, 4 Aug., 1710, Richard Christo-

[1] Rev. William Whittingham, pastor of the first Congregational church gath-
ered at Geneva, Switzerland, Dean of Durham, England, m. Catharine, sister of
John Calvin. Baruch Whittingham, son of William Whittingham and Catharine
(Calvin), died just as he was embarking for America; but his wife came, notwith-
standing, bringing their son (William), who married a daughter of J. Lawrence of
Ipswich. Their daughter, Mary Whittingham, married 1st, William Clarke of
Boston, and on his decease she married 2d, Gurdon Saltonstall, Governor of Con-
necticut, as his third wife.

G. Saltonstall.

pher,[1] b. 18 Aug., 1685 (son of Richard Christopher of New London, b. 1662); d. 9 June, 1726.

Children: —

1. Richard, b. 29 July, 1712; m. 1734, Mary, dau. of John Pickett; d. 28 Sep., 1736. Children: —
   - 1a. Mary, b. 23 March, 1734.
   - 2a. Elizabeth, b. 24 Dec., 1735; m. Captain Joseph Hurlbut; d. 11 March, 1798.
2. Elizabeth, b. 13 Sep., 1714.
3. Mary, b. 17 Dec., 1716.
4. Sarah, b. 6 Dec., 1719.
5. Joseph, b. 30 Nov., 1722.

She m. 2d, Isaac Ledyard, merchant, of New England.

151. 149. (VII.) MARY SALTONSTALL, dau. of Governor Gurdon Saltonstall by first wife, Jerusha Richards, was b. 15 Feb., 169$\frac{1}{2}$; m. 1771, Jeremiah Miller, M. D., of New London, grad. Yale Coll. 1709. She d. 1749. They had 7 children.

The record of their children is incomplete. Three are said to have died in infancy; Mary, the only daughter, died unmarried; Gurdon, died in 1751, aged 26; Jason, died in 1755. Their son Jeremiah (b. 1719, d. 1797), m. 1743, Margaret, dau. of John Still and Ann (Dudley) Winthrop, b. 1717, d. 1803, and his first child, John Still Miller (b. 1746, d. 1824), m. Henrietta Saltonstall (174), dau. of General Gurdon Saltonstall (158).

Dr. Jeremiah Miller m. 2d, Mrs. Ann (Dudley) Winthrop, relict of John Still Winthrop and daughter of Governor Joseph Dudley. He died in 1756, and was buried in the Saltonstall tomb at New London. (Part II. 151.)

152. 149. (VII.) SARAH SALTONSTALL, dau. of Governor Gurdon Saltonstall by first wife, Jerusha Richards, was b.

---

[1] Richard Christopher was Judge of the Superior Court 1711, Judge of the County Court, and in 1716 Judge of the Court of Probate. During the administration of Governor Gurdon Saltonstall, lasting from 1708 to 1724, he appears in the colonial records to have been a most diligent public servant, as he certainly was most prominent and trustworthy. He died on the 9th day of June, 1726, leaving a large estate. See Caulkins's *History of New London*, also Colonial Records.

8 April, 1694; m. 1st, John Gardiner, 2d, Samuel Davis, 3d, Thomas Davis, all of New London.

153. 149. (VII.) JERUSHA SALTONSTALL, dau. of Governor Gurdon Saltonstall by first wife, Jerusha Richards, b. 5 July; d. 12 Sep., 1695.

154. 149. (VII.) GURDON SALTONSTALL, son of Governor Gurdon Saltonstall by first wife, Jerusha Richards, b. 17 July; d. 27 July, 1696.

155. 149. (VII.) ROSEWELL SALTONSTALL, son of Governor Gurdon Saltonstall by second wife, Elizabeth Rosewell, grad. Harv. Coll. 1720; resided in Branford on the Rosewell estate (Part II. 155 A); d. at New London 1 Oct., 1738. (Part II. 155.) He m. Mrs. Mary Lord, dau. of Hon. John Haynes and great-granddaughter of Governor John Haynes and widow of Elisha Lord. She m. 3d, Rev. Thomas Clapp.[1] Rosewell Saltonstall had 5 children, but the names of only 4 are given, viz.: —

    160. Mary.
    161. Sarah.
    162. Catherine.
    163. Rosewell.

156. 149. (VII.) KATHERINE SALTONSTALL, dau. of Governor Gurdon Saltonstall by second wife, Elizabeth Rosewell, b. 19 June, 1704; m. Thomas Brattle of Boston.

157. 149. (VII.) NATHANIEL SALTONSTALL, son of Governor Gurdon Saltonstall by second wife, Elizabeth Rosewell, b. 1 July, 1707; m. 1733, Lucretia Arnold; removed to one of the southern colonies.

158. 149. (VII.) GURDON SALTONSTALL, son of Governor Gurdon Saltonstall, by second wife, Elizabeth Rosewell, b. 22 Dec., 1708; grad. Yale Coll. 1725; m. 15 March, 1733,

---

[1] Rev. Thomas Clapp, who married the widow of Captain Rosewell Saltonstall, on 5 Feb., 1741, was born 26 June, 1703. He was the great-grandson of Thomas Clapp who was born in Dorchester, England, in 1597, and emigrated to America in 1633.
Rev. Thomas Clapp was President of Yale College for many years, and was one of the most celebrated men of his day. President Styles, his successor, speaks of him as "standing in the first rank of the learned men of the age, and one of the first philosophers America ever produced."

Rebecca Winthrop, dau. of John Still and Ann Winthrop
and granddaughter of Hon. Waitstill and Mary (Browne)
Winthrop. He was a brigadier-general in the Revolution,
and after the war Collector of the Port of New London.
(Part II. 158.)

The children of General Saltonstall were 14 in number
(from whom resulted connections by marriage with the families of Mumford, Richards, Wanton, Christopher, Sage,
Huntington, Parkin, Coit, Stewart, Seabury, Ebbets, Dean,
Atwater, Manwaring, Miller, Starr, Buck, etc.), as follows:—

164. Gurdon.
165. Rebecca.
166. Catherine.
167. Winthrop.
168. Dudley.
169. Ann.
170. Rosewell.
171. Elizabeth.
172. Mary.
173. Richard.
173*a*. Martha.
174. Henrietta.
175. Gilbert.
176. Sarah.

159. 149. (VII.) Richard Saltonstall, son of Governor
Gurdon Saltonstall by second wife, Elizabeth Rosewell, b. 1
Sep.; d. 12 Sep., 1710.

160. 155. (VIII.) Mary Saltonstall, dau. of Rosewell
(155), m. Nathan Whiting of New London; grad. Yale Coll.
1743; d. 1771.

161. 155. (VIII.) Sarah Saltonstall, dau. of Rosewell
(155), m. Jonathan Fitch of New Haven, grad. Yale Coll.
1748; d. 1793.

162. 155. (VIII.) Catherine Saltonstall, dau. of Rosewell (155), m. Jonathan Welles of Glastonbury, Conn., grad.
Yale Coll. 1751; d. 1792.

163. 155. (VIII.) ROSEWELL SALTONSTALL, son of Rose-well (155), b. 1736; grad. Yale Coll. 1751; unmarried; d. in Branford 25 Jan., 1788.

164. 158. (VIII.) GURDON SALTONSTALL, son of Gurdon (158), b. 15 Dec., 1733; grad. Yale Coll. 1752; unmarried; d. at Jamaica, West Indies, 18 July, 1762.

165. 158. (VIII.) REBECCA SALTONSTALL, dau. of Gurdon (158), b. 31 Dec., 1734; m. David Mumford of New London, afterwards of New York. (Part II. 165.)

166. 158. (VIII.) CATHERINE SALTONSTALL, dau. of Gurdon (158), b. 17 Feb., 173$\frac{5}{6}$; m. John Richards of New London.

167. 158. (VIII.) WINTHROP SALTONSTALL, son of Gurdon (158), b. 1 June, 1737; grad. Yale Coll. 1756; m. 17 April, 1763, Ann, dau. of Hon. Joseph Wanton of Newport, R. I. (Part II. 167, and 167 A.) She d. 1784.

Children: —
178. Rebecca.
178. Gurdon.
179. Mary Wanton.
180. Ann Dudley.
181. Winthrop.

168. 158. (VIII.) DUDLEY SALTONSTALL, son of Gurdon (158), b. 8 Sep., 1738. A commodore in the war of the Revolution. He m. 1765, Frances, dau. of Dr. Joshua Babcock of Westerly, R. I. She d. in New London in 1787. He d. in the West Indies in 1796.

After his decease his family removed to Canandaigua, N. Y. (Part II. 168.)

Children: —
1. 182. Hannah.
2. 183. Frances.
3. 184. Dudley.
4. 185. Joshua.
5. Catherine.
6. Thomas Brattle, b. 1772; unmarried; d. 1795.
7. Luke, d. in infancy.

169. 158. (VIII.) Ann Saltonstall, dau. of Gurdon (158), b. 29 Feb., 17$\frac{39}{40}$; m. Thomas Mumford of Norwich. No issue.

Mr. Mumford was the owner of the sloop Hancock, a very successful vessel, capturing many prizes in the war of the Revolution. (Part II. 169.)

170. 158. (VIII.) Rosewell Saltonstall, son of Gurdon (158), b. 29 Aug., 1741 ; m. 4 March, 1763, Elizabeth Stewart,[1] dau. of Mathew Stewart of New London. He moved late in life to New York, where he d. 12 Jan., 1804, and his widow Elizabeth in 1817. They were buried in Trinity Churchyard.

Children : —

   1. 186. Elizabeth.
   2. 187. Richard R.
   3. 188. Rosewell.
   4. 189. Abigail.
   5. 190. Ann.
   6. 191. Hannah.
   7. 192. William.
   8. 193. Mathew Stewart.
   9. Mary, m. John Fell of New York.
  10. Francis Walter, d. in New York, unmarried.
  11. Frances, mentioned in letter of sister (189) as living with her in 1841.

171. 158. (VIII.) Elizabeth Saltonstall, dau. of Gurdon (158), b. 12 Jan., 174$\frac{2}{3}$; m. 1st, John Ebbets, 2d, Silas Deane, United States Commissioner to France during the Revolutionary War.

172. 158. (VIII.) Mary Saltonstall, dau. of Gurdon (158), b. 28 March, 1744 ; m. Jeremiah Atwater of New Haven, many years steward of Yale College.

173. 158. (VIII.) Richard Saltonstall, son of Gurdon (158), b. 1 Jan., 1776 ; d. unmarried.

173a. 158. (VIII.) Martha Saltonstall, dau. of Gur-

---

[1] The Stewart arms, once owned by Elizabeth Stewart who married Rosewell Saltonstall, are now in the possession of Francis G. Saltonstall of New York city.

don (158), b. 8 Oct., 1748; m. David Manwaring of New London and New York. (Part II. 173 A.)

174. 158. (VIII.) HENRIETTA SALTONSTALL, dau. of Gurdon (158), b. 19 March, 17$\frac{49}{50}$; m. 28 Feb., 1772, John Still Miller, b. 3 Aug., 1746, d. 2 Nov., 1824. He was the first child of Margaret Winthrop of New London (dau. of John Still Winthrop and Ann Dudley, b. 1717, d. 1803) and Jeremiah Miller, M. D., b. 1719, d. 1797. (Part II. 174.) They had 13 children.

175. 158. (VIII.) GILBERT SALTONSTALL, son of Gurdon (158), b. 27 Feb., 175½; grad. Harv. Coll. 1770; Captain U. S. Marines; m. Harriet Babcock. (Part II. 175.)
Children: —
    194. Gurdon.
    195. Gilbert.

176. 158. (VIII.) SARAH SALTONSTALL, dau. of Gurdon (158), b. 17 June, 1754; m. 3 Dec., 1775, Daniel Buck of Wethersfield, Conn. He was b. 13 June, 1744; d. 6 June, 1808. She d. 19 Nov., 1828. They had 7 children. (Part II. 176.)

177. 167. (IX.) REBECCA SALTONSTALL, dau. of Winthrop (167), b. 4 March, 1764, m. Peter Christopher of New London. (Part II. 177.)

178. 167. (IX.) GURDON SALTONSTALL, son of Winthrop (167), b. 3 July, 1765; m. Hannah Sage of Middletown, b. 28 Jan., 1769, dau. of General Comfort Sage; was largely engaged in commercial pursuits. He d. at St. Nicholas' Mole, Island of St. Domingo, 9 June, 1795. His wife lived in widowhood 58 years and died at the age of 84 in Chicago, Ill., 28 Jan., 1853, at the residence of her son, William Wanton Saltonstall, who had removed to Chicago 1838.
Children: —
    196. Mary H.
    197. William Wanton.

179. 167. (IX.) MARY WANTON SALTONSTALL, dau. of Winthrop (167), b. 14 March, 1769; m. 29 Nov., 1789, Dr.

Thomas Coit of New London, b. April, 1767, son of Thomas
H. and Mary (Gardiner) Coit. (Part II. 179.)

Children: —

1. Anna W.
2. Mary Gardiner.
3. Hannah Saltonstall.
4. Augusta Dudley.
5. Martha.
6. Thomas Winthrop.
7. Elizabeth Richards.
8. Gurdon Saltonstall.

180. 167. (IX.) ANN DUDLEY SALTONSTALL, dau. of Winthrop (167), b. 8 Jan., 1770; unmarried; d. 21 May, 1845,
at Hartford.   Her body was subsequently placed in the
Saltonstall Tomb at New London.   " Last Friday night
the corpse of Ann Saltonstall was brought from Hartford,
it was taken to Mr. Sistare's, and on Saturday put into the
Saltonstall Tomb.   Jonathan Coit and Mary Coit her niece
followed first, William and Margaret (Winthrop) next, Mrs.
Christopher[1] was not well, and I was not able to go."— Letter from Mrs. Mary Parkin (née Winthrop) to her son.

181. 167. (IX.) WINTHROP SALTONSTALL, son of Win-
throp (167), b. 10 Feb., 1775; grad. Yale Coll. 1793; M. D.
Columbia College, New York, 1796; d. 27 June, 1802. (Part
II. 181.)

182. 168. (IX.) HANNAH SALTONSTALL, dau. of Dudley
(168), b. 1767; m. Joseph Whalley (or Walley), an English-
man who settled in Canandaigua, N. Y.

183. 168. (IX.) FRANCES SALTONSTALL, dau. of Dudley
(168), b. 1769.

184. 168. (IX.) DUDLEY SALTONSTALL, son of Dudley
(168), b. 1771 ; grad. Yale Coll. 1791; settled in the South.

185. 168. (IX.) JOSHUA SALTONSTALL, son of Dudley
(168), m. Abbie Lewis, dau. of Thomas and Sarah Lewis of
Farmington, Conn.

---

[1] Mrs. Christopher was Rebecca Saltonstall. (See No. 177.)

Children : —
1. Thomas Lewis, m. Mary Andrews, *s. p.*
2. 198. Dudley Gilbert.
3. Frances Catherine, m. Judge C. Carpenter.
4. Edward Burke, lost at sea.

186. 170. (IX.) ELIZABETH SALTONSTALL, dau. of Rose-well (170), b. about 1765; d. at an advanced age, unmarried.

187. 170. (IX.) RICHARD R. SALTONSTALL, son of Rose-well (170), b. 1768; unmarried; d. Sep., 1798, of yellow fever. An able merchant.

188. 170. (IX.) ROSEWELL SALTONSTALL, son of Rose-well (170), d. unmarried, about 1840; lived in New York during his latter years.

189. 170. (IX.) ABIGAIL SALTONSTALL, dau. of Rosewell (170), m. 23 June, 1799, Dr. William Handy of Newport, afterwards of New York.

Children : —
1. Caroline, b. 1 Aug., 1800; m. William Erskin Gold.
   Children : —
   1a. William.
   2a. Fanny, m. D. F. Worcester.
   3a. Lizzie, m. Jno. R. Eliott.
   4a. Caroline, unmarried.
2. Elizabeth, b. 16 June, 1803; m. Jno. T. Dunbar.
   Child: Rosalie.
3. Ann, living in 1848.

190. 170. (IX.) ANN SALTONSTALL, dau. of Rosewell (170), m. Rev. Charles Seabury, Rector of St. James's Church, New London, Conn. He d. April, 1845. He was the son of the Rt. Rev. Samuel Seabury, who was ordained 21 Dec., 1753, as Deacon, 23 Dec., 1753, as Priest, both in London, and on 14 Nov., 1783, in Aberdeen, Scotland, as Bishop, and the first Bishop of the Protestant Episcopal Church in America. (For descendants see Part II. 190.)

191. 170. (IX.) HANNAH SALTONSTALL, dau. of Rosewell, d. unm. Sep., 1805.

192. 170. (IX.) WILLIAM SALTONSTALL, son of Rosewell,

m. Maria Hudson, an English lady.   He d. at Pensacola 26
Aug., 1842.
Children : —
   199. William.
   200. Mary Susan.
   201. Henry.
  193. 170. (IX.) MATHEW STEWART SALTONSTALL, son of
Rosewell (170), d. young.
  194. 175. (IX.) GURDON SALTONSTALL, son of Gilbert (175),
was Professor of Mathematics in the University of Alabama,
where he d. *s. p.*
  195. 175. (IX.) GILBERT SALTONSTALL, son of Gilbert (175),
b. in 1791; m. 3 July, 1814, Elizabeth, dau. of J. Starr of New
London; d. at Tuscaloosa, Ala., 6 Feb., 1833.
Children : —
   1. Harriet, d. unmarried.
   2. George, d. in infancy.
   3. Mary, d. in infancy.
   4. 202. Gurdon, d. unmarried.
   5. 203. Gilbert D.

  196. 178. (X.) MARY H. SALTONSTALL, dau. of Gurdon
(178), m. 21 July, 1812, Rev. Daniel Huntington. (Part II.
196.)
Children : —
   1. Anne Moore, m. 20 April, 1841, Alfred Hebard, then
     of Burlington, Iowa; in 1893 living in Red Oak,
     Iowa.   Children : —
     1a. Augustus Huntington, b. 21 June, 1842; m. Alice
       A. Partridge, 25 June, 1866, at St. Louis.   Child:
       Alfred Partridge, b. 16 Dec., 1867.
     2a. Adelaide Lockwood, b. 21 May, 1844.
     3a. Mary Saltonstall, b. 3 June, 1847.
     4a. Annie Moore, b. 9 Jan., 1852; d. 5 June, 1853.
   2. Hannah Saltonstall, b. 26 Aug., 1816; m. 10 Nov.,
     1841, Franklin Chappell of New London.   Chil-
     dren : —

1a. Frank Huntington, b. 1845.
2a. William Saltonstall, b. 6 April, 1847.
3a. Alfred Hebard, b. 12 May, 1849.

197. 178. (X.) WILLIAM WANTON SALTONSTALL, son of Gurdon (178), b. 19 Jan., 1793; m. 1826, Mary, dau. of Richard W. and Mary (Winthrop) Parkin of New London, Conn. He removed from New London to Chicago in 1838, and resided there till his death in 1862. He was appointed Register and Assignee in Bankruptcy in 1842 and held that office twenty years. He was most highly respected in Chicago.[1] She d. in Brooklyn, N. Y., 30 June, 1887, aged 90 years and 6 months.
Children: —

1. Gurdon Winthrop, b. 3 June, 1827; d. 19 Dec., 1893.
2. 204. Francis G.
3. 205. Mary Parkin.
4. Isabella Dudley, b. 19 Jan., 1832; d. Sep., 1832, bur. in Saltonstall tomb, New London.
5. William W., b. 16 April, 1834; d. 19 May, 1880, in New York.
6. Edward H., b. 24 April, 1836.
7. Richard Parkin, b. 29 Nov., 1838; d. in infancy.
8. Margaret Jane, b. 1840; d. in infancy.
9. 206. Lindall Winthrop.

198. 185. (X.) DUDLEY GILBERT SALTONSTALL, son of Joshua (185), b. 10 Sep., 1808; m. March, 1845, Sophia A. M. de Zocieur, b. 1819.
Children: —

1. 210. Dudley Edward.
2. 211. Gurdon Winthrop.

---

[1] A very just and feeling tribute to his memory appeared in the *Chicago Tribune* of 21 March, 1862. (Part II. 197.) His remains were interred in Graceland Cemetery, but removed in 1886 to the lot of his son, Francis G. Saltonstall, in Greenwood Cemetery, New York. In this lot also rest the remains of his mother, Hannah Saltonstall, of his wife Mary, of his children, William W., Gurdon Winthrop, Richard Parkin, and Margaret Jane.

Miniature likenesses of William Wanton (197) and Gurdon (178), his father, are in the possession of Francis G. Saltonstall (204).

3. 212. William Herbert, b. 18 Nov., 1851; lives in Toledo.
4. Lewis Francis, b. July, 1854.
5. Lillian Theodora, b. 1857; d. 1859.
6. 213. Richard Arthur, b. 12 Nov., 1859.
7. 214. Victor de Zocieur, b. Aug., 1862.

199. 192. (X.) WILLIAM SALTONSTALL, son of William (192), b. 1806. No record of the place of his birth; he went to the West and settled in Chicago about 1835; was engaged in business for many years. He m. 1st, —— Hogan, d. *s. p.*, in 1839 or 1840; m. 2d, —— Aiken. Living in 1894 in Chicago.

Children: —

1. Elizabeth, b. 28 Jan., 1841; m. Jan., 1858, William Miller of London, Eng.
2. Constance, b. 20 Aug., 1845; m. 30 Oct., 1878, Wm. L. Patton of New York.
3. 207. Brayton, b. 14 Jan., 1848; living 1893.
4. 208. Gilbert, b. 11 July, 1850; living 1893.
5. Grace Mabel, b. 10 April, 1858; m. 20 Jan., 1886, John L. Peirson of Chicago.
6. 209. Henry Lincoln, b. 8 July, 1860.
7. Gertrude, b. 1843; d. aged 7 years.

200. 192. (X.) MARY SUSAN SALTONSTALL, dau. of William (192), m. Thomas Marston Beare of Meriden, Conn.; d. 1 Oct., 1869.

Children: —

1. Thomas Marston, d. unmarried.
2. Charlotte, d. unmarried.
3. Isabel, m. Geo. Benj. Mickle of Bayside, L. I. Children: —
   1a. Andrew H., b. 5 Oct., 1856.[1]
   2a. George B.

---

[1] Andrew H. Mickle of Flushing, who, in conformity with legal requirements, adopted the surname of Saltonstall, his grandmother's maiden name, m. Susan S. Hunter of Berkeley Springs, W. Va., and has one child, Sophia Forest, b. 14 Aug., 1893.

4. James Johnston, d. unmarried.
5. Francis, d. in infancy.
6. Died in infancy.
7. Alice Van Wyck, m. Rev. William Seabury, 29 Oct.,
   1868. Children: —
   1a. Susan, b. 21 Dec., 1869.
   2a. Samuel, b. 22 Feb., 1873.
   3a. Lydia Winthrop, b. 6 April, 1874.
   4a. Muriel Gurdon, b. 3 Nov., 1875.
   5a. William Marston, b. 18 March, 1878.
8. Jane Johnston, m. Howard Phelps.   Child: Mabel
   Marston.
9. Louisa de Laguel, m. 21 Nov., 1871, Rudolph D.
   Townsend.   Child: Isabel D., b. April, 1874.

201. 192. (X.) HENRY SALTONSTALL, son of William (192),
d. about 1880.   He m. Grace —— of Meriden, who
was living in 1889.

203. 195. (X.) GILBERT D. SALTONSTALL, son of Gilbert
(195), M. D., m. Sarah, dau. of John Marseilles; lived in Jer-
sey City Heights, N. J.; Med. Inspec. Hudson Co. Board of
Health.
Children: —
   1. Florence, m. Dr. Henry Allers.
   2. Louisa Seabury.
   3. 215. Gilbert Dudley Gurdon.
   4. Laura.

204. 197. (XI.) FRANCIS G. SALTONSTALL, son of William
(197), b. 14 Nov., 1828, in New London, Conn.   Removed
with his father to Chicago in 1838.   In 1860 came to New
York, where he now resides.   He m. 1st, Jane C. Manning,
d. 1856, *s. p.;* m. 2d, Ella Borland Parkin, 18 April, 1872.
Children : —
   1. Grace M., b. 23 April, 1873.
   2. Ella Winthrop, b. 28 Nov., 1876.
   3. Mary Elizabeth, b. 21 July, 1881.
205. 197. (XI.) MARY PARKIN SALTONSTALL, dau. of Wil-

liam (197), b. 17 Oct., 1830; m. 19 May, 1851, W. S. Woodward of Brooklyn, L. I.; d. 15 Aug., 1890, in Brooklyn.

Children: —
1. William Rainey, b. 17 Jan., 1852 ; m. 30 Oct., 1872, Adelaide L. Phelps of Brooklyn.
2. Mary S., b. 1856; d. in infancy.
3. Cornelia Whipple, b. 15 Sep., 1859; m. 27 April, 1880, Dr. A. W. Catlin; d. 30 March, 1881.
4. Elizabeth L., b. 1862 ; m. 23 Sep., 1885, Dr. A. W. Catlin.
5. Frederick S., b. 19 Sep., 1865 ; m. 25 Sep., 1892, Mary Eva Woodward of Washington.
6. Clarence L., b. 23 Dec., 1868.

206. 197. (XI.) LINDALL WINTHROP SALTONSTALL, son of William (191), b. 3 Dec., 1843 ; Rector Christ Church, Hartford, Conn. He m. 2 Nov., 1892, Mrs. Frances M. Jasper of Dorchester, Mass.

210. 198. (XI.) DUDLEY EDWARD SALTONSTALL, son of Dudley (198), m. Annie, dau. of Samuel H. and Mary P. Satterlee. Living in Rye, N. Y., in 1892.

Children: —
1. 216. Satterlee, b. 19 July, 1870.
2. 217. Dudley, b. 22 June, 1874.
3. Clarence Sanford, b. 28 April, 1884 ; d. 5 Nov., 1888.

211. 198. (XI.) GURDON WINTHROP SALTONSTALL, son of Dudley (198), b. 23 Sep., 1848 ; m. 27 May, 1882, Florence M. Furguson in San Francisco, where he resided in 1888.

Child: —
Lillian Madeline, b. 6 June, 1883.

The Register of the Parish Church in Halifax begins in 1539, and contains baptisms, marriages, and burials of twenty-six townships or hamlets, all being within that parish. The entries are in Latin, and for the first seventy years are exceedingly difficult to decipher, in consequence of their being so closely written.

Forty-four marriages and one hundred and twenty baptisms of those bearing the name of Saltonstall are recorded in this register between the years 1540 and 1624, among the baptisms being that of Richard, son of Samuel (Sir Richard of New England) of Hipperholme, 4 April, 1586.

A somewhat remarkable circumstance is that no family bearing the name of Saltonstall is now known to exist in Great Britain.

In the record of burials we have that of "1598 Dec 29. Gibt Saltenstal (grandfather of Sir Richard of New England) Hipp 40ˢ in pecunijs 20ˢ anni redditq dedit et legavit scolæ gramāt vicariat de Hal"; of Richard Saltonstall of Warley, brother of the above, and of his daughter Agnes, 30 Nov., 1599, who signs herself in her will "of Saltonstall," and leaves legacies to her brothers Gilbert and Richard.

Church of St. John the Baptist, Halifax, Yorkshire.

(From a photograph taken for the Author)

PART II

HALIFAX, ENGLAND

" THE parish or vicarage of Halifax in the West Riding of Yorkshire and wapentake of Morley consists of twenty-six townships or hamlets, viz. : Barkisland, Brighouse, Eland, Eringden, Fixby, Greetland, Halifax, Heponstall, Hipperholme, Langfield, Linley, Midgley, Northouram, Norland, Ovenden, Rastrick, Rishworth, Stainland, Stansfield, Shelf, Skircoat, Sowerby, Soyland, Southouram, Warley, and Wadsworth. Saltonstall, Nether and Over, are in the township of Warley."

Hipperholme, the residence of many members of the Saltonstall family, " is perhaps so called from its being the higher Holme, in opposition to the lower and middle Holme, which lie beneath it. The word Holme denotes it to be on the top of the hill." [1]

The Rev. John Watson, in his " History and Antiquities of the Parish of Halifax," describing the Druidical House in that parish, says, pp. 26, 27 : —

In Warley, one of the townships constituting the parish or vicarage of Halifax in the West Riding of Yorkshire, lay the hamlet of Saltonstall, known to this day, though almost deserted, as Upper and Nether Saltonstall. " On a common called Saltonstall Moor is what the country people call the Rocking Stone. . . . It is a large piece of a rock, one end of which rests on several stones, between two of which is a pebble of different grit, seemingly put there for a support, and so

---

[1] See Watson's *History and Antiquities of the Parish of Halifax in Yorkshire*, 1775, pp. 314, 332.

placed that it could not possibly be taken out without breaking or removing the rocks, so that in all probability they have been laid together by art. . . . The other part of this stone is laid upon a kind of pedestal, broad at the bottom, but narrow in the middle; and round this pedestal is a passage, which from every appearance seems to have been formed by art, but for what purpose is the question. . . . In ancient Greece there was a custom of returning oracular answers by a voice uttered from a secret place without the inquirer seeing who spake to him. This was to give the greater sanction to what was delivered, as though it were some Deity who spoke. And why may not these artful Druids have practiced a juggle of this sort?"

"On Saltonstall Moor is also a large heap of stones, which, at a distance (for I had not an opportunity of viewing them near) looked like a carnedde rising to a considerable height, and which might possibly be the sepulchre of some considerable person, for human bodies have been actually found under such heaps."

A very interesting account of the Church of St. John Baptist in Halifax is given by Watson as follows: —

"The church was built in first part of twelfth century, and was dedicated to St. John Baptist, — 192 feet long, more than 62 feet broad, the tower being 117 feet to the top of the pinnacles." [1]

The records of this church from 1540 to 1624 contain 120 baptisms of the family of Saltonstall; from 1588 to 1599, 8 deaths; and from 1539 to 1639, 44 marriages.

In Domesday Book, Wakefield and Halifax are entered part of demesne lands of King Edward, where it continued till William I., who gave it (as some have asserted) by way of portion with his daughter Gundred to William, Earl Warren, or as others, with more probability, till Henry I. conveyed it, amongst others, to William, Earl of Warren and Surrey, etc.

[1] The pictures of this ancient church are from photographs recently taken for the author.

Interior of the Church of St. John the Baptist, Halifax, Yorkshire.

(From a photograph taken for the Author.)

6. GILBERT SALTONSTALL

WILL OF GILBERT SALTONSTALL OF SHELF IN THE PARISH OF HALIFAX[1]

In dei nōie Amen the XXVIIIth day of Marche in the yere of ou^r lorde MCCCCCXVIIth, I, Gilbt. Saltonstall of Shelfe in the poche of Halyfax holl of mynd and reason make my testament in this mañ.

First I bequeath my soull to Almighty God to ou^r Lady saynt Mary and to all the saynts in hevyñ, my body to be buryed in the churche of saynt John Baptyst in Halifax.

Also I bequeath to the vicar of the sayd churche in the name of my mortuary, my beast. Also I bequeath to the Seyllying of the said churche XX^s.

Residewe forsothe of all my goods not given nor bequeathede my detts thereof trewly content and paide, I give and bequeath to Edward Saltonstall and Wiłłm Saltonstall my sonnes which I ordeyne and constitute my executors, that they the same goods well and trewly dyspose as they shall thynk best for the spede by the ovᷤsyght of Edward Saltonstall my broder, Richard Saltonstall my son, John Drake and Richard Best.

In witness of which thyng to this my p̄nte testament I have sett to my sealle. Thies Witnesses, Sir Wiłłm Otts, prest, John Saltonstall, Richard Haldworth, and odders.

Provèd 28 April, 1518.

---

[1] Extracted from the Registry of the Prerogative Court of the Archbishop of York.

9. GILBERT SALTONSTALL (I.)

WILL OF GILBERT SALTONSTALL OF THE ROOKES

In the name of God Amen, the **XXIII** of November, in the yeare of our Lord 1598, I Gilbert Saltonstall of the Rookes, in the Countie of Yorke, gent, sicke in bodye, but of sounde and pfect memory, do make and sett downe this my p̃ente testament conteyning therein my last will in manner and sorte here after ensewing.

First I commend my soule into the hands of Almightie god my Creator from whome I did receive it, and my bodie to the earth whereof it was made, undoubtedly believing that this my body shall through the mightie power of Jesus Christ my redeemer being the resurrecc̃on and life itselfe be raised again at the sounde of the last trumpe and that then my soule entringe againe this my body shall wth theis eyes and no other behold that blessed savio^{r} that then shall come to iudge the worlde and receive from him throughe faith in his blood that most comfortable sentence of come ye blessed amongst the nomber of his elect and chosen children wch faith I humblie beseech him to strengthen and contynue in me so long as this my bodie and soule shall contynue together and grant me grace to direct this my will according and agreeing to and wth his most heavenlie and blessed will, so be it.

I give towards the repaire & mayntenance of the pish church of Halifax whereof it pleased god to make me a pishoñ, the sum of **XX**^{s} to be paid by my executor to the Churchwardens their for that use w^{th}in one yeare after my decease.

Item I give to the poore people inhabiting w^{th}in the towne of Halifax **XX**^{s} to be divided amongst them at the discretion of the church wardens there. Also I give to the poore people of the Townshipp of Hippholme ten pounds to be paid to them in ten years next after my death viz. eṽy year **XX**^{s} to be deliṽed to them at my house at the Rookes eṽy xpem-

nas even during the said ten yeares, and to the poor people
of the pish of wragbye ten shillings to be distributed amongst
them at and by the discretion of myne executo^r. Itm I give
unto Isabell my wife, ten pounds.

Itm, I give to Mary Saville my daughter ten pounds in full
satisfaction of all her filiall & childes part and porčon of all
my goods and chattells.

Itm, I give towards the repaire of the Chappell of Hippholme, otherwise called the East Field Chappell, or High-
cliff Chappell, XX^s.

The residue of all my goods and chattells as well reall as
personall my debts being paid and my funeralls discharged,
I give to Samuel Saltonstall my sonne whome I do ordeyne
and make executo^r of this my last will and testament, and I
do ordeyne and make Mr. Willm Ramsden of Longley and
my brother in lawe Samuel Ashton of Bissett Supervisors
thereof hoping that they will take some paines to see the
execucon thereof as my trust is in them.

In testimony whereof I have hereunto sett my hand and
seale the day and yeare first above written.

Signed and sealed in the pnce of theis whose names are
here under written.

Samuel Ashton, Mathewe Heather, Thomas Greene,
Thomas Walker.

Proved 9 January, 159⅞.

---

10. SAMUEL SALTONSTALL (II.)

EXTRACTS FROM WILL OF SAMUEL SALTONSTALL OF KING-
STON-UPON-HULL IN YORKSHIRE, FATHER OF SIR RICH-
ARD

" In the name of God Amen. the last day of December in
the tenth year of the Raigne of o^r soveraigne Lord James by
the grace of God Kings of England France & Ireland, Defender of the faith &c. & of Scotland the six and fortieth and

in the yeare of o^r lord god accordinge to the computaĉon of the church of England 1612, I Samuell Saltonstall of Kingston upon Hull, in the Countie of Kingston upon Hull, Esquire, beinge somewhat sicke in bodie but of good and perfect mynde and memorie thankes be to god, doe make and ordaine this my last will and testament in mañ & forme followinge that is to saye,

"First and principally I give & commende my soul into the hands of Almighty god my most mercifull father assuredly trustinge and faithfully beleevinge to have full and free remission of all my sinnes by the meritts, passion and precious bloudshedinge of my alone saviour and Redeemer Jesus Christ, and by him to have life everlastinge amongst the blessed Saints of God in the kingdome of heaven, and I comend my bodie to the Earth whereof it is made hopeinge that the same shall have a joyfull resurrection at the last daie, And I will that the same shalbe buried in decent & Christian buriall at the sight and discreĉon of my Executors."

Then follow a very large number of legacies and bequests dividing his estate of " Rogerthorpe in the parish of Badsworth and in Thorp Haamell and Thorp Audlen in the County of York," with a large personal estate, among his numerous children.   Prominent mention is made of his son Richard (Sir Richard 13), wherein he bequeaths to him an interest in "the Capitall Messuage or Tenement, grainge, or Hall, called Hasle, in the countie of Yorke, and of all the edifices buildings, orchards, gardinges, lands, tenements, meadows, pastures, feedings and other hereditament to the same belonginge or appertayninge wch I latelie had and purchased of Sr. Jarvis Clifton, Knight, and the ladie his wife." Providing for the care and tuition of his daughters; committing the tuition of his daughter Margaret, "during her minoritie, unto my good friend, Mr. John Kaye of Woodsome, Esquire," he being the father of Grace Kaye, the wife of Richard (39), son of Sir Richard.

The will concludes thus : —

" In witness whereof I the said Samuell Saltonstall have

The Old Chapel, Over Saltonstall.

hereunto sett my hand and seale the daie & yeare first above written. These beinge witnesses. John Graves, John Lister Junior, Edward Richardson, George Pease, Robert Hogg, William Foxley."

Proved 22 July, 1613.

WINTER-EDGE

"Winter-Edge," in Hipperholme, "so called from its being situated at the edge, or brink, of some lands called the Winters, or from being on the edge of an hill and subject to cold winterly blasts. This house is not at present the residence of any Gentleman; but everything shews that it has formerly been so. Under the garden-house is the following inscription : —

Garrulus insano crucietur mundus amore,
Dum mea perplacide vita serena placet.

Over the door of the garden-house, ' Meliora spero.' Still higher over the window, ' Contra vim mortis, non est medicamen in hortis.' In the said garden-house, and in an outbuilding are several specimens of curiously stained glass.

"This Winter-edge was held, 42 Eliz., of the crown in fee, by Samuel Saltonstall, of Huntwike, and has lately been in the possession of the Priestleys." [1]

---

12. SIR RICHARD SALTONSTALL, LORD MAYOR (II.)

EXTRACT FROM AN OLD FOLIO HISTORY OF LONDON PRINTED IN 1666

Under the head of " Sir Richard Saltonstall " is the following description of the Skinners Hall, the Guild or Company of which he was a member.

"In High St., called Dowgate, stands the Skinners Hall, a noble structure built of fine brick, and richly finished, the

[1] Watson's *History and Antiquities of the Parish of Halifax, in Yorkshire*, 1775, p. 235.

hall with right wainscot, and the great parlor with odoriferous wood (cedar). It is said to have cost £18,000 in building. This Hall was called Copped Hall by Dowgate in the Parish of St. John upon Wallbrook. In the 19th year of Edward the 2nd, Ralph Cobham possessed it with 5 shops, etc.

" The Skinners Company in London was incorporated by Edward 3rd in the first of his reign. They had two Brotherhoods of Corpus Christi, viz. one at St. Mary Spittle and the other at St. Mary Bethlem without Bishops gate. Richard the 2nd in the 13th of his reign granted them to make their two brotherhoods one by the name of the Fraternity of Corpus Christi of Furriers. Divers Royal persons were named to be Founders and Brethren of this Fraternity, viz. Six Kings, 5 Queens, 1 Prince, 9 dukes, 2 Earls, and 1 Lord; Kings Edward 3rd, Richard 2nd, Henry 4th, Henry 5th, Henry 6th and Edward the 4th.

"This Fraternity had also once every year on Corpus Christi day afternoon, a procession, which passed through the principal streets of the city wherein was borne more than one hundred lighted torches of wax (costly garnished) and about 200 clerks and priests in surplice and copes, singing, after which was the Sheriff, the mayor's sergeants, the council of the city, the mayor and aldermen in scarlet, and then the Skinners in their best liveries."

" Sir Richard was in Elizabeth's reign Sheriff, Lord Mayor, and Member Parliament for London."

EXTRACT FROM WILL OF SIR RICHARD SALTONSTALL

Bequests to the poor of St. Thomas' Hospital, St. Bartholomew's Hospital, and to the poor children of Christ's Hospital. " To thirty poor men which shall attend upon my body to my burial forty (sic) gowns of the price of ten shillings the yard. To the Company of Skinners in London ten pounds to be spent upon them in a dinner to be made at my burial day, to the Master Wardens and Commonalty of the same Company one hundred pounds (for loans to honest

PEDIGREE OF POINTZ (OR POYNTZ)

FROM THE VISITATION OF ESSEX

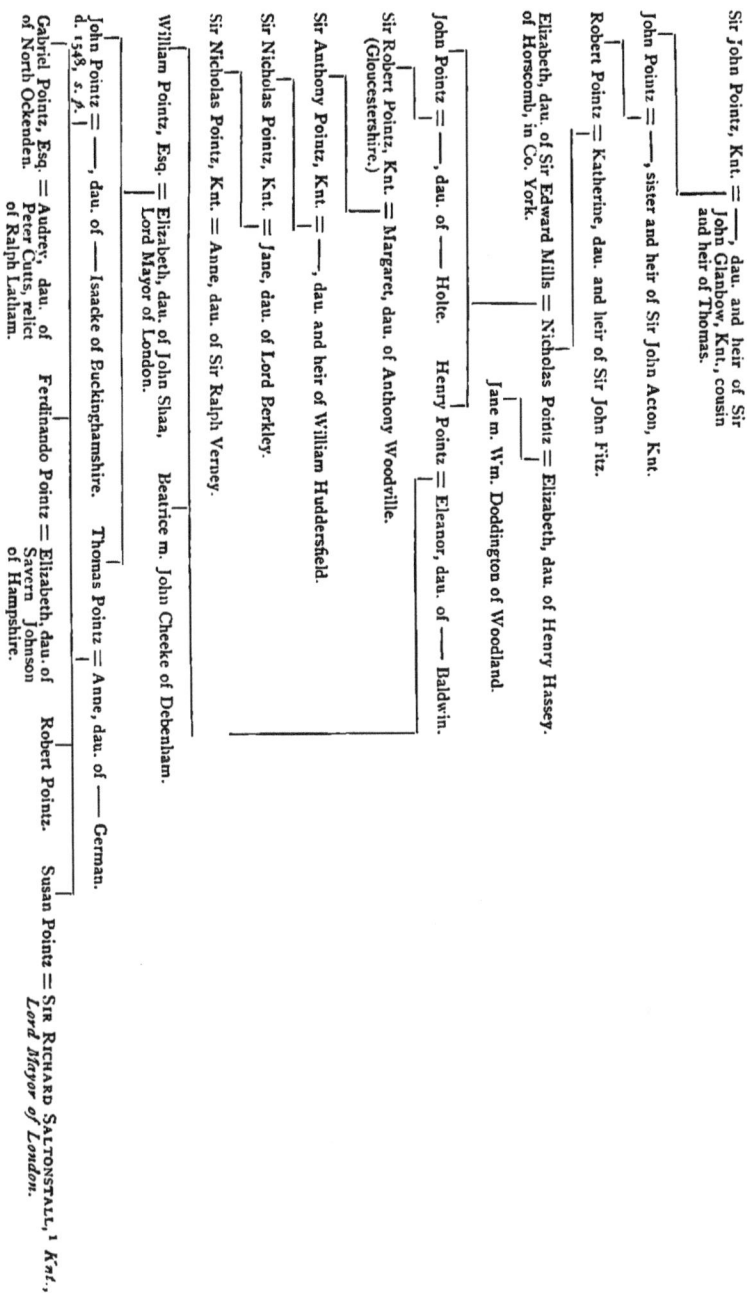

Sir John Pointz, Knt. = ——, dau. and heir of Sir John Glanbow, Knt., cousin and heir of Thomas.

John Pointz = ——, sister and heir of Sir John Acton, Knt.

Robert Pointz = Katherine, dau. and heir of Sir John Fitz.

Elizabeth, dau. of Sir Edward Mills = Nicholas Pointz = Elizabeth, dau. of Henry Hassey. of Horscomb, in Co. York.

Jane m. Wm. Doddington of Woodland.

John Pointz = ——, dau. of —— Holte.   Henry Pointz = Eleanor, dau. of —— Baldwin.

Sir Robert Pointz, Knt. = Margaret, dau. of Anthony Woodville. (Gloucestershire.)

Sir Anthony Pointz, Knt. = ——, dau. and heir of William Huddersfield.

Sir Nicholas Pointz, Knt. = Jane, dau. of Lord Berkley.

Sir Nicholas Pointz, Knt. = Anne, dau. of Sir Ralph Verney.

William Pointz, Esq. = Elizabeth, dau. of John Shaa, Lord Mayor of London.   Beatrice m. John Cheeke of Debenham.

John Pointz = ——, dau. of —— Isaacke of Buckinghamshire.   Thomas Pointz = Anne, dau. of —— German. d. 1548, s. p.

Gabriel Pointz, Esq. = Audrey, dau. of Peter Cutts, relict of Ralph Latham.   Ferdinando Pointz = Elizabeth, dau. of Savern Johnson of Hampshire.   Robert Pointz.   Susan Pointz = SIR RICHARD SALTONSTALL,[1] Knt., of North Ockenden.   Lord Mayor of London.

[1] This connection with the family of Pointz is given in Visitation of Hertfordshire in 1634, and also in Clutterbuck's History of Hertfordshire.

young men being merchant adventurers and free of said Company). I give and bequeath to some godly and learned
preacher ten shillings to make a sermon at my burial. One
hundred pounds to be distributed to the poor within the parish of Halifax, in ready money or in penny loaves of good
sweet and wholesome bread in remembrance of me the said
Richard Saltonstall, Alderman, and upon the necessary and
needful repairations and ornaments of the parish Church " —
beside providing liberally for his widow and numerous children.

Proved 19 May, 1601.

13. SIR RICHARD SALTONSTALL OF HUNTWICKE
(III.)

" The first time his (Sir Richard's) name appears in the
records of the Courts of the Massachusetts Bay Company
was Mar. 5, 162⅜, where it immediately succeeds the names
of the officers; and it will be found in those records that his
name almost invariably stands at the head of the Assistants.
When the proposition of Gov. Cradock to transfer the government of the Company from England to the Colony was
to be argued in a General Court of the Company, on the 29th
of Aug., 1629, Sir Richard was named first of those who
were designated to advocate the transfer. At a General
Court, held 15 Oct., 1629, two committees were appointed,
one on the part of the adventurers who were to remain in
England, and the other on the part of those to go over, in
order to draw up articles of agreement between the ' adventurers here at home and the planters that are to go over, as
well as for arranging and settling the joint stock, as for recon-
ciling any difference that may happen upon this change
[transfer] of government.' Sir Richard was appointed chair-
man of the committee on the part of the emigrant adventurers. At a General Court held September 29, 1629, ' were
read the orders made the 28th and 29th of August last, con-

cerning the transferring of the patent and government of the plantation into New England, but that business being of great and weighty consequences, is thought fit to be deferred for determination until Sir Richard Saltonstall, Mr. Johnson, and other gentlemen, be come up to London, and may be here present.' It is probable that his residence continued to be in Yorkshire until about the time he went to America, and for that reason he was not a constant attendant at the Courts of the Company.[1] At a General Court held Dec. 1, 1629, in order to fulfil those articles of agreement, the Company appointed five 'undertakers' among those about to go over, of whom Sir Richard was named next after the Governor, and five others among those that were to remain in England.

"Early in April, 1630, Sir Richard, with his sons and daughters, embarked at Yarmouth, on board the Arbella, and arrived at Salem on the 12th of June. Those passengers, by this and other ships, who landed at Salem, very soon proceeded to Charlestown, where their number was much enlarged by the arrival of passengers in other ships that came directly to Charlestown. Here this company was very soon divided into two portions. One of them, with Sir Richard as their leader, and Mr. Phillips as their minister, went to plant Watertown, and without delay (July 28) organized a church, and Sir Richard was the first subscriber to the church covenant. The other portion of the Company, with Gov. Winthrop as their leader, and Mr. Wilson as their minister, remained in Charlestown, and organized a church, which was soon afterwards transferred to Boston.

"Sir Richard remained in America less than a year. On the 29th of March, 1631, he with his two daughters and one of his younger sons embarked for England, and, it is said, fixed his residence in London, having sold his estate in York-

---

[1] In Thoresby's *History of Leeds*, Whitaker's second edition, 1816, mention is made of the purchase by Sir Richard Saltonstall of Ledsham, and subsequent sale by him of Ledsham Hall to the Earl of Stratford. Pedigrees of Yorkshire families, West Riding, Harleian MSS. 4630.

shire about the time he became one of the adventurers in the
Massachusetts Bay Company. He never returned to America ; yet we may presume that he proposed, and was expected
to return, as he was elected an Assistant by the General
Court in May, 1633. He continued to be a proprietor of
Watertown for several years. Mar. 3, 163⅚, the Court granted
him 100 acres of meadow in Watertown, and in the allotment of Beaver Brook plowlands, 1636, 30 acres were assigned
to him, among ' the townsmen then inhabiting.' This assign-
ment was made because his estate in Watertown was man-
aged by his servants, in his name, for whom he was responsible ; and this probably continued only until his sons Samuel
and Henry attained to their majority. In the list of possessions ordered to be made in 1642, Sir Richard's name does
not appear, but the names of those two sons.

" He, with Viscount Say and Seal, Lord Brooke, and
others, was one of the patentees of Connecticut, and he was
active in promoting its settlement. For this purpose he sent
over a bark of 40 tons, with 20 servants, which arrived at
Boston, June 16, 1635. His interest in the Connecticut
plantation did not, however, seem to diminish his regard for
Massachusetts Bay. This was evinced by his efficient super-
intendence of its interests in England, by the settlement of
three of his sons, and the education of the other, in Massachusetts, and by his legacy to Harvard College.

" Among those who subscribed the two letters, dated London, Aug. 29, 1629, one of them addressed to Gov. Endicott, and
the other to the ministers of Salem, and likewise that letter
dated on board the Arbella, April 7, 1630, addressed to their
Christian friends and brethren they were about leaving in
England, the name of Sir Richard Saltonstall stands first.
In addition to this circumstance, there is in them so much
Christian charity, such a courteous tone, a spirit so liberal
for that day, and so much in harmony with his admirable letter, addressed to the ministers of Boston a few years afterwards, that we may fairly conjecture, if not confidently assert,
that he was the author of all of them. Of that letter of

expostulation and rebuke to the ministers of Boston above referred to, Dr. Francis justly says, 'this letter is a noble testimony to his charitable and Christian feelings, and seems to me scarcely less to deserve the praise of being beyond the age, than the celebrated farewell address of John Robinson at Leyden.' A character in all points so exemplary, so good and so great, so exempt from any seeming blemish or defect, it is not easy to find among the early worthies of New England; and his honorable descent, and the superior social position, so evidently conceded to him by the other adventurers, are feeble claims to our respect, compared with his eminent personal worth.

" After he returned to England, he received marked tokens of the public confidence. His influence at court is shown by his success in thwarting the machinations of the enemies of Massachusetts Bay. In 1644 he was ambassador to Holland,[1] and while there his portrait was painted by the celebrated Rembrandt. It is now in the possession of the family of the late Hon. Leverett Saltonstall, and it is very highly valued as a work of art. Upon it is this inscription: 'Ætat. Suæ 58, A. D. 1644.'[2] In 1649 he was one of the High Court of Justice appointed to try Duke Hamilton, Lord Capel, the Earl of Holland, the Earl of Norwich, and Sir John Owen, for high treason, of whom the first three were condemned and executed, and the other two were condemned, but pardoned."[3]

THE HUMBLE REQUEST

The humble request of his Majesty's loyal subjects, the governour and company late gone for New England, to the rest of their brethren, in and of the CHURCH OF ENGLAND; for the obtaining of their prayers, and the removal of suspicions and misconstruction of their intentions.

London, printed for John Bellamie, 1630. (4to.)

[1] He was in Holland in 1644, as stated in Rosamond's letter to her brother Samuel, p. 106, but there is no proof that he was ambassador.
[2] It is in the possession of the author, and is here reproduced in heliotype.
[3] Bond's *Genealogies and History of Watertown*, vol. i. pp. 915, 916.

Reverend Fathers and Brethren:

The general rumour of this solemn enterprise, wherein ourselves with others, through the Providence of the Almighty are engaged, as it may spare us the labour of imparting our occasion unto you, so it gives us the more encouragement to strengthen ourselves by the procurement of the prayers and blessings of the Lord's faithful servants. For which end we are bold to have recourse unto you, as those whom God hath placed nearest his throne of mercy; which as it affords you the more opportunity, so it imposeth the greater bond upon you to intercede for his people in all their straits. We beseech you therefore, by the mercies of the Lord Jesus, to consider us as your brethren, standing in very great need of your help, and earnestly imploring it. And howsoever your charity may have met with some occasion of discouragement through the misreport of our intentions, or through the disaffection or indiscretion of some of us, or rather amongst us, for we are not of those that dream of perfection in this world; yet we desire you would be pleased to take notice of the principals and body of our company, as those who esteem it our honour to call the Church of England, from whence we rise, our dear mother; and cannot part from our native country, where she specially resideth, without much sadness of heart, and many tears in our eyes, ever acknowledging that such hope and part as we have obtained in the common salvation, we have received in her bosom, and sucked it from her breasts. We leave it not, therefore, as loathing that milk wherewith we were nourished there; but, blessing God for the parentage and education, as members of the same body shall always rejoice in her good, and unfeignedly grieve for any sorrow shall ever betide her, and while we have breath sincerely desire and endeavour the continuance and abundance of her welfare, with the enlargement of her bounds in the kingdom of Christ Jesus.

Be pleased, therefore, reverend fathers and brethren, to help forward this work now in hand; which if it prosper, you shall be the more glorious; howsoever, your judgment is with the Lord, and your reward with your God. It is an usual and laudable exercise of your charity to commend to the prayers of your congregations the necessities and straits of your private neighbours. Do the like for a church springing out of your own bowels. We conceive much hope that this remembrance of us, if it be frequent and fervent, will be a most prosperous gale in our sails, and provide such a passage and welcome for us, from the God of the whole earth, as both we which shall find it, and yourselves with the rest of our friends who shall hear of it, shall be much enlarged to bring in such daily returns of thanksgivings, as the specialties of his providence and goodness may justly challenge at all our hands. You are not ignorant, that the Spirit of God stirred up the apostle Paul to make continual mention of the church of Philippi, (which was a colony from Rome;) let the same spirit, we beseech you, put you in mind, that are the Lord's remembrancers, to pray for us without ceasing, (who are a weak colony from yourselves,) making continual request for us to God in all your prayers.

What we intreat of you that are the ministers of God, that we also crave at the hands of all the rest of our brethren, that they would at no time forget us in their private solicitations at the throne of grace.

If any there be, who through want of clear intelligence of our course, or tenderness of affection towards us, cannot conceive so much of our way as we could desire, we would intreat such not to despise us, nor to desert us in their prayers and affections; but to consider rather, that they are so much the more bound to express the bowels of their compassion towards us, remembering always that both nature and grace doth ever bind us to relieve and rescue, with our utmost and speediest power, such as are dear unto us, when we conceive them to be running uncomfortable hazards.

What goodness you shall extend to us, in this or any other Christian kindness, we, your brethren in Christ Jesus, shall labour to repay, in what duty we are or shall be able to perform; promising, so far as God shall enable us, to give him

no rest on your behalfs, wishing our heads and hearts may be
fountains of tears for your everlasting welfare, when we shall
be in our poor cottages in the wilderness, overshadowed with
the spirit of supplication, through the manifold necessities
and tribulations which may not altogether unexpectedly nor,
we hope, unprofitably befall us.

And so commending you to the grace of God in Christ, we
shall ever rest your assured friends and brethren,

JOHN WINTHROP, GOV.   RICH : SALTONSTALL,
CHARLES FINES,   ISAAC JOHNSON,
                       THO. DUDLEY,
GEORGE PHILLIPS, &c.   WILLAM CODDINGTON, &c.

From Yarmouth, aboard the Arbella, 7 April, 1630.[1]

"Soon after the removal of the emigrants from Salem to
Charlestown, a large portion of them, with Sir Richard Saltonstall as their leader, accompanied by Rev. George Phillips
as their pastor,[2] proceeded about four miles up Charles River,
and commenced a settlement, at first sometimes called Sir
Richard Saltonstall's plantation, but soon after, by the Court,
named Watertown.[3]   It is difficult to determine the date of

[1] Hubbard's "History," *Mass. Hist. Coll.* 2d series, vol. v. p. 126.
[2] Nathaniel Saltonstall (105) m. Anna, daughter of Samuel White of Haverhill,
whose wife Sarah was great-granddaughter of Rev. George Phillips.
[3] At the dedication of the Cambridge Hospital, 29 April, 1886, Dr. Morrill
Wyman in his interesting address speaks of the spot where Sir Richard landed, as
follows : —
"This spot is of historical interest. On the 12th of June, 1630, that excellent
Knight, Sir Richard Saltonstall, liberal far beyond his age, accompanied by John
Winthrop, the Governor, landed at Salem. After a short stay at Charlestown Sir
Richard in July moved up the Charles River in search of wider and better fields.
As he rowed he must have seen on either hand extensive and uninviting marshes
which forbade a landing." "As he turned the bend in the river just below, he
might have seen this high and well wooded bank, its southern slope descending
sharply to the water's edge. Here he landed, and from that time here has been
the public landing. Near at hand was a water brook, now shorn of its former
proportions, but still pouring its narrow stream into the river. Here, having found
both wood and water, he and those with him took up their abode." (This spot, known
until very recently as "Sir Richard's Landing," is in the immediate vicinity of
Mount Auburn, and of "Elmwood," the home of the late James Russell Lowell.)
Here was to be the 'town' (Watertown). Here was organized, on the 30th of July,
only forty-eight days after landing at Salem, a church of forty members, with Sir
Richard at its head. Thus was formed 'the first church in New England that

the removal from Salem to Charlestown, as it was probably a gradual process; nor is the exact date known when Sir Richard and his followers left the latter place for Watertown. But their stay in Charlestown must have been short; for only forty-eight days elapsed after the landing of Sir Richard at Salem, before Watertown affairs had become sufficiently matured to organize a church, when forty men, with Sir Richard at their head, signed the covenant.

"It seems clear that only three towns in the colony can claim priority of settlement over Watertown [Salem, Charlestown, and Dorchester]. . . . That a large number of settlers accompanied Sir Richard to Watertown, or very soon followed him, is evident from the following considerations: In the first place ' about forty men ' signed the covenant on the 30th of July. It is known that some of them, probably most of them, had families. . . . There is good reason to believe that others, some of them having large families, did not then sign the covenant, not being titled to church membership. In the next place, on the 30th of November, only four months later, the Court of Assistants passed an order to collect of the several plantations, except Salem and Dorchester, £60 for the maintenance of the two ministers; and the portion of the several towns was as follows: Boston £20, Watertown £20, Charlestown £10, Roxbury £6, Medford £3, Winnesemet £1. When it is considered that at this time most of the office holders and men of large estates, except Sir Richard, belonged to Boston and Charlestown, and that assessments were made according to estates or possessions, it is not unreasonable to suppose that the population of Watertown was then equal to that of Boston and Charlestown. . . .

distinctly adopted the Independent Congregational order.' Here was its home-stall. Near Elmwood Avenue stood the house built by Sir Richard for that learned minister, that staunch advocate of independent Congregationalism and of civil rights, the Rev. George Phillips, the first minister of Watertown. In this immediate neighborhood was the first meeting-house. Where else than upon this homestall, with such surroundings, and such associations, could better be built this temple, dedicated to God in the name of humanity? Here all may lay their gifts upon the same altar, and in communion listen to the Divine words, ' Inasmuch as ye have done it unto one of the least of these my brethren, ye have done it unto me.' "

" Until the end of the first year (1630) all the plantations
and people in the colony, excepting Salem and Dorchester,
appear to have been regarded as two churches or congregations, with their two pastors, between whom the assessment
for pastoral maintenance was to be equally divided. One of
them was the church organized in Charlestown, embracing
Boston, and probably the few people of Roxbury, Medford,
and Winnesemet. Here Governor Winthrop engaged to
provide accommodation for the minister, Mr. Wilson. The
other church was that organized in Watertown, where Sir
Richard engaged to provide for the minister, Mr. Phillips." [1]

THE WATERTOWN COVENANT

July 30, 1630.

We whose names are hereto subscribed having through
God's mercy escaped out of the pollutions of the world, and
been taken into the society of his people, with all thankfulness do hereby, both with heart and hand, acknowledge his
gracious goodness and fatherly care towards us ; and for further and more full declaration thereof to the present and
future ages, have undertaken (for the promoting of his glory
and the Church's good, and the honor of our blessed Jesus,
in our more full and free subjecting of ourselves and ours,
under his gracious government, in the practice of and obedience unto all his holy ordinances and orders, which he hath
pleased to prescribe and impose upon us) a long and hazardous voyage from East to West, from Old England in Europe
to New England in America ; that we may walk before him,
and serve him without fear in holiness and righteousness all
the days of our lives ; and being safely arrived here, and thus
far onwards peaceably preserved by his special providence,
that we may bring forth our intentions into actions, and perfect our resolutions, in the beginnings of some just and meet
executions, we have separated the day above written from all
other services, and dedicated it wholly to the Lord in divine
employments, for a day of afflicting our souls, and humbling

[1] Bond's *Genealogies and History of Watertown*, vol. i. pp. 978, 979.

ourselves before the Lord to seek him and at his hands
a way to walk in by fasting and prayer that we might know
what was good in his sight; and the Lord was intreated
of us.

For in the end of that day, after the finishing of our pub-
lick duties, we do all before we depart, solemnly, and with
all our hearts personally, man by man, for ourselves and ours
(charging them before Christ and his elect Angels, even them
that are not here with us this day, *or are yet unborn*, that
they keep the promise unblameably and faithfully unto the
coming of our Lord Jesus) promise, and enter into a sure
covenant with the Lord our God, and before him with one
another by oath and serious protestation made, to renounce
all idolatry and superstition, will worship, all human traditions and inventions whatsoever, in the worship of God; and
forsaking all evil ways, do give ourselves wholly unto the
Lord Jesus, to do him faithful service, observing and keeping all his statutes, commands, and ordinances, in all matters
concerning our reformation; his worship, administrations,
ministry, and government; and in the carriage of ourselves
among, and one towards another, as he hath prescribed in
his holy word.

Further swearing to cleave unto that alone and the true
sence and meaning thereof to the utmost of our power, as
unto the most clear light and infallible rule, and all-sufficient
canon in all things that concern us in this our way. In
witness of all, we do examine, and in the presence of God
hereto set our names or marks in the day and year above
written.

(Signed by Sir Richard Saltonstall and forty others.)

SIR RICHARD AND THE SETTLEMENT OF WATERTOWN

"Sir Richard Saltonstall early engaged in the New England enterprise, and in the charter of Charles I. is the first
named Associate to the six original patentees of Massachusetts Bay, and was appointed the first Assistant. On board

the Arbella, at Yarmouth, he, with Gov. Winthrop and others, signed that 'Humble request of his Majesty's loyal subjects the governour and company late gone for New England to the rest of their brethren in and of the Church of England,' in and which they take so affecting a leave of their native land on their departure for their 'poor cottages in the wilderness.' He arrived at Salem in the Arbella, 12th June, 1630. On the 17th of June the Governor, and some of the principal persons, left Salem and travelled through the woods to Charlestown. Prince says the want of good water and other conveniences at Charlestown, 'made several go abroad upon discovery. Some go over to Shawmut. Some go without Charlestown neck and travel up into the main, till they came to a place well watered, whither Sir Richard Saltonstall with Mr. Phillips and several others went and settled a plantation, and called it Watertown.' Johnson says 'this town began by occasion of Sir Richard Saltonstall, who at his arrival, having some store of cattel and servants, they wintered in those parts.' There they entered into a very liberal church covenant, 30 July, 1630, which Dr. Mather has published at large, adding, 'about forty men, whereof the first was that excellent knight, Sir Richard Saltonstall, then subscribed this instrument.'

"He was present as first Assistant, at the first Court of Assistants, which was held at Charlestown, 23 Aug., 1630, at which time various orders and regulations were made concerning the planting and government of this infant colony.

"The suffering of those who engaged in this new settlement in the wilderness was extreme the first winter, and Sir Richard Saltonstall became discouraged from remaining himself, but left his two eldest sons. Gov. Winthrop has recorded in his journal, that '29 March, 1630, he, with his two daughters, and one of his younger sons, came down to Boston and stayed there that night at the governour's, and the next morning, accompanied with Mr. Pierce and others, departed for their ship at Salem.'[1]

[1] When Newtown (Cambridge) was settled, says Rev. Lucius R. Paige in his

"Sir Richard Saltonstall always continued to be the friend of the colony, and was actively engaged in their behalf. Two of his sons continued here, and he was largely interested as a proprietor. When Sir Christopher Gardner attempted to injure the colony by misrepresentations, and on other similar occasions (for Massachusetts was troubled from its infancy by the false accusations of enemies), he rendered the colony great assistance, and interceded with the government in its favor.[1]

"Sir Richard Saltonstall was a man of singular liberality in religion, for a Puritan of the age in which he lived, and was offended at the bigotry of his associates, who were no sooner secure from prosecution themselves, than they began to prosecute in their turn. He remonstrated against this inconsistency, and wrote from England to Mr. Cotton and Mr. Wilson a letter, which Hutchinson highly commends for its catholic spirit, and which deserves a place in this memoir.

"This letter, Gov. Hutchinson says, must have been written between 1645 and 1653, fourteen years at least after Sir Richard Saltonstall left this country, and it shows that he con-

---

History of Cambridge, pp. 7, 8, "It would seem that Sir Richard Saltonstall intended to build a house, and a lot of land was assigned to him for that purpose; but he went to England in the spring of 1631, and did not return." "The Proprietors' Records show that what is now known as Winthrop Square was allotted" to him; "but when it was ascertained that he would not return from England, the lot was assigned for a 'Market Place,' by which name it was known for more than two centuries."

[1] "Sir Christopher Gardner, Thomas Morton, and Philip Ratcliffe, being sent back to England for several misdemeanors, endeavored what they could to undermine the plantation of the Massachusetts, by preferring complaints against them to the king and council; being set on by Sir Ferdinando Gorges and Capt. Mason, which had begun plantations about Pascataqua, and aimed at the general government of New England, for their agent, Capt. Neale, as was said.

"Their petition was affirmed to contain many sheets of paper, wherein, among some truth represented, were many false accusations laid to their charge; as if they intended rebellion, having cast off their allegiance, and that their ministers and people did continually rail against the State, Church, and Bishops of England. But *Sir Richard Saltonstall*, Mr. Humphry, and Mr. Cradock, the first governor of the company, being then in England, gave a full answer to all those bold allegations and accusations."— Hubbard's "History," *Mass. Hist. Coll.* 2d series, vol. v. p. 145.

tinued his connection with the principal settlers, and felt a lively interest in the honor and welfare of the colony.

" Sir Richard Saltonstall was also one of the patentees of Connecticut with Lord Say and Seal, Lord Brook, and others, and a principal associate with them in the first settlement of that colony. They appointed John Winthrop governor, and commissioned him to erect a fort at the mouth of Connecticut River. In 1635, Sir Richard Saltonstall sent over twenty men to take possession of land for him under this patent and to make settlements." [1]

COPY OF THE LETTER FROM SIR RICHARD SALTONSTALL TO MR. COTTON AND MR. WILSON

Reverend and deare friends, whom I unfeignedly love and respect.

It doth not a little grieve my spirit to heare what sadde things are reported dayly of your tyranny and persecutions in New England, as that you fine, whip, and imprison men for their consciences. First, you compell such to come into your assemblyes as you know will not joyne with you in your worship, and when they show their dislike thereof, or witness against it, then you styrre up your magistrates to punish them for such (as you conceyve) their publicke affronts. Truely, friends, this your practice of compelling any in matters of worship to doe that whereof they are not fully persuaded, is to make them sin, for soe the Apostle (Rom. 14 and 23), tells us, and many are made hypocrites thereby, conforming in their outward man for feare of punishment. We pray for you, and wish you prosperitie in every way, hoped the Lord would have given you so much light and love there, that you might have been eyes to God's people here, and not to practice those courses in a wilderness which you went so far to prevent. These rigid wayes have layed you very low in the hearts of the saynts. I doe assure you I have heard them pray in the publique assemblies that the Lord would

[1] A Sketch of Haverhill, by Hon. Leverett Saltonstall of Salem, *Mass. Hist. Coll.* 2d series, vol. iv. p. 156.

give you meeke and humble spirits, not to strive so much for uniformity as to keepe the unity of the spirit in the bond of peace.

When I was in Holland, [1644] about the beginning of our warres, I remember some Christians there, that then had serious thoughts of planting in New England, desired me to write to the governour thereof to know if those that differ from you in opinion, yet houlding the same foundation in religion, as Anabaptists, Seekers, Antinomians, and the like, might be permitted to live among you, to which I received this short answer from your then governour, Mr. Dudley. God forbid (said he) our love for the truth should be growne soe could that we should tolerate errours ; and when (for satisfaction of myself and others) I desired to know your grounds, he referred me to the books written here between the Presbyterians and Independents, which if that had been sufficient, I needed not have been so farre to understand the reasons of your practice. I hope you doe not assume to yourselves infallibilitie of judgement, when the most learned of the Apostles confesseth he knew but in part and saw but darkely as through a glass, for God is light, and no further than he doth illumine us can we see, be our parts and learning never so great. Oh that all those who are brethren, though yet they cannot thinke and speake the same things, might be of one accord in the Lord. Now the God of patience and consolation grant you to be thus mynded towards one another, after the example of Jesus Christ our blessed Savyor, in whose everlasting arms of protection hee leaves you who will never leave to be

Your truly and much affectionate friend in the nearest union,

RIC. SALTONSTALL.

For my reverend and worthly much-esteemed friends, Mr. Cotton and Mr. Wilson, preachers to the church which is at Boston, in New England, give this.

SIR RICHARD AND HARVARD COLLEGE

President Quincy says: " Second only to Harvard and Winthrop, in order of time, amount of benefactions, and value of services, stands Sir Richard Saltonstall; that excellent Knight, as he is called by Mather, that much honored and upright hearted servant of Christ, as he is denominated by Johnson. . . . During a life protracted beyond the middle of the seventeenth century he continued the faithful, active, devoted friend of the colony and the college. He defended both against the assaults and aspersions of their respective enemies, and, on all occasions, vindicated their character and interests. He was not, however, blind to the failings nor insensible to the inconsistencies of the ecclesiastical leaders of the colony. His kind and catholic spirit was touched with sorrow at the persecutions they were carrying on against liberty of conscience. Nor could the interest which he took in the honor and welfare of New England be in any way more strikingly manifested than it is in that deep and solemn tone of remonstrance in which he addresses John Cotton and John Wilson, the most powerful of all those ecclesiastical leaders, on the tyranny and persecutions in New England.

" We pray for you, says he, that the Lord will give you light and love. These rigid ways are laying you very low in the hearts of the saints. By compelling any in matters of worship you make many hypocrites. ' Do not assume to yourselves infallibility of judgment, when the most learned of the Apostles confesseth he knew but in part, and saw but darkly, as through a glass.' During life he had contributed by his purse and influence to the foundation and advancement of the Seminary. At his death he made a liberal bequest for its support." [1]

[1] Quincy's *History of Harvard University*, vol. i. p. 163.

GRANTS OF LAND IN WATERTOWN TO SIR RICHARD
SALTONSTALL

25 July, 1636. A grant of the Great Dividents lotted out
by the Freemen to all the Townsmen then inhabiting being
120 in number, the land being divided into foure Divisions,
every Division being 160 rods in breadth. Beginning next
to the small Lots, and bounded with Cambridge Line on the
Northside & the Plowland on the South, to be laid out successively one after another (all the Meddows and cartwaies
only being excepted) for them to inclose or feed in common.
Sr Richard Salteston, one hundred acres.

28 Feb., 1636. A grant of the Plowlands at Beverbroke
Planes, devided and Lotted out by the Freemen to all the
Townesmen then inhabiting, being 106 in number, &c.
Sr Richard Salteston, thirty acres.

26 June, 1636. A grant of the Remote or Westpine Meddows, &c.
Richard Saltenstall, thirty acres.

Sr Richard Saltenstall. 1. An Homestall of Sixteen Acres
by estimation, bounded the Northeast wth Thomas Brigan &
Robert Keies the Southeast with the River, the Southwest
wth the Highway & the Northwest wth George Phillips granted
to him.

2. Foure Acres of Vpland by estimation, bounded the
Northwest wth George Phillips, the South wth Isaac Hart &
the East wth Joseph Cooke granted to him.

3. Twenty Acres of Vpland by estimation bounded the
Southeast wth the highway, the Southwest wth Pequsset Med-
dow, the Northwest wth William Hammond and Thomas
Boydon granted to him.

4. One Hundred Acres of remote Meddow by estimation
bounded wth the Farmeland granted to him.

5. One Hundred Acres of Vpland by estimation being a
great Divident adioyning to his meddow and bounded wth the
Farmeland granted to him.

6. Two Hundred Acres of Vpland by estimation adioyn-

ing to his great Divident, & bounded wth the farmeland granted to him.

7. Twenty Acres of Plowland by estimation bounded the South wth Edward How, the North wth the highway, the West wth John Whitney & the East wth John Knights granted to him.

8. Ten Acres of Meddow in Plaine Meddow by estimation bounded the East wth the brooke, the West wth William Paine, the North wth the highway and the South wth common land granted to him.

9. Thirty Acres of Remote Meddow by estimation bounded wth the great Dividents & the seventy one lott granted to him.

10. Thirty Acres of Plowland by estimation in the hither Plaine bounded the South wth the River, the North wth the highway the East wth Simon Eire and the West wth John Traine granted to him.

11. Twenty eight acres & an halfe of Vpland by estimation beyond the further plaine and the thirty nine lott granted to him.[1]

SIR RICHARD AND THE CONNECTICUT SETTLEMENT

Quite an interesting episode was the undertaking of Sir Richard to establish a settlement in Connecticut under the patent granted to Lord Say and Seal, Lord Brook, himself, and others. After the appointment by them of John Winthrop the younger as governor of the new colony, Sir Richard in 1635 sent out a bark, according to his own narration, in his letter of complaint to Governor John Winthrop, at his own expense.[2] The bark was owned and provisioned by himself, and between twenty and thirty men were in the company, employed by him, with cattle, material for building, and plen-

[1] *Watertown Records, Prepared for Publication by the Historical Society,* 1894, pp. 5, 6, 10, 69.
[2] This letter, in the author's possession, is in Sir Richard's handwriting, is signed by him, has his seal with arms and crest nearly perfect, and is endorsed by Governor Winthrop "Sr Richard Saltenstall 1636." It was printed in the *Mass. Hist. Coll.* vol. vi. pp. 579–581. It is also printed on pp. 77–79 of this volume, and is given in facsimile.

tiful supply of provision. Sir Richard signified his intention to come out himself as soon as " a house was prepared against his coming."[1]

The appearance of Francis Stiles with Sir Richard's party was the first assertion of the claims of the Connecticut patentees. The party, according to Sir Richard's letter, seem at first to have been repelled by some " Dorchester men," who had settled near the Falls at Windsor, where they intended to plant, and who refused to recognize the authority of the patentees. The party under Francis Stiles seem, however, afterwards to have established themselves at Windsor, whether through the intervention of Governor Winthrop of Connecticut, or through the better judgment of Roger Ludlow and his Dorchester men, cannot now be told. The land taken possession of by Stiles for Saltonstall was said to have been bounded on the south by the north line of Windsor.

The following affidavit, taken before the Governor and Council at Hartford, 25 June, 1710, is of much interest in this connection : " Henry Stiles [2] sen[r] of Windsor aged about 79 years and Daniel Hayden [3] sen[r] of Windsor aged about 69 years jointly testifie and declare as follows: — that is to say, That they very well knew, and was intimately acquainted with M[r] Francis Stiles, formerly of said Windsor, and that they have often heard the said Francis Stiles declare and say, that he was sent over from England into New England by Sir Richard Saltonstall, Knight, to take up a tract of land for him of about 2,000 acres upon Connecticut river, and to fence it in for a park ; and that accordingly he the said Francis Stiles had taken up that quantity of land for the said Saltonstall on the East side said river, at and near the place called

[1] " A bark of forty tons arrived, set forth with twenty servants, by Sir Richard Saltonstall to go plant at Connecticut." Winthrop's *History*, vol. i. p. 192.
[2] Henry Stiles was born in England, a son of John, brother of Francis Stiles, who had charge of the expedition. Henry was four years old when he came to Connecticut with the Stiles party in 1635.
[3] Daniel Hayden, Senr., was born in Windsor, 1640, a son of William Hayden who lived less than half a mile above Mr. Francis Stiles. Saltonstall Park was three miles above and on the opposite (east) side of the river from the ground occupied by the pioneers.

Warehouse Point, at the foot of the falls between Windsor
and Enfield; and the same Park was one mile in breadth
from North to South, at the said river, and did run east with
that breadth from the river until it included the quantity of
2,000 acres, and that the said river was the West bounds
thereof. Also that a certain brook running upon the said
tract of land, commonly called Saltonstall's brook, and the
said place called Warehouse Point are both comprehended
and contained within the said Park. And that he said
Francis Stiles had purchased said tract of land for a park of
one Ne-row-we-nock, an Indian Sachem: — and the said deponents also testifie and say that they have formerly heard
the ancient inhabitants of Windsor tell and declare that the
said Francis Stiles was agent for Sir Richard Saltonstall, and
that he did take up the aforementioned tract of land for a
park for him, and that the said brook was first named Saltonstall's brook by reason of its being within the said Park.
And the said deponents further testifie and say that to their
certain knowledge the said brook hath been commonly called
Saltonstall's Brook, and the said point commonally called
Warehouse Point for above 50 years last past, and that they
never heard or knew of any person whatsoever who did ever
yet improve or manure any part of the Park or tract of land
aforementioned to this day. And the said Daniel Hayden
further testifies and says that about 60 years ago he saw a
company of men going towards the said Park to work, and
that his Father Wm. Hayden then told him they were going
to fence in the said Park. And the said Henry Stiles also
further says that he hath seen an high palisado fence that was
set up and standing near the South side of the said Park
about 60 years ago. The above named Henry Stiles and
Daniel Hayden made oath to their above written evidence
severally before the governor[1] and council in Hartford, June
25th, 1710."[2]

[1] Gurdon Saltonstall, Governor of Connecticut from 1708 to his death, 1724.
[2] *Colonial Records of Connecticut*, pp. 579–581; Stiles's *Hist. of Ancient Wind-sor*, vol. i. pp. 736, 737.

It would thus appear that a tract of land a mile wide on the river and extending east about three miles was purchased by Francis Stiles for Sir Richard Saltonstall of the Indians, that the title was confirmed to Sir Richard by the assembly of Connecticut in 1640.

It would appear, too, that the territory taken by Sir Richard was claimed also by Massachusetts, for we find that on 6 May, 1646, Robert Saltonstall, son and attorney of Sir Richard, has 2,120 acres of land allowed him "above Connecticut Falls, provided he accepts it as part of that proportion dew to Sir Richard Saltonstall." (See Mass. Records.)

This grant was evidently obtained to make the title secure, whether the land should prove to belong to the one or the other colony. Massachusetts claimed that the Park was within her jurisdiction.

The Park remained, as we have seen, for seventy years unsettled and uncultivated, perhaps owing to disputed claims to the territory on the part of the two colonies.

Massachusetts finally gave (in 1713) to Connecticut, as an equivalent for accepting the line as it was fixed, several thousand acres north of the line claimed by Massachusetts farther east, and granted an extra 2,000 acres to Connecticut as the equivalent of Saltonstall Park, as appears by the following order, General Assem. of Connecticut, May Session, 1714: "The Governor (Gurdon Saltonstall) having shown that the government of Massachusetts has allowed 2,000 acres equivalent to this Colony for a grant of land formerly made by them to his ancestor, Sir Richard Saltonstall, Knight, which happens to fall within the bounds of Windsor, in this Colony, and having declared in this assembly that he is content the said town of Windsor should enjoy the said grant provided he may take up the equivalent for it instead thereof where it may best suit him in the lands given for equivalent by the said government of Massachusetts, It is therefore granted by this Assembly that the Governor, Gurdon Saltonstall, Esqʳ., may take up to his own use the same quantity of acres among the equivalents allowed this Colony, where it shall best suit him, provided the said tract shall be in one entire piece."

Later on they say the 2,000 acres may be taken up in parcels of not less than 500 acres each, in the northeast corner of this colony, east by Woodstock, north of the supposed old line.

It would appear that the heirs of Sir Richard Saltonstall might have held the Park, — for it had never been occupied, but they chose to abandon it to the colony, and there is nothing to show that the Governor selected either of the other tracts as its equivalent.

"*Warehouse Point.* — As early as 1636, when Springfield, Mass., was settled, Mr. William Pyncheon undertook to send his supplies thither, around by water from Boston ; and finding that his vessels could not pass the falls at this point, he was obliged to provide land carriage 14 miles to Springfield. It was probably years before boats were provided suitable for running the rapids ; and Mr. Pyncheon erected a warehouse, at the highest point his vessels could reach, on the east side of the river, wherein to store his goods while awaiting transit by land. This warehouse probably stood about forty rods south of State Street and about forty-five to fifty rods below the present ferry landing between West Street and the river bank. It consequently gave to the place the name by which it has ever since been known, — ' Warehouse Point.'

" The antiquity of this name, as well as the interesting fact that *the whole Warehouse Point district was originally designed and set apart as the private domain and park of an English nobleman,*[1] who was largely and honorably (though not profitably for himself) concerned in the early planting of the Connecticut colony, is fully proven by the following evidence given in Dr. Charles J. Hoadly's lately published (xv.) volume of ' Colonial Records of Conn.' pp. 579–581.[2]

" ' The following remarks upon this very interesting point

---

[1] Sir Richard Saltonstall was a knight, but not a nobleman. — AUTHOR.
[2] Stiles's *Hist. of Ancient Windsor*, vol. i. p. 736.

in our East Windsor history are from the pen of Mr. Jabez H. Hayden of Windsor Locks : —

"'" Sir Richard Saltonstall, one of the original patentees of Massachusetts, came over with Governor Winthrop 1630, and returned to England 1631, where he died in 1658. He probably expected to return, as he was appointed Assistant by the Massachusetts General Court in 1633, and was a proprietor at Watertown many years. (Bradford's Hist. Mass., and Bond's Watertown Genealogies.) His sons, Richard[1] and Robert, came over to Massachusetts soon after their father's return, and the latter was his attorney here. (H. S. Sheldon.) Sir Richard was one of the principal 'Lords and Gentlemen' who were patentees of Connecticut; and his attempt to establish a colony at Windsor, through his agent, Mr. Francis Stiles, has been already narrated. . . . Indeed, this and that portion of our history must be studied in connection to fully understand them aright, — the former having reference rather to Sir Richard's actions as one of the patentees; the latter, to his individual plans and purposes. Saltonstall Park was 'a tract at the Falls,' the highest point reached by Pyncheon's vessels when carrying supplies for the new settlement at Springfield in 1636. This park was described in 1710 as one mile in breadth on the river, extending east three miles ; 1,500 acres of it was set to Francis Stiles, 400 acres 'by allotment' and 1,100 by purchase from the town (Windsor Town Rec.), but it was nearly ten years before Stiles transferred it to Robert Saltonstall, as agent for his father, Sir Richard. The petition of Robert (Conn. Col. Rec. i. 62) in 1640 was probably for authority to him to hold this land taken up by Stiles, which the Court authorized their Commissioners to grant, provided the town of Windsor consent thereunto."'"[2]

In 1642 the Court confirmed this to Saltonstall, and ordered that the north line of Windsor (Conn. Col. Rec. i. 72) should run on Mr. Saltonstall's land, "and what prejudice Mr.

[1] Richard came over with his father in the Arbella in 1630, returned the next year, and came here again with his wife, Muriel Gurdon, in 1635.
[2] Stiles's *History of Ancient Windsor*, vol. i. pp. 737, 738.

Saltonstall shall sustain thereby the country shall make good; " at the same time the Court released Mr. Saltonstall from the conditions attached to " the said grounds formerly granted which was to have been impaled within three years."

Saltonstall Park, as described seventy years after (see Stiles and Hayden's affidavit), included Saltonstall's Brook and the warehouse (about a mile apart). The south line of it evidently was on the north bounds of Windsor as originally set at Kettle Brook. The same affidavit claims that this is the ground Stiles took up for Saltonstall and extinguished the Indian title. The land which Stiles transferred to Saltonstall (1647) was described in the deed to Stiles (1640) as sixty rods wide on the river, extending east three miles, and there in breadth four hundred and forty-four rods. Possibly the town line of 1636 ran through Saltonstall's land (then in Stiles's name), and the Court in 1642, recognizing the town line of 1636, made Saltonstall's land a parallelogram containing 1,500 acres; to which the Massachusetts Court (1641) (Mass. Col. Rec. i. 331) added 500 acres, " if it fall within our patent, making the 2,000 acres (1,500, 500, and 120, total 2,120 acres); and later on Massachusetts (1645) (Mass. Col. Rec. iii. 66) threw her shield over the whole."

LETTER FROM SIR RICHARD SALTONSTALL TO GOVERNOR WINTHROP OF CONNECTICUT

GOOD MR. WINTHROPP,

Being credibly informed (as by the inclosed may appeare) yt there hath bene some abuse & Injury done me by Mr Ludlow & others of Dorchester who would not suffer ffrancis Styles & his men to empayle grounds wheare I appoynted them at Connecticute   Although both by pattent wch I took aboue 4 yeares since & prepossession Dorchester men being then vnsettled & seekeing vp the river aboue the falls for a place to plant vpon but finding none better to their likeing they speedily came backe againe & discharged my worke men casting lotts vpon yt place where he was purposed to begin his worke notwithstanding he often told them what great

charge I had bene at In sending him & soe many men to
prepare a house against my coming & enclose grounds for
my cattle & how the damage would fall heavy upon those
that thus hindered me, whom ffrancis Styles conceiued to
haue best right to make choyce of any place there   Notwithstanding they resisted him slieghting me wth many vnbe-
seeming words such as he was vnwilling to relate to me, but
Justifie vpon his oath before Authority when he is called to
itt   Therefore we haueing appoynted you to be our gouern-
our there, the rest of the Company being sensible of this
affront to me would haue signified their minds In a generall
letter vnto you but I told them sith itt did concerne my selfe
In particular & might perhaps breed some Jelousies In the
people and soe distast them wth our Gouernment, where vpon
they Aduised me to write vnto you to request you wth all speed
& diligence to examine this matt^r & if (for the substance)
you find it as to vs it appeares by this Informacion herewth
sent you yt then in a faire & gentle way you giue notice to
Dorchester men of this great wronge they haue done me
Being the first yt to further this designe sent my pinnace
thither at my owne great charge of Almost 1000L wch now
is cast away by their detaininge her soe longe before she
could vnlaid & for wch in Justice I may require Satisfa͡con,
as alsoe for my [provisions] which cost aboue fiue hundred
pounds & are now (I heare) almost al spent by this meanes &
not any payling as yet set up at that place where I appoynted
them wch had I but Imagined they would haue thus greedily
snached up all the best grounds vpon yt river my pinnace
should rather haue sought a pylate at new Plymoth then to
haue staid ten days as she did in the Bay to haue giuen them
such warning thus to prevent me   And let them spaire as
(I am told) they may very well forth of yt great quantity they
have Ingroced to themselues soe much as my [proportion]
comes to & if they have built any houses there vpon I will
pay them their reasonable charges for the same   But I pray
you ether goe yor selfe wth some skilfull men wth you or send
Sergieant Gardiner & some wth him to set out my grounds

Facsimile Letter of Sir Richard Saltonstall to Governor John Winthrop, Jr. of Connecticut

Facsimile of envelope for Sir Richard Saltonstall's Letter to Governor John Winthrop

where it may be most conuenient betwene Plymoth Trucking house & ye falls accordinge to my directions giuen both to the Mr of my pinnace & to ffrancis Styles wch I thinke they will not now deny me vnderstanding what charge I am at (wth others of the Company) to secure this Rivers mouth for the defence of them all wherin we hope you will neglect noe meanes according to our great trust reposed in you thus beseeching the lord to [prosper] the worke begun I comend you wth all our affayers vnder your charge to the gratious direction and protexion of oᵣ good god In whom I am,

Yᵣ most assured ffrend

Ric : Saltonstall

I pray you comend [me] after yoᵣ selfe to yoᵣ good wife & Sergieant Gardiner wth his fellow souldier whom I purpose god willing to visit this suῆer if he will [provide] an house to receive me and mine at my landinge.

ffor my worthyly Respected Friend Mᵣ John Winthrop Governour of the plantãcons vpon Connectacut Ryver in Newe England.

(Labelled) Sᵣ Richard Saltenstall 1636.[1]

Sir Richard Saltonstall stood high in the estimation of all who knew him. In England before the departure of the Company so much reliance was placed on his judgment that important meetings of the Company were adjourned, in his absence, till he could be present. After his return to England he was held in the highest respect as a friend and effective supporter of the colony, and, as Dr. Bond says, "he received marked tokens of the public confidence," and was called upon to fill important and responsible offices. At a period when narrowness and bigotry prevailed, the qualities he possessed were of inestimable value to the community; especially his broad and charitable views upon religious questions. His undaunted courage, his sincerity of purpose, his purity of life, combined with his perfect self-control and a most persuasive manner, gave him a lofty and enviable position, with an influence most salutary and enduring.

[1] *Mass. Hist. Coll.* 2d series, vol. viii. p. 42.

His reasons for returning to England cannot be positively stated; that he fully intended to remain here cannot be doubted, for he was one of the first and most honored at the inception of the enterprise, and embarked in it after disposing of his estates, and bringing with him all his children, evidently with no intention of ever leaving; but the dreadful suffering experienced by the colonists during the first severe winter doubtless had much to do with his return. His two daughters, taken from luxurious homes, were very young; and deprivation of every comfort, even of proper and sufficient food, with the extreme cold and wretched shelter, must have rendered life here almost unendurable. But may not the difference of his views on civil and religious questions from those of his associates have had much to do with his departure? He was too liberal for the time and the place, and there is strong ground for the opinion that this had much influence upon him. His letter, already quoted, afterwards written from England to the ministers of Boston shows what were his convictions, and therein he distinctly avows what he conceived to have been the intentions of the leaders of the enterprise. In that letter, too, he says that he had before written to Governor Dudley on the same subject, complaining of the intolerance which prevailed here.

The reasons, then, for Sir Richard's departure are not far to seek, and would seem quite conclusive. He probably intended to return to Massachusetts, though of this there is no proof, except his election as Assistant in May, 1633,[1] his services were of the utmost value to the colony after his departure, and he never ceased to regard it with almost parental interest; but the Connecticut Patent, in which, with Lord Say and Seal, Lord Brook, and others, he had so large an interest, certainly engrossed a large part of his time and attention, and his unfortunate efforts to establish a settlement on his land, the abuse of his men, the loss of his bark, and his failure to obtain redress after being the " first (as he says

[1] See, also, postscript to his letter to Governor Winthrop of Connecticut (1636), wherein he declares his intention to visit Connecticut that year.

Woodsome Hall, Yorkshire, formerly Seat of the Kaye family.

in his letter to Governor Winthrop) to further the design of settlement," must have quenched all intention or desire he may have had to return to New England.

WOODSOME HALL

The family of Kaye, to which Grace Kaye, the wife of Sir Richard Saltonstall, belonged, was very ancient in Yorkshire. Woodsome, the family seat, is now in possession of the Earl of Dartmouth. The following description is taken from "Old Yorkshire," edited by William Smith, F. S. A. S.

"Woodsome Hall, the home of Grace Kaye, where she was married to Sir Richard Saltonstall, is situated near Huddersfield, and is described by a recent writer as one of the most charming places in Yorkshire. It looks towards the east. Its gabled front with long stone windows stands on a paved terrace from which there is a beautiful view down the wooded valley. There is an air about the place not only of unbroken antiquity, but of most complete repose and quiet, contrasting delightfully with the bustle of the surrounding district.

"The mansion of Woodsome consists of a central hall, flanked with gabled projections on either side, of Elizabethan style and date. A stone porch in the centre bears the date of 1600 over the entrance arch, and has stone sedilia. A muniment room was at one time over the porch, which has the date of 1600 on the apex. The interior is as little changed as the outside.

"On entering the house, on the left hand side is a room entirely wainscoted, containing, besides old furniture and an antique pier glass, two oil paintings representing probably Sir John Kaye in style of Charles I., with iron breastplate, flowing wig, and lace necktie; the other representing a beautiful young lady partially veiled, bearing a torch, probably of the same period. This was most likely the library or drawing-room of the 'belted squire' and Worshipful Justice of the Peace. Beyond, are the kitchens and other offices, and a long passage leading to the court-yard or quadrangle behind. On the right hand side of the entrance is the great hall ten

yards square, high, lofty, and airy, with its broad windows.
On the walls are hung various articles of olden warfare;
matchlocks, cullions, halberts, battle-axes and rapiers.   A silver trumpet of the date of the Restoration formerly 'hung
upon the wall,' but has also been removed and 'speaks of war
no more.'

"But the principal objects of interest are the paintings,
large portraits of probably the Sir John Kaye of Charles II.
days, in silk robes, black wigs, and lace bands. On each side,
Lord Lewisham and the heiress who carried the estates to
the present noble family (of the Earl of Dartmouth) in the
costume of the early part of the last century.   But the greatest curiosities are the two boards hung on cranes under the
gallery.   These boards have painted upon them a collection
of portraits of the Kaye family.   Old oak chairs with cane
seats, cabinets, and other old furniture surround the hall.   In
the windows, which occupy the whole east side, are in glass
the crest and coronet of the present noble owner, whose judicious care has restored and repaired the whole structure without, according to the hope of the writer to whom we have
referred, 'imparing its original style.'

"Leaving the great hall, we enter what was formerly the
dining-room, but now the drawing-room, also wainscoted
throughout, 12 yards by 9 yards, filled with antique furniture,
china, mirrors, and ornaments.

"On leaving the present drawing-room (formerly the dining-room), we enter on two smaller wainscoted rooms.   Over
the fireplace of the first is an old painting representing the
finding of Moses in the bulrushes.   Ascending an oak
staircase, we reach the principal bedrooms, also wainscoted,
and a large number of other chambers, with much ancient
furniture, especially an old four post bedstead, with an inscription in ornamental old English character,

"'Miserere mei Deus et Salve Me.'

"On the north side of the court-yard, in the rear of the
principal port, is a lofty wing of three gables of a later date,

Woodsome Hall (Dining-Room).

attributable to Robert Kaye, son of John and grandson of Arthur Kaye. In it are, on the first floor, a large dining-room recently restored. Over the stone fireplace are the arms of Kaye and Finchenden impaled with the stagshead of Legge, and, above, the crest of the latter family."

The following description of Woodsome Hall is taken from Murray's " Handbook for Yorkshire," 1882 : —

" Woodsome Hall, a seat of the Earl of Dartmouth [formerly of the Kayes], one of the most charming old places in Yorkshire.

" The house, re-fronted in 1600, and again somewhat altered in 1644, low, gabled, and with long stone windows, stands on a paved terrace with a balustrade in front. Tufts of autumnal crocus push upward between the chinks of the pavement ; and masses of old-fashioned greenery rise against the gray walls themselves.

" From the terrace there is a beautiful view down the valley, which is much wooded. There is an air about the whole place, not only of unbroken antiquity, but of the most complete repose and quiet, contrasting most delightfully with the bustle of the surrounding district. The interior is as little changed as the outside. A gallery runs along one side of the hall, which, with its old portraits, armor, cabinets, and enormous fireplace (above which are the names Arthur Kay, Beatrix Kay), affords an admirable study for the artist. A daughter of Arthur and Beatrix Kay married Lord Lewisham, and thus brought Woodsome into the family of its present owners. Curious portraits of an earlier John Kay and his wife (temp. Henry VIII., the builders of the house) hang on cranes in the hall, so that they can be turned on either side. On the reverse of John Kay's portrait are the arms of many Yorkshire families, 'kin to Woodsome,' by John Kay and his. wife, and on the reverse of his wife's portrait are the 'portraitures' of the descendants of an earlier Arthur Kay. Many edifying verses are inscribed on either picture, including the ' Vita uxoris honesta.'

> " 'To live at home in howswyverie
> To order wel my famylye
> To see they lyve not idyllye
> To bringe upe children vertiuslye
> To relyeve poore foulk willinglye
> This is my care with modestye
> To leade my life in honestye.'

" The house is built round a square court-yard, into which the main entrance formerly led.   There are many gables, and an external staircase of stone affords access to the upper chambers.   Woodsome is altogether an admirable specimen of a good (though not large) Yorkshire house of the 16th cent.; and it is much to be hoped that it is destined to undergo no changes.   At the back are some pleasant woods with a space of green field (*ham*-woods-*ham*) between them and the house."

25. SIR RICHARD SALTONSTALL OF SOUTH OKENDEN (III.)

The will of Sir Richard Saltonstall of South Okenden (or Wokendon) in the county of Essex, dated 30 Nov., 1618, proved 6 May, 1619, mentions wife Jane, and children, Richard (49), Susan (52), Bernard (50), and John (51), also his mother, sister to Sir Gabriel Poyntz, and speaks of his manor in Chipping Warden in Northamptonshire, his chief mansion house called Grooves in the parish of South Wokendon, etc., also his " great bason and ewer of silver, all gilt and graven with my father's arms, and my mother's thereupon engraven and amelled, she being the sister of Sir Gabriel Pointes of North Wokendon Essex, Knight, which I would also have my son Richard to leave to his eldest son after his decease, in remembrance of that worthy knight, Sir Richard Saltonstall, his grandfather, deceased."

PEDIGREE OF KAYE

FROM THE VISITATION OF YORKSHIRE IN 1612

William Kaye =

John Kaye =

Cicely, dau. of = Lawrence = Elizabeth, dau. of   James.   William.   John.   Peter.   Richard.
Wm. Bradshaw. | Kaye. | Thomas Amyas.

John Kaye of Woodsome = Jane, dau. of   Thomas Kaye = Elizabeth, dau. and heir
| Peter Scargill. | of Robt. Turner.

John Kaye of Woodsome = Jane, dau. of John Lacye of
in Yorkshire, living 33 | Cromwelbotham in Yorkshire.
H. VI.

William Kaye of Woodsome =

George Kaye of Woodsome, Esq. = Matilda, dau. and heir of —— Racliffe
| of Langley in Lancashire.

Arthur Kaye of Woodsome = Beatrice, dau. of Matthew
| Wentworth, Esq., of Bretton.

John Kaye, of Woodsome 1585. = Dorothy, dau. of Robert   George Kaye.   Anne m. William Ald-   Margaret m. Francis
| Mauliverer of Wothersome.   burgh of Aldburgh.   Woodroff of Wolley.

1. Robert Kaye, of Woodsome = Anne, dau.   Dorothy m.   2. Arthur.   6. George.   Anne m.   Jane m.
1612; Justice of the Peace and | of John Flower   Thomas Blythe,   3. Richard.   7. Matthew.   Richard Marks   Bryan Thornhill
Treasurer for Lame Soldiers | of Whitewell in   cousin and heir   4. Edward.   8. John.   of Beverly.   of Fixbye.
in the time of Queen Elizabeth. | Co. Rutland.   of John Blythe   5. Francis.   9. Thomas.
                                              of Quenby.

John   Kaye = Anne, dau. of Sir John   Grace m. Sir Richard   Dorothy m. John Carvill of
aged 7, 1585; | Ferne, Knt.; one of   Saltonstall of Huntwicke   Normanton, Esq.; Counsellor
living in 1612. | the Council of York.   in Co. York. N. E. 1630.   at Law, of the Inner Tem-
                                                                      ple, London.

Sir John Kaye of Woodsome,
Knt. and Baronet.

Elizabeth Kaye, 3 years old 1612;
m. Sir Ralph Ashton of Middleton
in Lancashire.

DESCENT OF GRACE KAYE

FROM WILLIAM THE CONQUEROR

Maud or Matilda = William the Conqueror, d. 1087.

Gundrada = William, Earl Warren and Surrey.

William, Earl Warren = Elizabeth of Valois.

William, Earl Warren = Ellyn, dau. to Montgomery, Earl of Shrewsbury.

Lady Ella Warren = Sir William Fytz William of Sprotborough.

Sir William Fitz William = Albreda, dau. of Earl of Lincoln.

Sir Thomas (or Wm.) Fitz William = Anne, dau. of Lord Grey.

Sir Thomas Fitz William = Agnes, dau. of Lord of Mytford.

Sir William Fitz William = Agnes, dau. of Sir John Metam.

Sir William Fitz William = Isabell, dau. of Lord Dencourt.

Sir John Fitz William = Jane, dau. of Adam Reresby.

Sir William Fitz William = Lady Elizabeth, dau. of Earl of Huntington.

Sir William Fitz William = Maud, dau. of Ralph Cromwell, Lord of Tatershall.

Sir John Fitz William = Elenor, dau. of Sir Henry Greene.

Sir John Fitz William = Margaret, dau. of Thomas Clarell.

Sir William Fitz William = Elizabeth, dau. of Thomas Chaworth.

Isabella Fitz William = Richard Wentworth.

Beatryce Wentworth = Arthur Kaye.

John Kaye = Dorothy Maleverer.

Robert Kaye = Anne Flower.

Grace Kaye = Sir Richard Saltonstall.

This Pedigree is taken from the Yorkshire Visitation, published by the Harleian Society.

27. SIR PETER SALTONSTALL (III.)

Sir Peter Saltonstall of Barkway in the County of Herts, by his will dated 12 July, 1651, directs his body " to be buried in the chancel of the parish Church of Barkway," and mentions "my nephew, Sir John Saltonstall," "my grand child Anne Chester," " my nephew Captain Charles Saltonstall," and others.

Epitaph on Christian, second wife of Sir Peter Saltonstall, in the Chancel of Barkway Church :—

> Here lyeth burried the body of the Lady
> Saltonstall, daughter of Sir
> John Pettus, of Norfolk, Knt, wife
> of Sir Peter Saltonstall, Knt, owner
> of the Rectory of Barkway, by whom
> he had three sons and five daughters ; they
> lived together married 39 years;
> She departed this life June the 21st
> 1646, aged about 60.

> Lo here that jewell of sincerity
> Who was in truth the same she seemed to be,
> Mirrour of charity and godly life ;
> She died and rose with Christ, yet lived with us,
> Now dead she lives with Christ more glorious.

Sir Thomas Pettus, by his will dated 14 Oct., 1618, proved 3 Nov., 1618, left a legacy to " my sister Dame Christian Saltonstall, the wife of Sir Peter Saltonstall Knight," and to James, her son, a legacy.[1]

29. SIR SAMUEL SALTONSTALL (III.)

Sir Samuel Saltonstall appears to have taken an interest in the settlement of Virginia, and to have befriended Capt. John Smith, who mentions him as executor of his will, etc., in the following work, " The Adventures and Discoveries of Captain John Smith sometime President of Virginia and Admiral of New England, newly ordered by John Ashton, with

[1] *Genealogical Register*, October, 1894.

illustrations taken by him from original Sources." We find the will of John Smith executed " the one and twentieth daie of June in the Ssaventh year of the reigne of our Soveraigne Lord Charles, by the grace of God King of England Scotland France and Ireland, defender of the faith, &c. . . . Item, I give and bequeath to my much honored and most worthy freind, Sr. Samuel Saltonstall, Knight, the sume of fyve poundes, . . . I give unto Thomas Packer . . . my trunck standing in my chamber at Sr. Samuel Saltonstall's house in St. Sepulchres Parish . . . Item I nominate appoint and ordain my said much honered friend, Sr. Samuel Saltonstall and the said Thomas Packer, the elder, joynt executors of this my last will and testament."

In the third charter of King James to the Treasurer and Company of Virginia appears the name of Samuel Saltonstall who was knighted at Whitehall 23 July, 1603, Collector of Customs 4 March, 1618. A bill of adventure was granted him for three shares in the Virginia Company of London. The charter signed at Westminster 12 March, 9th year of King James, contains names of 325 persons, of whom about 25 were in the Peerage, 111 Knights, 10 Doctors, Ministers, etc., 66 Esquires, 30 Gentlemen, and 83 citizens, with others, not classified, but mostly merchants. (See " Genesis of the United States," by Alex. Brown.)

---

39. RICHARD SALTONSTALL OF MASSACHUSETTS
(IV.)

" Richard Saltonstall, Jr., eldest son of Sir Richard (13), b. at Woodsome, Co. York, in 1610; matriculated ' Mr. Fellow-commoner,' in Emmanuel College, Camb., Dec. 14, 1627. He accompanied his father to New England, in 1630, before taking a degree; was adm. freeman, May 18, 1631, then of Wat., aged 21, with the title ' Mr.' This was only a few weeks after his father departed for England. He embarked for England Nov. 23, 1631, where he remained about four

Deare S^r

The best thing that I have to begg your thoughts
for at this present, is, a motto or 2 that Mr Prin hath
writt vpon his chamber walls, (in the Tower:)

Carcer probat amicos, detegit inimicos, expellit mundum,
includit deum; alit virtutes, extinguit libidines, docet
temperantiam, cohibet luxuriam, mortificat carnem, sancti=
=ficat hominum, ingenerat gratiam, Vnthesaurizat gloriam

Psal: 61. 3. Deus est turris etiam in turre.
Turris libertatis, in turre angustiæ; Turris consolationis in turre
tristitiæ; turris quietis in turre molestiæ; Turris fœlicita=
=tis in turre miseriæ; Turris honoris in turre dedecoris; Turris
Splendoris in turre obscuritatis; Turris securitatis in turre
perturbationis; Turris salutis in turre perditionis; Turris spes,
in turre desperationis; Turris gaudij in turre afflictionis; turris
pacis in turre belli; Turris protectionis in turre periculi,
Turris vitæ in turre mortis; Turris gloria in turre perpessionis;
& in turre precati, turris Gratia.

Turris } protegendo, } a malis; in malis; } Semp,
{ Consolando, } Contra malos, } abundanter,
{ Eripiendo, } Inter malos, } vbiq;
Citò, tempestivè, sapienter, optimè; Fortissimè
Suavissimè
Gratissimè

Arctari non potest qui in ipsa dej infinitate in carcere clausus
spatiatur. Mortalium procul dubio beatissimus qui
mundi exul, christiq captivus turris: Turris christianos
fideles ficte incarcerat, verè liberat. Nil crus sentit in
nervo si animus sit in cœlo; nil cortus patitur in ergas=
=tulo, si anima sit in christo. I have nothing els (beeing in
great hast) but my best love, which is (as my selfe) alwayes be
yours Richard Saltonstall iunior.

To his worthily endeared, Mr
John Win-throp junior:&c

NEngland::

his mother

Present::

William Brimer
are mine

years and a half, and, it is conjectured, gave some attention
to legal studies. About 1633, he married Meriell [Muriel]
Gurdon, dr. of Brampton Gurdon, of Asson., Co. Suffolk,
Esq. (who, it is said, 'had eight sons, Parliament men').[1] He
embarked at London, in Ap., 1635, with wife Meriell, aged
22 yrs., and dr. Meriell, aged 9 months. Upon his arrival,
then aged 25, he settled in Ipswich, and immediately began
to receive tokens of public respect and confidence; and there
is not probably in the early colonial history another instance
where so young a man received so many. The Colonial
Records show that he was truly a worthy son of a very worthy
father.

"Mr. Saltonstall was elected Deputy of Ipswich, to the
first General Court held after his return, and was at five
courts between Mar. 3, 1635-6, and April, 1637. He was
elected Assistant, June 1, 1637, and continued to be elected
annually until 1649. In Oct. of that year, another man was
appointed in his place on a commission, which he could not
attend to, 'in regard of his intended voyage,' bound to England, probably for the benefit of his wife's health. Sept., 1649,
'being by God's Providence, upon a voyage to England,' he
appoints the present Pastor and the Deacons of the Church
of Ipswich, his attorneys, 'with power to act,' about all of
his estates in Ipswich. (Essex Deeds, ii. p. 6.) When he returned has not been ascertained, but he was in England in
the spring of 1662. (See Hutchinson's State Papers, p. 371.)
In 1672, he went back to England, where his three daughters
were [living] married. He returned to Massachusetts again
in 1680, where he remained about three years; and then, at
the age of 73, went again to England, where he died, at
Hulme, Ap. 29, 1694, aged 84. He was elected Assistant in
1664, and again, upon his second return to Ipswich, in 1680,
81, and 82. Sept. 6, 1636, the Court appointed a committee

---

[1] Extract from letter of Lucy Downing to John Winthrop, Jr., 22 June, 1633:
"Last night ould Msr. Gurdon came to me to desire my house for his lodgeing,
and his daughter is heer to be maryed the next week to Sir Richard Saltonstall's
sone: The youngest daughter: next spring they intend for new Eng." — *Mass.
Hist. Coll.* 5th series, vol. i. p. 8. p. 8.

to examine the accounts of Mr. R. Saltonstall, executor of the estate of John Dillingham, deceased, and of Edward Dillingham, his son. This estate was not finally settled until 1645. May 25, 1636, he, with two others, was appointed 'to keep court' at Ipswich. In 1644, 1646, and 1647, he was appointed (desired) 'to keep court' at Piscataqua. Sept. 8, 1636, he was one of those deputed to require the last rates of each town in the plantation ; to find out the true value of every town in the plantation, and to make an equal rate for £600. The next year he received a similar appointment. In 1638, he was appointed a referee 'in business, between Henry Sewall and the town of Newbury.' Mar. 12, 1637–8, he was one of the committee appointed to report upon 'excessive prices,' and to report 'their thoughts for remedying the same.' At the same time he was appointed on a committee 'to consider of a levy, petitions, and other trivial matters.' May 29, 1644, he, with two others, was appointed 'with full power to hear and determine all businesses at Hampton, both about their differences, offences, and a new plantation, according to their several petitions.'

"Oct. 7, 1641, he was, by the Court, appointed Sergeant Major in Col. Endicott's Regiment. Although he received so many offices and appointments (and the preceding are only a part), he does not seem to have been ambitious for office. Winthrop says that in 1644 Mr. Saltonstall 'moved very earnestly that he might be left out of the next election (of Assistants), and pursued his motion after to the towns;' and he supposes that it was because Mr. S. found himself in a small minority, among the Assistants, on some points of public policy. Like his father, he had more correct views of public justice, and of civil and religious liberty, than were then and there prevalent. Oct. 1, 1645, the Court granted a charter for 20 years, after any discovery made within three years, to the following gentlemen, as a trading company or company of adventurers, viz., ' Richard Saltonstall, Esq., Mr. Syman Bradstreet, Mr. Samuel Symonds, Mr. Richard Dumer, Mr. Willie Hubbard, Capt. Wm. Hathorne and Mr. Wm. Paine.'

He was one of those persons who were privy to the conceal-
ment of the regicide Judges, Whalley and Goffe, and in 1672
he gave them £50.

"There are three events in the life of Mr. Saltonstall of
some importance, as illustrative of his regard for civil liberty,
public justice, and humanity.

"The greatest blemish, the charge which it is most difficult to meet satisfactorily, in the conduct of the planters of
Massachusetts Bay, is undoubtedly their bigoted attachment
to the minutia of their religious dogmas, their seeming to be
the disciples of Moses more than of Christ, their intolerance
of any variation from their views, even on speculative points
of no practical importance, and the severity of their dealings
with those who conscientiously differed from them. In such
a condition of the public sentiments, or rather of those who
bear rule, there can hardly fail to be a proneness towards the
assumption of arbitrary power. This was manifested in the
early attempt of the Court to tax the people without their
consent, which, however, was so met by the Rev. George
Phillips, the uncompromising Elder Richard Browne, and
other people of Watertown, that it was not afterwards attempted. This occurred while Mr. Saltonstall was in England.
The next important manifestation of this tendency was on
the 3d of March, 1635–6, when the Court passed an order,
that the General Court, at their next meeting, 'shall elect a
certain number of magistrates for term of their lives, as a
standing council.' This order was obnoxious to the people,
and awakened among them a jealousy of the designs of their
rulers. They looked upon it as an infringement of their
rights, as an attempt to introduce into the government an
almost irresponsible body, which was not warranted by their
charter. Such was the excitement produced, that at the
end of three years (May 22, 1639), the Court virtually, but
not formally, almost annulled the force of that order. The
obnoxious Standing Council, however, still subsisted, and to
allay the excitement, the Court authorized 'every freeman to
give their advice to any of the deputies concerning the institution and power of the Standing Council.'

"Mr. Saltonstall, although an Assistant, with a very fair prospect of becoming a member of that Council, if he desired it, coincided in sentiment with those freemen, and such of the Elders as disapproved of the Standing Council, differing in this respect from most of the other Assistants; and he wrote a book, maintaining that the institution of such a body for life was not warranted by the charter, and was a sinful innovation. It is evident from Winthrop that his remarks were cogent and pointed. Mr. Saltonstall put the book into the hands of Mr. Hathorne, a Deputy, and from him it passed into other hands, and not until after the lapse of considerable time was it laid before the Court. The book gave great offence, especially to some of the high officials, those most interested in the institution which was attacked, and they would gladly have censured or otherwise punished the author. But such was the character and influence of Mr. Saltonstall, and so cogent and unanswerable his argument, that they did not succeed, and he was 'discharged from any censure or further inquiry by this or any other court.' This vote was passed May 3, 1642. Yet so much rankling did the book leave in certain persons interested, that on the 14th of the next month the Court voted 'to vindicate the office of the Standing Council, as it is now ordered, and the persons in whom it is now vested, from all dishonor and reproach cast upon it or them, in Mr. Saltonstall's book.' For this purpose the book was referred to the Elders, the very persons who had advised the institution of such a Council. 'The Elders all met at Ipswich,' Oct. 18, 1642, and took the book into consideration. They 'differed much in their judgment about it,' but finally agreed to report that three propositions are laid down in it, and, 'in their answer they allowed the said propositions are sound;' but they made some nice distinctions about the application of them, intended to lessen the odium attached to the institution and the authors of it.

"The Government of Massachusetts Bay, through their own weakness and the artifice of La Tour, became dishonorably, not to say dishonestly, implicated in 'the French business,' — the controversy between D'Aulney and La Tour. In an early stage of this business (in May, 1643), 'those about Ipswich, &c., took great offence at these proceedings,' protesting against them 'with divers arguments, some whereof were weighty.' (Winthrop, ii. 128; Hutchinson's State Papers, p. 115.) In this protest, it is fair to presume that Mr. Saltonstall was the leader, not only from his social and official position, his being the first subscriber, and his known sentiments, but from his subsequent conduct.

"This protest, dated July 14, 1643, was signed by Richard Saltonstall, Simon Bradstreet, Samuel Simonds, Nath. Warde, Ez. Rogers, Nath. Rogers, John Norton. (See Hazard's State Papers, i. p. 502.) Mr. Bradstreet speaks of it as a joint production, — 'we writ the letter,' 'our letter,' and he defended it against the strictures of Gov. Winthrop.

"At the General Court, in May, 1645, a commission was granted to the Governor (Dudley), Lieut. Atherton, Mr. Pelham, Capt. Cooke, Mr. Saltonstall, and Mr. Hathorne, with power to summon witnesses, &c., to search out the truth about 'the French business;' yet, at the same Court, a pass was granted to La Tour for seven armed vessels; and a small amount of provision was allowed them 'on the country charge.' This was a manifest violation of the spirit, if not of the letter, of the 9th Article of the Confederation of the four New England Colonies, entered into in May, 1643; and in August, 1645, a solemn and formal protest was delivered to the Commissioners of the United Colonies, in the handwriting of Mr. Saltonstall, and signed by himself and Mr. Hathorne, who were a minority of those commissioners of inquiry, appointed the preceding May. This protest, for pertinence, perspicuity, just sentiments, and comprehensive views, will compare most favorably with any state paper of that period. (See Winthrop, ii. pp. 381–3.) From this paper we may infer the ability displayed in Mr. Saltonstall's book against a Standing Council for life.

"Mr. Saltonstall is entitled to a high place among those Christian philanthropists who have entertained a consci-

entious regard for 'the higher law,' and have spoken and
acted promptly and boldly against the nefarious slave trade.
Capt. James Smith, of Boston, and his mate, Thos. Kaezar,
in the ship Rainbow, went to the coast of 'Guinea to trade
for negroes.' Upon their return, bringing only two negroes
to Boston and reporting their doings, Mr. Saltonstall, in Oct.,
1645, presented to the General Court a petition representing
in strong terms the heinous conduct of Smith and Kaezar,
declaring that 'the act of stealing negroes, or taking them
by force (whether it be considered a theft or a robbery), is
(as I conceive) contrary to the law of God and the law of
this country,' and he 'requested that the several offenders
may be imprisoned by the order of this Court, and brought
to their deserved censure in convenient time.' The petition,
written with Mr. Saltonstall's peculiar terseness, perspicuity,
and boldness, was signed by himself only. (Winthrop, ii.
p. 379.) The petition was granted, and it was ordered that
Capt. Smith (a member of Boston Church), and Mr. Kaezar,
'be laid hold on, and committed to give answer.' The Court
ordered the two negroes to be delivered up, and one, if
not both of them, to be sent back to Guinea at the public
expense." [1]

"Perplexity about our Sir Richard Saltonstall, called by
Hutchinson (who is not often either so indistinct or erroneous) 'son or grandson of Sir Richard Saltonstall, Lord
Mayor of London,' was relieved by finding in Thoresby's
History of Leeds, ed. 2, by T. D. Whitaker, LL. D., &c.
vol. ii. 236: 'Gilbert Saltonstall of Halifax had son, by his
first wife, Samuel, who was father of Sir Richard Saltonstall,
Knight, who married Grace, d. of Robert Kaye, Esq., and
by her had son Richard, born at Woodsome 1610, obiit
1694, married Mariel, d. of Brampton Gurdon, of Assington
in Suffolk, Esq.' "[2]

[1] Bond's *Genealogies and History of Watertown*, pp. 918–921.
[2] Savage's "Gleanings," *Mass. Hist. Coll.* 3d series, vol. viii. p. 313.

DESCENT OF MURIEL GURDON

FROM THE ROYAL LINES OF ENGLAND AND SCOTLAND

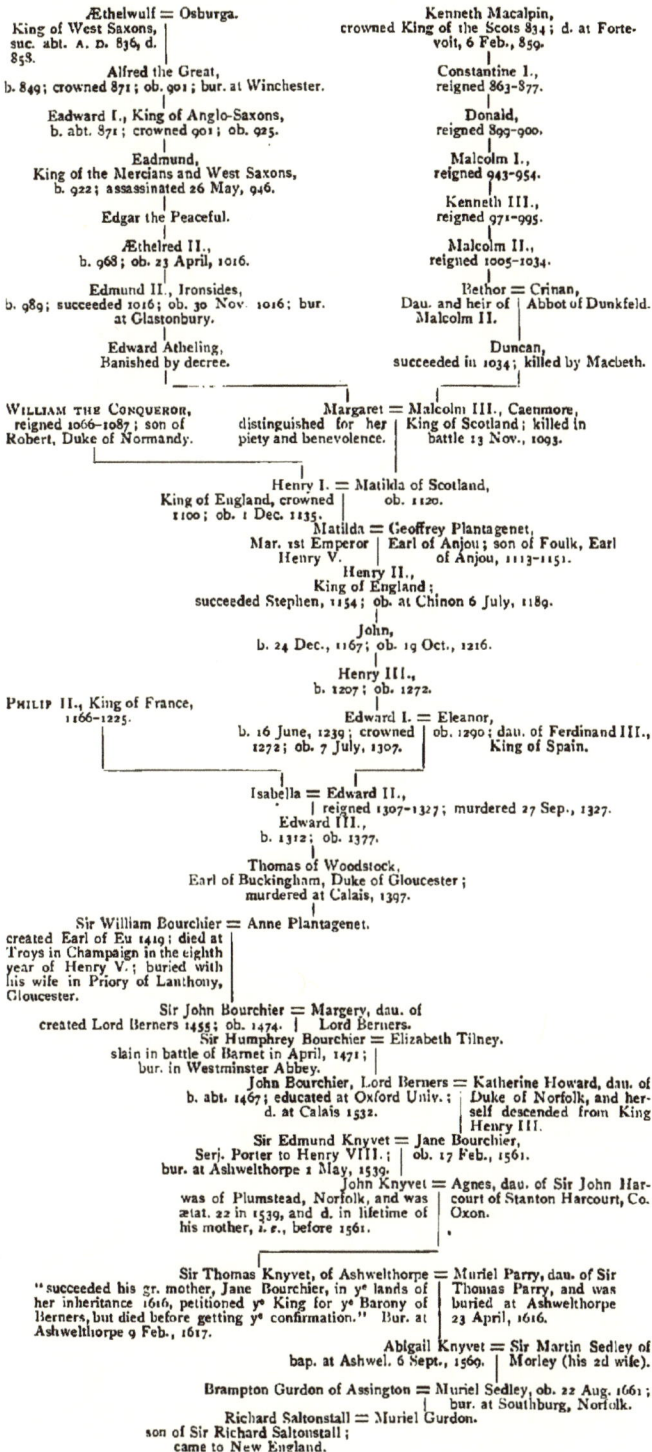

Æthelwulf = Osburga.
King of West Saxons,
suc. abt. A. D. 836, d.
858.

Alfred the Great,
b. 849; crowned 871; ob. 901; bur. at Winchester.

Eadward I., King of Anglo-Saxons,
b. abt. 871; crowned 901; ob. 925.

Eadmund,
King of the Mercians and West Saxons,
b. 922; assassinated 26 May, 946.

Edgar the Peaceful.

Æthelred II.,
b. 968; ob. 23 April, 1016.

Edmund II., Ironsides,
b. 989; succeeded 1016; ob. 30 Nov. 1016; bur.
at Glastonbury.

Edward Atheling,
Banished by decree.

Kenneth Macalpin,
crowned King of the Scots 834; d. at Forte-
voit, 6 Feb., 859.

Constantine I.,
reigned 863-877.

Donald,
reigned 899-900.

Malcolm I.,
reigned 943-954.

Kenneth III.,
reigned 971-995.

Malcolm II.,
reigned 1005-1034.

Bethor = Crinan,
Dau. and heir of | Abbot of Dunkfeld.
Malcolm II.

Duncan,
succeeded in 1034; killed by Macbeth.

WILLIAM THE CONQUEROR,
reigned 1066-1087; son of
Robert, Duke of Normandy.

Margaret = Malcolm III., Caenmore,
distinguished for her | King of Scotland; killed in
piety and benevolence. | battle 13 Nov., 1093.

Henry I. = Matilda of Scotland,
King of England, crowned | ob. 1120.
1100; ob. 1 Dec. 1135.
Matilda = Geoffrey Plantagenet,
Mar. 1st Emperor | Earl of Anjou; son of Foulk, Earl
Henry V. | of Anjou, 1113-1151.
Henry II.,
King of England;
succeeded Stephen, 1154; ob. at Chinon 6 July, 1189.

John,
b. 24 Dec., 1167; ob. 19 Oct., 1216.

Henry III.,
b. 1207; ob. 1272.

PHILIP II., King of France,
1166-1225.

Edward I. = Eleanor,
b. 16 June, 1239; crowned | ob. 1290; dau. of Ferdinand III.,
1272; ob. 7 July, 1307. | King of Spain.

Isabella = Edward II.,
| reigned 1307-1327; murdered 27 Sep., 1327.
Edward III.,
b. 1312; ob. 1377.

Thomas of Woodstock,
Earl of Buckingham, Duke of Gloucester;
murdered at Calais, 1397.

Sir William Bourchier = Anne Plantagenet.
created Earl of Eu 1419; died at
Troys in Champaign in the eighth
year of Henry V.; buried with
his wife in Priory of Lanthony,
Gloucester.

Sir John Bourchier = Margery, dau. of
created Lord Berners 1455; ob. 1474. | Lord Berners.
Sir Humphrey Bourchier = Elizabeth Tilney.
slain in battle of Barnet in April, 1471; |
bur. in Westminster Abbey.
John Bourchier, Lord Berners = Katherine Howard, dau. of
b. abt. 1467; educated at Oxford Univ.; | Duke of Norfolk, and her-
d. at Calais 1532. | self descended from King
| Henry III.

Sir Edmund Knyvet = Jane Bourchier,
Serj. Porter to Henry VIII.; | ob. 17 Feb., 1561.
bur. at Ashwelthorpe 1 May, 1539. |
John Knyvet = Agnes, dau. of Sir John Har-
was of Plumstead, Norfolk, and was | court of Stanton Harcourt, Co.
ætat. 22 in 1539, and d. in lifetime of | Oxon.
his mother, i. e., before 1561.

Sir Thomas Knyvet, of Ashwelthorpe = Muriel Parry, dau. of Sir
"succeeded his gr. mother, Jane Bourchier, in ye lands of | Thomas Parry, and was
her inheritance 1616, petitioned ye King for ye Barony of | buried at Ashwelthorpe
Berners, but died before getting ye confirmation." Bur. at | 23 April, 1616.
Ashwelthorpe 9 Feb., 1617.

Abigail Knyvet = Sir Martin Sedley of
bap. at Ashwel. 6 Sept., 1569. | Morley (his 2d wife).

Brampton Gurdon of Assington = Muriel Sedley, ob. 22 Aug. 1661;
| bur. at Southburg, Norfolk.
Richard Saltonstall = Muriel Gurdon.
son of Sir Richard Saltonstall;
came to New England.

Johnson, in his "Wonder Working Providence," says of Richard and his father Sir Richard : —

"Also at this time Christ sent over the much honoured and upright hearted servant of his, Richard Saltingstall Esquire, Son of the before-named Sir Richard Saltingstall, who being weary of this Wildernesse worke returned home again not long before, and now his Son being chose to the Office of a Magistrate, continued for some good space of time, helping on the affaires of this little Common wealth to the honour of Christ, who hath called him: both Father and Son are here remembered.

"Thou worthy Knight, Saltingstall hight, her's gaine doth gold exceed.
Then trifle not, its to be got, if thou can'st see thy neede.
Why wilt thou back, and leave as wreck, this worthy worke begun.
Art thou back-bore, Christ will send more, and raise instead thy son.
His Father gon, *young Richard* on here valiantly doth War,
For Christ his truth, to their great Ruth, Heathens opposers are :
To study thou, thy mind dost bow, and daily good promote,
Saltingstall why, then dost thy fly, let all Gods people note.
That thou wilt stand, in thy own Land, Christ there then strengthen thee
With grace thee heate, that thy retreate, may for his glory be :
At ending day, he thee array, with Glory will not faile,
Breaking graves bands, with his strong hands, and free dust from death's gaole."

President Quincy says: "His [Sir Richard Saltonstall's] son Richard of the same name, a kindred spirit, and of like moral worth, imbibed his father's attachment to the College and displayed equal zeal and self-devotion in advancing its interests. This country being the place of his principal abode, he had opportunities of rendering frequent useful services, of which he never failed to avail himself.

"It appears by the records of the College, that of two hundred and fifty pounds sterling, subscribed in 1654 for the repairs of its buildings, by twenty-six individuals, his subscription amounted to one hundred and four pounds. Subsequently being in England, he transmitted three hundred and twenty pounds for its benefit. Whether this was a donation of his own, or was his father's legacy, has been made a question. It is a point, however, of little consequence. The deed belongs to the honors of the name of

Saltonstall, emblazoned in every period of our history by its public spirit and its private charities.

"Richard Saltonstall, not less than his father, was distinguished for fixedness of purpose and independence of opinion, and was as much in advance of his age and country in his views of civil, as was his father in his of religious liberty. . . . 'Notwithstanding his political predilections were in favor of Winthrop, yet his principles of liberty were so repugnant to the idea of a Standing Council, composed of members elected for life,' that he wrote a book expressly against it; denominating the Council 'a sinful innovation, which ought to be reformed.' The boldness and spirit which characterized the work displeased Winthrop and the ecclesiastical leaders, deeming it an attempt to undermine the essential foundations of the Government.

"Governor Winthrop twice moved that the matter of that book should be taken into solemn consideration of the General Court. Such, however, was the popularity of Saltonstall, and probably so congenial were the principles of the work with the views of the majority, and so satisfied were they of 'the honest intention of the writer,' and that his design was in favor of popular liberty, that the Court would not even inquire into the subject until they had first 'voted an indemnity to the author against any censure.' . . .

"Nor does the truth permit us to fail in remembering that this family, distinguished in every age for intellect, faithfulness, and honor, as well as for intense attachment to Harvard College, is at this day especially fortunate, that the heir of their house is also the heir of their affections and virtues."[1]

LETTER FROM RICHARD SALTONSTALL TO EMANUEL DOWNING

In 1890 the author was informed by a lady in England that an interesting letter addressed by Richard Saltonstall

[1] Quincy's *History of Harvard University*, vol. i. p. 164. President Quincy refers to Hon. Leverett Saltonstall of Salem, Class of 1802.

from Massachusetts, to Emanuel Downing, Esq., in London, had been found in a certain collection of old papers, which upon further inquiries proved to be the Coke MSS. preserved at Melbourne Hall, Derbyshire, and that a copy of this letter could be obtained upon certain conditions, which being complied with, the copy was subsequently received.

The letter, which was indorsed, " Mr. Saltonstall's of the 4 of Feb^r. 1631. Rcd 10 May 1632 (in another hand) Acc^t of Massachusetts Bay," and signed by Richard Saltonstall, is as follows : —

To my very worthy friend Emanuell Downing Esq. at the Byshop's Head in Fleet Street, near the Conduict in London d. d.

    Worthy S^r.

Since my arriuall in New England I have endeuored to giue a trew & fathfull relation of such things as came within mine observation & might answere the desires of such as expected letters from mee.   That which I know will bee most gratefull to you in regard of your desire of a common good, & my debt vnto you thereby, I will briefly sett doune : The countrie abounds with good creatures needfull for sustenation of the life of man ; and after some time of libertie from building and inclosing of grounds for ye safetie of our cattell from the wolfe, I doubt not but we shall rayse good proffit not only by o^r fishing Trade (which is sufficiently knowne) but by Hempe, flaxe, pitch, tarr, pottashes, sope ashes, masts, pipe staues, clapboard (& Iron as we hope) for we find there are mineralls ; but for want of skill & time cannot yet certainly satisfie either ourselues or you, of what kind they are.   Therefoer good S^r incourage men to come ouer for heare is land & meanes of lively hood suffitient for men that bring bodys able, & minds fitted to braue the first brunts, which the beginnings of such works necessarily put men vpon.   Without hands nothing can bee don nor anything with any great profit vntill multitudes of people make labour cheape ; it is strange the meaner soart of people should bee soe backward hauing assurance that they may liue plentifully by their neighbours; & that the better soart of people should not helpe ye poorer, with meanes to transport them, that in time might returne their adventures with answerable advantage in any of the afoar named commodities & diuers others not mentioned.   If gentlemen of abillitie would transplant themselues, they might in time much advance their owne estates & not only supply the want wee labour vnder, of men fitted by their estates to beare common burdens and the giufts of their minds to nurse vp this infant plantation, but allsoe might improve their tallents & times for the honor & benefit of Old England, (to which wee owe the frute of our best endeuours) and their owne eternall glory, in being worthy instruments of propagating the gospell to these poore barbarous people, The trewest object of Christians bowell-compassions, that the world now affoards.   Oh that it might please God to mooue either the generall state or at least (by the fauour & encouragement of our gratious soueraigne) some large harted men, to contribute (if it were) but the tythe of what was bestowed upon Virginia for the educating of our poore Indeans, in the supporting of their bodilie necessities, till they might attain such abilities whereby they might feed themselves and others with spirituall foode.

I pray you send over by some of your East-contrie merchants to gett some few mayster-workmen for the ordering of our potash work.   Wee have great store of Hemp growing naturally in some pts of the contrie, a sample whereof you may call for from this bearer.   Certainly the ground would admirably well agree with it planted, that offers it vnto vs without our labours.   The hast of the bearer enforceth mee to take an abrupt leaue; & with my best respects to y^r selfe & Mrs. Downing doe rest,

Your very louing Friend
RICHARD SALTONSTALL
From the Matachusetts bay this 4th Feb. 1631.

The letter on being read by Mr. Leverett Saltonstall, at

Assington Hall, Suffolk, Seat of the Gurdon family.

(From a photograph taken for the Author.)

the May meeting of the Massachusetts Historical Society in 1890, excited much interest, being dated 4 Feb., 1631, it was at once suggested that, being Old Style, it was 1632, and that neither Sir Richard Saltonstall nor his son were in this country at that time. A communication from Mr. Leverett Saltonstall was read at the May meeting in 1893, in regard to the same.

Who was the writer of this letter is an interesting question, and it is one which has not yet been settled; whether there was at that time another Richard Saltonstall in this country, or whether Richard Saltonstall, Jr., who is reported to have sailed for England in November, 1630, could have returned to this country, and sailed again for England before his marriage.

An interesting debate ensued which will be found in " Proceedings of Massachusetts Historical Society," 1893, p. 202.

Richard was certainly the oldest son of Sir Richard Saltonstall, and must have been the one whom Governor Winthrop records as having sailed in November, 1631.

THE GURDONS

" ASSINGTON, SUFFOLK. A parish in the hundred of Babergh, Union of Sudbury, 61¼ miles from London.

"John Gurdon left £100 in 1777 for the instruction of the poor children of the parish.

"North is Assington Hall, the seat of John Gurdon, Esq. This family was originally from Gourdon, near Cahors, on the borders of Perigord, and came over with William the Conqueror; the name may still be found on the roll of Battle Abbey.

"Sir Adam de Gurdon was bailiff of Alton in the time of Henry III., but, being considered a member of the Montford faction, was outlawed for rebellion and treason. He was, however, on the accession of Edward 1st, restored in quality and made, in 1272, Warden of Wolmer Forest.

"He married three wives and had two sons by the last, the second of whom settled in London and had a son, John, who became eminent as a merchant.

"The sixth in lineal descent from that gentleman who married Rose, the daughter and heiress of Robert Letton, Esq., of Lavenham in Suffolk, served the office of High Sheriff and purchased Assington Hall.

"John Gurdon, Esq., the great grandson of that gentleman sat in the Long Parliament for the county, and was appointed one of the Committee to sit in judgment on Charles 1st, but did not attend the trial.

"The present proprietor succeeded to the estate in 1817, on the death of his father."[1]

At Assington are the following inscriptions relating to Brampton Gurdon, John his father, and Robert his grand-father: —

"Hic jacent Robertus Gurdon ar: et Rosa uxor ejus (filia Roberti Sexton de Lavenham in hoc Com: Ar.) qui obiit V^to die Aprilis, anno dñi 1577, annoque ætatis suæ LXIII^tio et habuerunt Johannem et Robertum filios, et Elizabetham filiam unicam."

"Hic jacent Johannes Gurdon filius Roberti Gurdon, qui duxit uxorem amiciam filiam et hærediem Gulielum Brampton de Letton in Com: North: Arm: qui obiit XX° die Sept: anno dñi 1623 et duos reliquit liberos Bramptonum filium et Elizabethem filiam."

"Erected, June, 1648. In memory of Brampton Gurdon of Assington in the County of Suffolk, Esq: who married first Elizabeth ye dau: of Edward Barret of Belhouse in the parish of [blank in original], in Essex, Esq: and Coheyre with her mother. She departed this life the 5th of Aprill in the year 1603, and after her the said Brampton for his second wife married Meriell, the dau: of Martin Sedley of Morley in the County of Norfolk, Esq."

By the will of Brampton Gurdon he leaves his Suffolk property to his eldest son John, and his Norfolk property to

[1] Clarke's *British Gazetteer*, 1852, vol. i. p. 120.

PEDIGREE OF GURDON

The name of Gurdon appears in the Roll of Battle Abbey, but no record appears of the family until the reign of Richard I., when there were two brothers.

THE ASSINGTON BRANCH,

descendants of John Gurdon (the eldest son of Brampton Gurdon by his first wife, Elizabeth Barrett) and Anne, dau. of Sir Calthorpe Parker of Erwarton, Suffolk.

THE LETTON BRANCH,

descendants of Brampton Gurdon (the eldest son of Brampton Gurdon by his second wife, Muriel Sedley) and Mary, dau. of Henry Polsted.

BERTRAM,
the Archer who shot Richard I. at the siege of Chalez; played alive 1189.

JERRY=
d. 1238.

Sir Adam == **Constantia, dau. of Thomas**
(A celebrated outlaw and the lieutenant of Mackard of Selborne.
Simon de Montfort. He carried on a
guerrilla warfare after the battle of Eve-
sham, but, being vanquished in single
combat by Edward I. (see White's History of Selborne), was pardoned and appointed Keeper of Wolmer Forest. He
died at a great age in 1310.)

Robert ==
(Of London, d. 1343.)
John ==
(Of London, d. 1365.)
John ==
(Of Clyve, Kent, d. 1456.)
John ==
(Of Clyve.)
John == Mathilda.
(Of Dedham, Essex, d. 1465.)
John == Joan.
(Of Dedham, d. 1494.)
John == (1) Mary, dau. of John Butler.
Robert == (2) Anne, dau. of John Coleman.
Rose, dau. and heiress of Robert Sexton of Layenham
and widow of William Appleton of Little Wadingfield.
Her son, Thomas Appleton, m. Mary, dau. of Edward
Raeke o Kent and had 4 sons.

Sir Isaac of == **John.** **Thomas,**
Little Wadingfield.

John == **Amy, dau. and heiress of**
(Of Assington; High William Brampton of
Sheriff for Suffolk Letton, Norfolk.
1581; d. 1623.)

Brampton == (1) Elizabeth, dau. of
John Barrett of Bel-
houe, Essex.
(2) Muriel, dau. of Mar-
tin Sedley of Morley,
Norfolk.

(By first wife, with other issue.)

John m. Ann,
dau. of Sir Cal-
thorpe Parker,
M. P. for Ips-
wich with and
folk; a Member
of the
Council
dered for life and to be
dragged on each anni-
versary of the execu-
tion of Charles I. from
Newgate to Tyburn and
back on a sledge with
a rope round his neck.
(See Pepys's Diary.)

Robert; m.
Abigail m.
Alice. Lucas
Letters
M. P. for
Ipswich
M. P. for
West
Nor-
folk; d. 1681.

Brampton m. Mary,
Abigail m. Roger Manwaring,
dau. of Henry Po-
sted; M. P. for
Sudbury; Col. of
Suffolk Horse at
the
siege of Colchester,
Naseby and at the
siege of Colchester,
afterwards Baron
of the Exchequer;
d. 1669.

Brampton,
M. P. for West Nor-
folk, m. Henrietta So-
sannah, dau. of Lord
Colborne; d. 1681.

John,
M. P. for Colchester,
m. (1) Mary dau. and
heiress of Gen. Horton
(2) Georgina, dau. of
the Earl of Norbury;
d. 1870, leaving is-
sue.

Robert Thornhagh
M. P. for South
Norfolk.

(By first wife.)
Amy.
Harriet.

(By second wife.)
Muriel.
Louisa.

Bertram.
Francis.

(1) Harriet Eden, dau.
of Sir W. Ellis; M.
P. for W. Somerset-
shire.
(2) Emily Frances, dau.
of Rev. Boothby
Herthcote.

Charlotte = Honore, son of Lieut.
Gen. Broke.

Philip
m. Hy. Henriette
Laura, dau. of ——
Polkeney; d. 1874,
leaving issue.

Anne
m. Hy. Wodehouse,
late County Court
Judge and Recorder
of Bury.

William,
late County Court
Judge and Recorder
of Bury.

Edward
(Rev.), m. (1) Fred-
erica, dau. of U. S.
Sergt. Frick; (2)
Catherine, dau. of
Frere; Canon Temple
Frere; d. 1871, leav-
ing issue.

Amy Louisa,
d. 1864.

William Brampton ==
K. C. B.

John, Lord Wodehouse,
created Earl of Kimberly 1866; Secretary of
State for India.

ROBERT ==
(of Assington in Suf-
folk), m. Elizabeth,
dau. of Philip, Visc.
Lyssle, eldest son of
the Earl of Leicester;
(1. of Wight) in the
Long, Barebones, and
Rump Parliaments; a
member of the Com-
mittee of State and one
of the Upper House
nominated by Crom-
well in 1657; d. s. p.

PHILIP,
M. P. for Sudbury;
d. s. p. 1690.

NATHANIEL,
(Rev., D. D.), d. 1696,
m. Eliza, dau. of the
Rev. E. Arundel of
Stoke, Northants.

BRAMPTON ==
Elizabeth, dau. of Col. Thorn-
hagh, eldest son of Sir Francis
Thornhagh and M. P. for East
Retford. He commanded the
Northamptonshire Horse in the
Parliamentary Army and was
killed at the head of Cromwell's Car-
airy. (See Hutchinson's Me-
moirs.)

Sir W. Cooke == **Jane Stuart of Brown Hall.**
John == Letitia, dau. of Sir W.
M. P. for Sudbury; Cooke, M. P. for Nor-
d. 1758. folk.

(Of Letton in Norfolk.)

Brampton Philip;
d. s. p.

John == **Bridget Aurora, dau. of Melton Lombarde**
of Stevenson, Kent;
(2) Anne, dau. of Col. Leslie. M. P. d. Glas-
Jorgh, Monaghan.

John Barrett == Sophia Katharine, dau. of
Philip, late Grenadier Guards
(now of Assington.)

Nathaniel,
d. s. p.

Philip (Rev.) == Elizabeth, dau. of Herbert
Philip (Rev.) == Sarah, dau. of ——
Richardson.

John == **Mary, dau. of Philip Bed-
ingfeld of Ditchingham;
(2) Mary, dau. of Samuel Howard of Brookfish in Norfolk.**

Thornhagh == **Sarah, dau. and heiress of Theophilus Dillingham of Shelton**
d. 1793. Reds.

Theophilus Thornhagh == **Anne, dau. of William Mellish,
Col. W. Norfolk Militia.** of Blyth, Notts; M. P. for
Midlleses.

Thornhagh == **Elizabeth, dau. of Sir v. m.
Cooke, M. P. for Norfe s.**
Receiver-General of the
Co. of Norfolk and au-
thor of the History of
Parliament and other
works; d. 1733.

This pedigree is taken from the Heralds' Visitation of Suffolk; from Davy's Collection of Suffolk Pedigrees; Additional MS. No. 19133, British Museum, and from manuscript sent the author by Sir William Brampton Gurdon.

[1] From Robert Gurdon, inclusive, there is an unbroken series of portraits at Letton.
[2] Sir Henry Mildmay was the second son of Sir Thomas Mildmay by his wife Agnes, dau. of Adam Winthrop of Groton, Suffolk, ancestor of the first Governor of Massachusetts.

Brampton, the eldest son of Muriel Sedley, his second wife. He gives to " Muriell " his wife his " best Coach, 5 horses with all ye harness and furniture belonging to it," and all his " plate marked with Sedley's and Knyvetts coats," with many other articles, such as silver bowls, plates, tankards, spoons, cup, and salts. The other articles of furniture were divided between his sons and daughters; his various suits of arms to his son Brampton. He leaves to his son Saltonstall £50, and to his daughter Saltonstall £50, to be paid within six months after his death.

" LETTON, NORFOLK. A parish in the hundred of Mitford, Union of Mitford and Laundritch, at the source of the Black-water River, 126 miles from London.

" Letton Hall, the seat of Theophilus Thornhaugh Gurdon, Esq., the descendant of a very ancient family, originally from Gourdon near Cahors on the borders of Perigord in Normandy, and one of whom came into England with William the Conqueror.

" One of his descendants, Sir Adam de Gurdon, was reign bailiff of Alton in the time of Henry 3rd, and was, in 1272, constituted Keeper of the Forest of Wolmer. From him was descended Brampton Gurdon, Esq., who founded the family at Letton, and was Colonel of a regiment of horse during the Civil War, and served the office of High Sheriff of Norfolk in 1625. The son of that gentleman, Brampton Gurdon, Esq., was a barrister at law, and represented Ipswich in Parliament from 1640 till 1654. From him the present proprietor of the domain is the lineal descendant.

" Mr. Gurdon, who inherited the family estate on the death of his father, the late Brampton Gurdon, Esq., in 1820, High Sheriff in 1824, was formerly Colonel of the West Norfolk Militia, and is now a Magistrate and deputy Lieutenant of the county."[1]

Southberg Church, on the Letton Estate, Norfolk, now owned by Robert Thornhaugh Gurdon, M. P. for W. Somer-

[1] See Clarke's *British Gazetteer*, 1852, vol. ii.

setshire, is the resting-place of many of the earlier members of the Gurdon family, among whom was Muriel (Sedley) Gurdon, mother of Muriel (Gurdon) Saltonstall, with this epitaph : —

"Here lyeth Muriell Gurdon second wife of Brampton Gurdon, of Assington, in the County of Suffolk, Esq: and daughter of. Martin Sedley of Morley, in this County of Norfolk, Esq :   She survived her said husband 10 years, and departed this life at Letton 22 August, Año Dñi 1661, Ætatis 78."

Letton, inherited by Brampton Gurdon from his mother, Amy Brampton, has been the inheritance of the descendants of Brampton Gurdon, through Brampton, his eldest son by his second wife, Muriel Sedley, while Assington in Suffolk has descended through the heirs of John, the eldest son of Brampton Gurdon by his first wife, Elizabeth Barrett.

The interesting old portrait of Brampton Gurdon is surrounded with a tree which is indistinctly defined in the heliotype.   On the tree are the arms of Gurdon impaled with those of the families of his sons and daughters-in-law, with their names, while below are the names and arms of his two wives, Barrett and Sedley.   The names on the left, reading from the lower, are Parker, Harvey, Mildmay, and those on the right are Polsted, Hill, Saltonstall.[1]   These names can be seen with the aid of a magnifying glass.

---

[1] The author has in his possession photographs of the portraits at Letton of : —
  1. Robert Gurdon (in armor) of Assington, Suffolk, High Sheriff of the county, d. 1577; father of John and grandfather of Brampton Gurdon. He (Robert) married Rose, dau. and heiress of Robert Sexton of Lavenham and widow of William Appleton of Little Waldingfield, and grandmother of Sir Isaac Appleton and his younger brother Samuel, who died at Ipswich, Mass., in 1670, aged 84.
  2. John Gurdon of Assington, d. 1623; son of Robert aforesaid.
  3. Amy Brampton, wife of John Gurdon of Assington (son of Robert), daughter of William Brampton of Letton, and mother of Brampton Gurdon.
  4. Muriel Sedley, 2d wife of Brampton Gurdon, mother of 'Muriel (Gurdon) Saltonstall.
  5. Brampton Gurdon, son of Brampton, Colonel of Suffolk and Norfolk Horse; M. P. for Sudbury, and brother of Muriel Saltonstall.

Y bery louing frend
Brampton Gurdon

Epitaph to Jane (Bourchier) Knyvet at Ashwelthorpe : —

Jane Knyvet resteth here, the only heir by right,
Of the Lord Berners, that Sir John Bourchier hight,
Twenty years & three a widdow's Lyff she ledd,
Always keeping House, where Rych & Poor were fedd.
Gentyll, just, quyet, void of Debate & stryff,
Ever doying Good ; Lo ! thus she ledd her Lyff,
Even unto the Grave, where Erth on Erth doth lye,
On whose Soul God grant of his abundant mercy,
The xvii of February, A°. Dm°. MDLXI.

On Martin Sedley's tomb in St. Peter's Chapel, Morley, is an inscription which runs in part as follows : — "toke to his second wife, Abigail, descended of the Worshipfull and antiente Famelye of the Knyvettes of Ashwell-Thorp and had issue by her . . . Meriell who married to Brampton Gurdon of Assington in Suffolk, Esquire."

An inscription on the tomb of her brother Robert in St. Botolph's, Burford, Norfolk, reads, " Robert second son of Martine Sedley of Morley, Esq. by his second wife, Daughter of Tho. Knyvett of Ashwell-thorp, Esq. died June 30, 1613."

39 A. IPSWICH, MASSACHUSETTS

The pretty little town of Ipswich, so intimately associated with the earliest history of the family, Richard Saltonstall, son of Sir Richard, being one of the first settlers, with his friend the younger Winthrop, and where he built a house which is still standing, and brought his young wife, Muriel Gurdon, celebrated its 250th anniversary in 1884. The houses of the old settlers were distinctly marked, and were visited by a large number of their descendants.

Services of much interest were held in the morning, and a great banquet brought together a happy throng of inhabitants and visitors, most of whom bore in their veins the blood of the sturdy pioneers. It was an occasion which stirred the blood and warmed the hearts of those who think of their ancestors with pious affection and reverence.

On being called upon, as one of their descendants, to

respond to a sentiment to the first settlers, Mr. Leverett Saltonstall (120), in the course of his speech, said : " There are few men living who by character and attainments so admirably illustrate the virtues and talents of their ancestors as the excellent gentleman whose letter has just been read.[1] Would that he had felt able to be here to-day to add by his rare eloquence force to what he has written in response to the sentiment, a duty for which I so painfully feel my own insufficiency, but which in his absence I consider it a high honor to be called upon to perform. And as Governor Winthrop with Sir Richard Saltonstall came over in the Arbella, and as their sons four or five years later came hither together to found this ancient town, so now my heart throbs with fervent sentiment while following my honored friend in laying a small tribute upon the shrines of those good men and their co-workers.

" The sentiment carries us back two hundred and fifty years to those admirable men and women from whom not we alone, nor New England, but thousands of the bravest and best throughout our great country, love to trace their blood and their virtues, whose piety, wisdom, and incredible courage laid deep the foundation of those twin columns, religion and civil liberty, upon which so vast and majestic a temple has been reared.

" How should we rejoice, and, with gratitude all the more profound as the years roll on, celebrate these great anniversaries and centennials which recall to us our fathers and mothers of former generations, and which so tend to strengthen the ties between the past and the present, to fill our hearts with thankfulness and our minds with wonder as we reflect on their trials and sufferings, their religious faith and zeal, as well as on their far-seeing and prudent management of public affairs. They seem to have seen through the long vista of years away ahead the blossoming and fruiting of those great republican institutions which they here planted and watered with their very life's blood.

[1] Hon. Robert C. Winthrop.

PEDIGREE OF KNYVETT AND BOURCHIER.

THROUGH CATHERINE HOWARD TO EDWARD I. OF ENGLAND, AND THROUGH SIR JOHN BOURCHIER, LORD BERNERS, TO EDWARD III. OF ENGLAND

Edward I. of England = Margaret, dau. of Philip III. of France.

Thomas Plantagenet, Earl of Norfolk = Alice, dau. of Sir Roger Halys.

Margaret Plantagenet = John, Lord Segrave.

Elizabeth Segrave = John, Lord Mowbray.

Thomas, Lord Mowbray = Elizabeth, dau. of Earl of Arundel.

Margaret = Sir Robert Howard.

Sir John Howard, Duke of Norfolk = Margaret, dau. of Sir John Chedworth.

Catherine Howard = Sir John Bourchier, Lord Berners.

Edward III. of England = Phillippa, dau. of William, Count of Holland.

Thomas, Duke of Gloucester = Eleanor, dau. of de Bohun, Earl of Northumberland.

Anne Plantagenet = William Bourchier, Earl of Ewe.

Sir John Bourchier = Margaret, dau. of Sir Richard Berners.

Humphrey Bourchier = Elizabeth, dau. of Sir Fred Tilney.

Jane Bourchier of Ashwellthorpe, dau. of and eventually sole heir of John (Bourchier), Lord Berners, ob. 17 Feb., 1561. = Edmund Knyvet, Esqre, Serj. Porter to Henry VIII.; buried at Ashwellthorpe, Norfolk, 1 May, 1546.

John Knyvet of Plumstead, Norfolk, Esqre., was æt. 22 in 1559, and died in the lifetime of his mother, s. p., before 1601. = Agnes, dau. of Sir John Harcourt of Stanton Harcourt, Co. Oxon.

Sir Thomas Knyvet of Ashwellthorpe succeeded his grandmother, Jane Bourchier, in the lands of her inheritance A.D. 1616. He petitioned the King for the Barony of Berners, but died before getting the royal confirmation; buried at Ashwellthorpe 9 Feb., 1617. = Muriel, dau. of Sir Thomas Parry, master of the Court of Wards; bur. at Ashwellthorpe 23 April, 1616.

Elizabeth, dau. of Sir Nathaniel Bacon of Stiffkey, Co. Norfolk. = Sir Thomas Knyvett "ye younger"; died vita patris; buried at Felixwell 20 Sep., 1605.

Abigail, baptised at Ashwell 6 Sep., 1569. = (2) Sir Martin Sedley of Morley. (His 1st wife was Anne Shelton.)

Muriel Sedley ob. 22 Aug., 1661; bur. at Southburg, Co. Norfolk. = Frampton Gurdon of Assington.

Muriel Gurdon = Richard Saltonstall.

"We are prone to picture to ourselves the early settlers as stern old Puritans, men of middle age or older, who had laid aside with their youth the desire to enjoy the sweets of life, and who from long forbearance had lost the very faculty and sense of enjoying anything but a long sermon preached through the nose. But this was not so. There were many young men of gentle blood educated at the university, some owning estates in England. They brought with them their young wives tenderly nurtured and accustomed to all refinements and luxuries of life, to nurse their babes to sleep with the howling of wolves and ofttimes the war-whoop of the savage Indian for a lullably.

"Two centuries and a half is a long time to review, but in many ways how near it seems to us!

"I doubt if there be any people who have so reverently and so devoutly cherished the memory of their ancestry. Fireside traditions have been supplemented by anniversary discourses and sermons, and by days of public thanksgiving which have been observed from the first settlement. Few there are among those of New England extraction who do not feel this interest, for few there are who do not trace their descent from one or more of the first settlers. The late Colonel Thomas H. Perkins of Boston, whom I well recollect, used to relate that in his youth he had seen an old man who had conversed with Peregrine White, the first child born in the Plymouth Colony, — one link only between the landing of the Pilgrim Fathers and him who was living thirty or forty years ago.

"I had as a visitor from England last year a descendant and bearing the name of Brampton Gurdon, whose daughter Muriel came to this town when eighteen years of age with her young husband, Richard Saltonstall. We called each other cousins, going back eight generations to the time of the settlement of this town for a common ancestor. So the knowledge we have of the men who settled this and other towns, of their characters, and of the parts they and their descendants took in the great work of founding and forming this mighty nation, in a certain way, makes us feel the great history to be much briefer than of two centuries and a half.

"At the Endicott festival a few years ago, at the dinner succeeding the oration, the accomplished orator (the Honorable William C. Endicott of Salem) said that he had occasion in the morning to allude to the "four good men" — Conant, Woodbury, Balch, and Palfrey — who were already settlers in Salem at the landing of Governor Endicott in 1628, and received him, and to Governor Endicott welcoming Governor Winthrop and Sir Richard Saltonstall in 1630. 'Now,' said he, ' I see before me descendants of those four men who live in Salem, and still bear their names; while on my right sit Winthrop and Saltonstall, the latter born and formerly resident in Salem.' The late Dean Stanley, who was one of the guests, turned to me and exclaimed, ' What an astonishing statement! Nothing like it could be said in any town in England.' Is it not quite natural, then, that we feel such honest local pride? and that thousands upon thousands descended from our forefathers who cover the prairies and fill the cities of our broad land, and who have so imparted of their inheritance to the homes of their adoption, all recur to their ancestry with deeper sentiment as they grow older?"

After referring to his ancestors, Mr. Saltonstall continued: " I have this morning seen the old house where Saltonstall is said to have lived. This may or may not be so. But as, in visiting the Holy Sepulchre, that particular spot may be a matter of doubt, yet one thing is certain, here is Mount Zion, there the Mount of Olives, here the Pool of Siloam, and there the garden of Gethsemane: so here are the same hills, the same fields, and the same gentle river winding through them which my ancestors beheld, — the one, from early manhood to old age, the other from infancy to manhood, — and where they had their varied experiences of joy, of suffering, and of anxiety, and where they exercised their brave spirits, contending against privation and the various dangers of the time.

House built by Richard Saltonstall at Ipswich; still standing (1895).

" May we never forget the founders of this town, and what they dared and endured for posterity, nor neglect to cherish and hand down to our children and children's children their sacred memory."

THE SALTONSTALL HOUSE AT IPSWICH

" Among the most conspicuous of the old houses histori- cally and architecturally is that erected by Richard Salton- stall, built where it now stands in 1635.

" For upwards of two hundred and fifty years humanity has found shelter beneath this roof. Its front and sides are bleached by the rains and snows, the suns and the winds, but there still remains a sturdy unwithering show of vitality. The construction is quite different from any that I have ever seen. The lower, overlapping beams that traverse the side project- ing were once modelled like a moulding, and the junction of cross beams were headed with an ornamental capital or bracket. The house was originally painted with white lead, the corner strips being decorated with red paint, as were also the projecting beams. There can be no doubt about these colors having been applied when the house was finished, de- spite the fact recorded that there were no painted houses in the colonies for nearly a century after their settlement. The paint was used as much for its preserving qualities as for dec- oration when it could be afforded. There is a massive beam which terminates in the front hall, and through its centre has been bored a hole large enough to admit a gun-barrel. This was doubtless used by the inmates to protect the main en- trance, and woe to the Indian who first showed his grim vis- age in this vicinity. The partitions are filled with clay and bricks, being made arrow and bullet proof, as well as to keep out the winds and cold of winter. The house as it originally stood was in the open field, and commanded a considerable view, so that any one approaching within musket-shot could be distinctly seen."[1]

[1] *New England Magazine*, September, 1894, p. 105.

40. ROSAMOND SALTONSTALL (IV.)

There is in the archives of the American Antiquarian Society at Worcester, an autograph letter of Rosamond Saltonstall to her brother, so warm with sisterly affection, and so imbued with an earnest Christian spirit, — so creditable to her mind as well as her heart, — that it seems worthy of insertion.

April 22, 1644,
From Warwick House.

DEAR BROTHER : —

I am not a little glad to receive any intimation of your health and happiness, either by word or writing, and both your own letter and my brother Henry's intelligence hath lately assured me of it.   I should be much more glad to see you that I might know you better, and enjoy more intimate acquaintance with your spirit, especially in spiritual things, which I trust you have seen and heard so much the beauty of, where you are, that they have really challenged your heart from all the world.   I can desire nothing so much as your soul's prosperity, and that you would interest yourself in all the ways and means that might add to your growth for an eternal welfare.   I am sure 't is the best counsel, and you will find it so one day, when all your days on earth must be concluded by death.   Consider that time much, and what kind of provision eternity will require, and then the world and carnal things will not take up your thoughts more than needs must.

Dear brother, I am glad to hear of you so well as I do, and, therefore I desire you would go farther, and not be a hindrance to the good of your own soul by any indisposition of nature.   Put forth yourself and trust God in his own way and work, if you can find, in any true measure, anything of Christ savingly wrought in you; and what he will own, man dares not reject, nor any that desire to draw near to God in any ordinance.   All his ordinances are precious and highly to be valued, and surely God will never draw so near, or

Ma 22 1654
from warwwick house

Deare Bro

I am not a litle glad to receaue any
intimation of your health and hapines ether by
word or writing and both your owne letter and
my Bro: Henerys intelligence hath lately assure
me might I should be much more glad to see your
chountance a new you here and inioye more intimate
acquantance with your spirit in spieretuall thinges
I trust you haue [s]eene and heard so much the
buty of wheare you are ether haue really challenged
youre hart from all the woreld of can desire nothing
so much as your soule resperavity and if you would
intrest your selfe in all the ways and meanes that
might add to your trowth for an eternall wellfare
am sure tis the best counsell and you will find it so
one day when all your days on earth must be concluded
by death Consider of time much and what kind of
prouision eternety will require and then the needs
and carnall things will not take up your thoughts
more then needes must, Deare [fleer] I am glad
heare of you so well as I doe and theirfore I loue
you would you further and not be a kinderance to
the good of your owne soule by any indisposition
in nature put y[our]selfe with your selfe and trust god
any true measure any thinge of Christ sauingly
wrought in you and what he will giue men here
not reiect nor any of desire to draw neere to an
ordinance all his ordinances are precious and
to be vallued and surely god will neuer drawe
to neare or desire in any of dos not make it theire
desire and indeauore to drawe neare to him in euery
ordinance Consider your condition seariously put your
selfe to triad let god se you willing to deny yourselfe
in all carnall Resconings and sinnfull obiections and
you may of giue up your selfe fully to be one of Christs
flocck of his may wholy rule ouer you Deare Bro:
you are Likely to be a Constant settleer wheare you
are theirefore with out gi[f]kten you haue liberty to
dispose of your selfe into church fellowshipe and I pray
god you may be so fitted for it as interested in it
for our conditions neare I neede not tell you how
we are dispersed my father and Bro: Henery in
holland my father hath onc necesity to be theire
now because of his whites brething by whome my
father hath lost more of his estate herselfe
left for the present of am and haue beene 2 yeares
in me Lord of warwwicks family my sister and
me Lady manchester and thus we ...

For my Deare Brother
Mr Samuell Saltonstall
at Wa—ower— in
New en— nd give
thes

delight in any that do not make it their desire and endeavor to draw near to him in every ordinance. Consider your condition seriously, put yourself to trial, let God see you willing to deny yourself in all carnal reasonings and sinful objections, that you may give up yourself fully to be one of Christ's flock, that he may wholly rule over you.

Dear brother, you are likely to be a constant settler where you are; therefore, without question, you have liberty to dispose of yourself into church-fellowship, and I pray God you may be so fitted for it, as interested in it.

For our conditions here, I need not tell you how we are dispersed: my father and brother Henry in Holland. My father hath some necessity to be there now, because of Mr. White's breaking, by whom my father hath lost more of that little estate he hath left. For the present I am, and have been two years, in my Lord of Warwick's family; my sister is with my Lady Manchester, and thus we are dispersed about. The Lord give us all a gathering in Christ, and there we shall meet without separations to all eternity.

Dear brother, farewell, only remember me, and I shall never [forget] you . . . Your truly affectionate sister

ROSAMOND SALTONSTALL.

. . . .

For my dear brother, Mr. Samuel Saltonstall, at Watertown in New England give these.

The officers of the American Antiquarian Society kindly consented that a photograph should be taken of this letter, which is here reproduced.

---

41. ROBERT SALTONSTALL (IV.)

Robert Saltonstall " was probably the 2d son of Sir Richard, as he must have attained his majority at least as early as 1636; for on the 23d Sept., 1637, Mr. Hugh Peters presented to the Court a deed, by which Robert Saltonstall assigned to him all the estate that he hath or shall have, to satisfy his creditors. This implies that he had some time before attained his majority. It appears by a deed dated about 1642, that he had resided some time in Watertown, and he probably went to reside in Boston as early as 1638 or 40; and was adm. mem. An. and Hon. Art. Co., 1638. He was the superintendent of his father's interest in this country, and it appears by the Colonial Records, that in 1645 Sir Richard had granted to him irrevocably all his dues or claims in this country, which was allowed by the Court. His name often occurs in the Colonial Records, in connection with business transactions. June 2, 1641, it was certified to the Court, that Connecticut colony had sold to Mr. Robert Saltonstall ' a great quantity of land, not far below Springfield.' June 20, 1645, for £100, he sold to his brother Richard 2,100 acres of land on Connecticut River, ' between Springfield and Windsor Ferry.' (Essex Deeds, i. p. 7.) He was one of those purchasers of the two patents of Wecohannet (Dover), and Pascataquack (Portsmouth), who, on the 14th of June, 1641, ' gave up and set over ' all their power of jurisdiction to the government of Massachusetts Bay. Oct. 1, 1645, the Court granted to him 3,200 acres, in right of his father, which had been granted to Sir Richard as an adventurer. Previous to May 26, 1647, he had sold to Adam and Dean Winthrop, 1,000 acres at Cochituit, which had been granted to his father, to be laid out by Capt. Pelham and Mr. Pendleton. There were repeated contests between him (as agent of his father) and Watertown, respecting titles to lands. They were finally terminated by arbitration in Oct., 1647. May 29, 1644, he was fined 5s. for presenting a petition, respecting land in Watertown, on so small and so bad a piece of paper. . . .

" He was never admitted freeman, probably because he was not disposed to conform to the rigid discipline of a Puritan church. He was enterprising and energetic, and his father seems to have reposed entire confidence in his integrity; yet he seems not to have possessed the public spirit and the high-toned religious and moral characteristics which were

so admirably illustrated in his father and his brother Richard.
He d. unm. about July, 1650.

" His will, dated June 13, proved Aug. 15, 1650, mentions
his father; his brothers, Richard, Samuel, and Henry; his
sisters, Rosamond and Grace; his uncle John Clarke, whom
with George Munnings he appointed executors; his aunt
Clarke, and her son, then in Barbadoes. He made bequests
also to Henry Walton, Adam Winthrop, and Thomas Lake.
On the day the will was proved, John Clarke renounced the
executorship. (See Geneal. Reg. vii. 334.) It is supposed
that Martha, wife of John Clarke, of Boston, was a sister of
Sir Richard; but it seems to me more probable that their
wives, Grace and Martha, were sisters." [1]

ABSTRACT OF THE WILL OF ROBERT SALTONSTALL

Unto bro. Samuel Saltonstall £20 sterlinge. To each of
my (executors ?) £10 sterlinge. also ( ) pounds sterlinge
towards releasinge Aunt Clarkes Sonne from Capt. Miditon
in the Barbadoes. To Henry Walton £10 sterlinge. Estate
in England after debts are satisfied unto my ffather Richard
Saltonstall, and my bro. Richard. Out of it to be paid to
Sister Rosamond £20, to bro. Henry £20, to Sister Grace
£10. Uncle John Clarke and Geo. Munninges Exectrs.
To Uncle John Clarke my best black suit and plush cassock.
Unto George Munnings my gray cloake, my Sadd colored
cloth suit and cloake, unto Henry Walton. Unto Mr. Adam
Winthrop the black beavor hat I am to receive from Capt.
Kim. The rest of my bootes, shoes, stockins & lynnen, to
George Munninge — 13 June 1650. Postscript, I give to
Mr. Thomas Lake out of that Estate due me either from Mrs.
Whitinge or Capt. Wiggins.

(Signed) ROBERT SALTONSTALL.

In presence of John Sanford Will Norcutt Henr. Walton.
Testified on oaths of Henry Walton and John Sanford 15 (6)
1650.

[1] Bond's *Genealogies and History of Watertown*, vol. ii. p. 917. According to

I John Clarke renounce the executorship of this will of my cosen R. Saltonstall and desire the court to enter it upon Record 15.6 1650.

JOHN CLARKE.

EXTRACTS FROM THE WATERTOWN RECORDS

At a General Towne Meeting the 8 (9) 1647, ordered that John Sherman shall goe to the Courte to answer the complaynt of Robert Saltonstall.

At a generall Towne-Meetinge the 8 (9) 1648 . . . m^r Pendleton is chosen to prisse for the Towne the pay that Robt. Saltonstall is to haue.

At a General Towne Meeting the 17 (7) 1649 . . . agreed that there shall be a Rate of 90£ made for to pay Robert Saltonstall; and to Build a School house; and to Build a gallery in the Meeting-house and to pay other debts the Towne oweth.[1]

---

42. SAMUEL SALTONSTALL (IV.)

Samuel Saltonstall, brother of Richard, Rosamond, and Grace, etc., son of Sir Richard (13) was in 1542 "proprietor of a homestall in Watertown, and 7 other lots, and probably had the land of his brother Henry after his return to England. Watertown was his permanent residence, where he d. Jan. 21, 1686, and administration was granted Oct. 7, 1696, to his nephew Col. Nathaniel Saltonstall. It is supposed that he was the 'Mr. Samuel' sometimes mentioned in the records, omitting the family name. Although he lived so long in Watertown, there is no record of wife or children,

the pedigree of Kaye given in the Heralds' Visitation (see Part II. 13), Grace Kaye had no sister Martha, nor had Sir Richard Saltonstall a sister named Martha, so that it is hard to explain this mention by Robert Saltonstall of his "uncle John Clarke" and of his "Aunt Clarke." John Clarke in renouncing the executorship of this will calls Robert "my cosen R. Saltonstall."

[1] *Watertown Records, Prepared for Publication by the Historical Society*, 1894, pp. 10, 16, 18.

and he appears to have had little or nothing to do with the municipal affairs of the town."[1] He is mentioned in the long document of settlement, Nov. 11, 1647, between Robert and Watertown, Mass. Records, Oct. 17, 1649.

EXTRACTS FROM THE WATERTOWN RECORDS

1642. Ordered that all the Townes Men that had not Farmes laid out formerly shall take them by Ten in a Division & to cast Lotts for the severall Divisions allowing 13 Acres of Vpland to every head of persons & cattle.

Samuel Saltenstall, One hundred fifty seven acres.

1. An Homestall of Sixteen Acres more or les bounded the Northeast with Thomas Brigan and Robert Keyes, the Southeast with the River, the Southwest with the Highway & the Northwest with George Phillips.

2. Seven Acres of Vpland bounded the East with the high way the West & North with Thomas Boyden & the South with John Braybrook.

3. Twenty Acres of Plowland in the hither Plaine bounded the South with the River the North with the highway, the East with Abram Browne and the West with John Whitney.

4. Thirty Acres of Meddow in the remote Meddowes & the 71 Lott.

5. Twenty eight Acres & halfe of Vpland beyond the further Plaine and the 39 Lott.

6. A Farme of One hundred fifty seven acres of Vpland in the 7 Division.

7. Six Acres of Meddow in Plaine Meddow bounded the East with the Brooke the West with William Paine the North with highway and the South with Common Land.

8. Foure Acres of Plowland in the further Plaine & the 58 Lott.

9. Foure Acres of Meddow in the remote Meddowes and the 110 lott.

[1] Bond's *Genealogies and History of Watertown*, pp. 415, 416.

10. Twenty Acres of Vpland, being a great Divident in the 2 Division & the 26 Lott.[1]

---

43. HENRY SALTONSTALL (IV.)

" Henry Saltonstall and William Stoughton, sons of our own college, we know were created fellows of New College at Oxford, and that the latter is not named in the Fasti: but of the former is this notice: II. 172 sub an. 1652, 'June 24 Henr. Saltonstall, a knight's son, fellow of New Coll. by the favour of the visitors, and Doct. of phys. of Padua was then incorporated. The said degree he took at Padua in Oct. 1649.' This made me curious to see the records of New College, which Dr. Williams, the Warden, exhibited, and permitted extracts from the list of Fellows: ' Henr. Saltonstall 1653–1657, Med. Dr. Patavii and Oxoniæ, Equ. aurati filius Author. Parl. 1650.' "[2]

EXTRACT FROM THE WATERTOWN RECORDS

1. A Farme of Three Hundred Acres of vpland and bounded with the Farme Land.
2. Four Score & Eight Acres of Meddow adioyning to the Farme & bounded with the great Dividents.[3]

---

49. SIR RICHARD SALTONSTALL OF SOUTH OKENDEN (VI.)

Sir Simond D'Ewes in his autobiography, vol. i. p. 121 (London, 1845), writing of his college life at Cambridge, says: —

---

[1] *Watertown Records, Prepared for Publication by the Historical Society,* 1894, pp. 13, 48.
[2] Savage's " Gleanings," *Mass. Hist. Coll.* 3d series, vol. viii. p. 251.
[3] *Watertown Records, Prepared for Publication by the Historical Society,* 1894, p. 49.

" Mine own exèrcises performed during my stay here, were very few, replying only twice in two philosophical acts : the one upon Mr. Richard Saltonstall in the public schools, it being his bachelors act; the other upon Mr. Nevill, a fellow Commoner and prime student of St. John's College in the Chapel." And vol. i. p. 139, "in the afternoon of this instant March, the last day save one being Thursday, I hastened to the schools, where was kept the latter act of the bachelors Commencement, and was performed singularly well on all hands. Mr. Richard Saltonstall my very entire friend, a fellow commonor of Jesus College being senior brother, upon whom at his keeping his act but a little before, I had replied in the same place publicly with very good success to mine own content."

---

66. SUSANNAH SALTONSTALL (IV.)

EPITAPH IN BARKWAY CHURCH

[Arms. — Azure, on a bend, argent, three castles embattled, sable, with a label of three points, Castell ; impaling, or, a bend between two eagles displayed, sable, Saltonstall.]

Neere to this place
lyeth interred the
body of Mrs. Susannah Castell, wife
of Robert Castell, of East Hartley, in the
Countie of Cambridge Esq. she was the
eldest daughter of Sir Peter
Saltonstall, Knt. and Christian his wife; she
departed this life the 21st of June an. Dom. 1633,
expecting a joyfull and glorious
resurrection at the coming of Christ.

The lodging of all heavenly virtues is
Lodg'd here on earth, whose soule hath traviled
To Heaven in childbirth, and being brought to the bed
Of rest eternall, left behind her this
Her precious body, which interred is
The fourth day after baptisme had begun
The resurrection of her new borne son;
She now hath found it true, that child-birth paines
By faith through death, life and salvation gaines.

57. BRIDGET SALTONSTALL (IV.)

INSCRIPTION IN BARKWAY CHURCH

" Here lyeth the bodies of Bridget and Elizabeth Saltonstall, daughters of Sir Peter Saltonstall, Knt. and of Christian
his wife, daughter of Sir John Pettus of Rackheath, in the
County of Norfolk, Knt. Bridget being aged 25 years, dyed
February 1639; Elizabeth dyed the May following, aged 17
years. "

58. CHRISTIAN SALTONSTALL (IV.)

INSCRIPTION IN THE CHANCEL OF BARKWAY CHURCH.

" Here under lyeth the body of Christian Saltonstall,
daughter of Sir Peter Saltonstall Knt. and of Christian his
wife, who departed this life the 23d of December 1639.

Nature she saith weepe
Grace a meane doth keepe. "

59. ANNE SALTONSTALL (IV.)

[Arms. — Chester, impaling Saltonstall.]

Here lyeth buried the Lady Anne Chester,
second wife of Sir Edward Chester, Knt. of this
parish ; she was daughter of the worthy Knight
Sir Peter Saltonstall, and the virtuous Lady
Christian. She departed this life the 14th of January
anno Dom. 1647, being 30 years of age, and left
behind her two sonns and one daughter.

Pedigree given from Sir Richard, Lord Mayor, 1597–8,
shows that Anne Saltonstall, dau. and heir of Sir Peter Saltonstall, Knt., bap. 29 Oct., 1618, d. 14 Jan., bur. 17 Jan.,
1647, aged 30, married Sir Edward Chester of Royston. Part
of the ancient manor house, the residence of the Saltonstall
family, is still remaining on the south side of the churchyard at Barkway.

61. WYE SALTONSTALL (IV.)

Wye Saltonstall was "'born of a knightly family in Essex, but descended from those of his name, as it seems (which are ancient), in Yorkshire.' After leaving Queen's College, Oxford, [he] spent some time in the study of the law at Gray's Inn, but in 1625 returned to Oxford, and 'was a sojourner there for several years, purposely for the benefit of the public library and conversation with learned men.' Where he died we know not; but he 'was living in good repute for his learning, in 1640 and after.'" Allibone, further quoting Bliss's Wood's Athen. Oxon. ii. 676–680, says he was the author of 1. "Picturæ Loquentes," 1631; 2. "Ovid's Heroical Epistles," 1626; 3. "Ovid's Tristia," 1633; 4. "Clavis ad Portam," 1633–4; 5. "Historia Mundi," 1635; 6. "Four Books of Elegies of Ovid de Ponto," 1639; 7. "Funerall Elegies in English, Latin, and Greek," upon the death of his father, Sir Samuel Saltonstall, Knight, still in MS. He also translated Eusebius' Life of Constantine. (See Allibone's Dict. of Authors for an extended description of his works.)

Harleian MS. No. 509 (No. 7, above) is a small quarto volume of about forty pages, six lines of poetry on each page. On the title-page in gilt letters on a black ground is the following: —

"Obijt 30 June An' 1640,
Flere meum nihil est nisi me flere
hoc sciat alter.
Diquum laude Virum Musa vetat
Mori.
Beati mortui, qui in Domino moriuntur
Memoria insticum
Laudibus, Prov. 10."

On the opposite page, also in gilt letters on a black ground: —

"The Dedication
These Funeral Eligies sacred to
the Memorye of the Right Wor¹
Sir Samuell Saltonstall
Knight
His Sonn Wye Saltonstall
Devoteth and Dedicateth."

67. RICHARD SALTONSTALL OF CHIPPING WARDEN
(V.)

Richard Saltonstall of Chipping Warden in the County of Northampton, Esquire, by will dated 18 Aug., 1688, proved 2 Oct., 1688, gives to daughter Elizabeth four thousand pounds, to wife Margaret "all my plate, her jewels and gold, my coach, chariot, and furniture and horses and all my stock of cattle. To my son Richard, and to my daughter Silence, his wife, I give an hundred pounds apiece to buy them mourning."

71. RICHARD SALTONSTALL OF CHIPPING WARDEN
(VI.)

Edward Griffen, Esq., sold the manor, advowson, and hundred of Chipping Warden to Sir Richard Saltonstall (25), great-grandfather of Richard (71), prior to 1619, in which year he died seized of them. From him they descended to Ricarda Posthuma Saltonstall, first wife of the Hon. George Montagu, afterwards second Earl of Halifax, by whom she had an only surviving daughter and heiress, Lucy, first wife of Francis North, first Earl of Guilford. In 1792, by the death of his father, Lord North succeeded to the Earldom of Guilford, which has since been enjoyed by his successors in title.

87. NATHANIEL SALTONSTALL (V.)

Nathaniel Saltonstall, son of Richard, graduated at Harvard College 1659, and settled in Haverhill upon that beautiful estate half a mile east of the bridge which remained in the possession of the family until about twenty years since, and is still known as the "Saltonstall Seat." This spot, exceeded perhaps by none in New England in fertility of soil and beauty of prospect, was conveyed to him (together with

other lands) by the Rev. John Ward, first minister of Haverhill, in consideration of his marriage with his daughter.

" As Washington " on his visit to Haverhill in 1789 walked
through the town, and his eye "took in the then unobstructed
view for miles up and down the Merrimac, he almost invol-
untarily exclaimed, ' Beautiful, beautiful!' He especially
admired the situation of the Saltonstall residence, just below
the village, . . . and pronounced it a most charming and picturesque location for a home." [1]

" About this time [1737] the long row of sycamore-trees
[buttonwood] that for a century afterward added so much to
the natural beauty of the ' Saltonstall Seat' . . . were set out.
The work was done by one Hugh Talent, an 'exile of Erin '
and a famous fiddler withal. Tradition says that the village
swains and the lasses did not allow the catgut and rosin of
this musical talent to rust for want of use. He lived with
Colonel Saltonstall in the capacity of a servant. Poor Hugh!
For nearly three generations after he had ' hung up his fiddle
and his bow ' the beautiful trees he planted were the pride of
our village and the admiration of all who beheld them.
Many an one whose head is sprinkled o'er with frosts of
many winters, as he reads these lines [1860], will call to mind
the days and scenes of the time when the ' Old Buttonwoods '
were flourishing in all their glory, and will embalm their
memory with a sigh, perhaps with a tear." [2]

Mr. Saltonstall was chosen an Assistant from 1679 to
1686, under the old charter, of which he was a firm friend ;
and from 1689 to 1692 under the new one. Edward Randolph, the implacable enemy of New England, and a principal instrument of depriving this colony of its charter,
included him among those whom he called a faction of the
General Court in 1681, and against whom he exhibited articles
of high misdemeanor to the Lords of the Council. In 1686,
when the charter was taken away, he was named in the commission as one of the " Council for the government of Massachusetts Bay," but as he had a few days before taken the

[1] Chase's *History of Haverhill*, p. 445.   [2] *Ibid.* p. 309.

oath of Assistant under the old charter, he refused to accept the appointment. After the seizure and removal of Sir Edmund Andros he was invited to join the Council, which took the government into their hands, and continued in this office until the charter of William and Mary, in which he was appointed one of his Majesty's Council.

In August, 1680, he went with the deputy governor and others, " with 60 soldiers in a ship and sloop from Boston to still the people at Casco Bay and prevent Governor Andros' usurpation." Randolph, in answer to " heads of inquiry concerning the state of New England," mentions his name among the most popular and well principled military men.

In 1683 Charles II. appointed him one of the commissioners " to examine and inquire into the claims and titles as well of his Majesty as others to the Narragansett country," to which important commission he attended.

Colonel Saltonstall possessed superior powers of mind, and was free from the prevailing bigotry and superstition of the age. He was opposed to the proceedings against the witches in 1692, and expressed his sentiments freely upon the subject. Mr. Brattle in his account of the witchcraft says, " Maj. N. Saltonstall, Esq., who was one of the judges, has left the court, and is very much dissatisfied with the proceedings of it." Upon this Mr. Bentley in his History of Salem remarks : " Saltonstall left the bench, but ought he not, as the friend to justice, to have been upon it?" Had he remained there to have raised his voice against the proceedings of his brethren, his conduct would doubtless have been more heroic, but it would have been in vain. So universal was the madness, that his attempts to resist the torrent might have been fatal to himself, without relieving the unfortunate victims of this delusion. It is no small honor to his memory and satisfaction to his descendants, that he was not carried away by this dreadful fanaticism, and was clear of the innocent blood.

Colonel Saltonstall lived to a good old age, and died 21 May, 1707. He left three sons, Gurdon, Richard, and Nathaniel. His only daughter was married to the Rev. Roland Cotton of Sandwich.[1]

In Mass. Records, vol. v. p. 295, is this entry: "13 Oct., 1680, And it is further ordered that the rest of the tounes in s͞d county, viz. Newberry, Rouley, Bradford, Andiver, Topsfeild, as also Salisbury, Amesbury, & Hauerill, together wth such troop's as either are already or which here after shallbe listed in sajd tounes to belong to the sajd regiment, & that the sajd regiment to be under the com͞and of Major Nathaniel Saltonstall, and he to haue com͞ission for y^s second diuission accordingly, any law, custome, or vsage to the con- trary notw^thstanding."

Judge Sewall, in his Letter Book, makes this curious entry; "July 24, 1690. Writt to Major Saltonstall, and sent him a *barrel of Salt* in Token of my Remembrance of him and sympathy with him in his dangers and confinements, dwell- ing in a fronteer Town as he does &c."

In the same, he writes Mrs. Elizabeth Saltonstall, widow of Colonel Nathaniel, sending her a book and says, " I can- not but Acknowledge the Obligation you lay even upon the Province, by denying your self, and continuing to live in a frontier Town, where our Enemies have often made formid able Impressions. By the sentiments of my dear Mother I conjecture you desire to ly by your honoured Consort and Parents. I pray, that in the most convenient Season, you may be brought to them in peace." [2]

" Col. Nathaniel Saltonstall, one of the firmest pillars of the town and a prominent man in the Colony, died on the 21st of May (1707), after being ill with consumption half a year. He possessed a vigorous, well cultivated intellect, was beloved by his neighbors, and proved comparatively free from the bigotry and superstition of the age in which he lived He was born in 1639 and graduated at Harvard College in 1659, and soon after settled on that beautiful estate conveyed

---

[1] *Mass. Hist. Coll.* 2d series, vol. iv. p. 160 ; Bond's *Genealogies and History of Watertown*, p. 92 ; Trumbull's *Connecticut*.
[2] *Mass. Hist. Coll.* 6th series, vol. i. pp. 110, 395.

to him by Rev. John Ward in consideration of his marriage to his daughter. It was known for many years by the name of ' Saltonstall Seat.'

" He was opposed to the proceedings of the Court against the witchcraft mania that commenced in 1692. He was then one of the judges; but he vacated his seat, and openly expressed his dissatisfaction at the violence of the Court. We are astonished at his independence, his moral energy, and his fearlessness in declaring his sentiments, though in opposition to the united opinion of his contemporaries of the bench, and against that of nearly the whole colony. A torrent of madness and delusion had overwhelmed it, and swept onward, carrying terror to every heart, and leaving death and desolation in its pathway. The judges of the land, the ministers, whose voices were heard in the sacred desks, the high and gifted in mind, were victims to this terrible fanaticism, and it is deemed an honor to Mr. Saltonstall, which will ever be attached to his memory, that he went forth from among them, and stood aloof from their councils." [1]

The following letter, the original of which is now in the possession of the author, is in this connection of great interest: [2]

GENTLEMEN

I do not remember that, since I belong^d to any Court, I had a greater or so strong a designe to give my personall appearance at any time than now. Business, tran(s)ient business hinders me not; the affaires of ye Court (all y^t I yet heare of) divert me not: My heart is wth you, and my prayer shall be for you. Were I wth you I could not sit in Court to hear any case, & besides that, this very day I have mett wth such a fall that puts me by any possibilitie of moveing this day. If I may be capable of serving ye Country to-morrow, I purpose to come, & do w^t I can, tho: I know I must, & some will say can't but be unhandsome. I'l try in y^e morning.

Gentlemen. Proceed I beseech you, & if in any case there

[1] Myrick's *History of Haverhill* (1832), pp. 112–116. See, also, Sibley's *Harvard Graduates*, pp. 1–8, and authorities cited.
[2] See facsimile of the original letter.

Haverhil March 29. 1692

Gentlemen

I do ____ ___ ___ that, since I belong'd to any
Court I had a greater or ____ ___ a designe to give my
personall appearance ___ at ___ ___ than now. Businesse, transibit
businesse hindreth me not, the ____ of ye Court (all ye I yet
heard of) divert me ___ ___ the heart it is ___ you, & my prayer
shall be for you. Alas ___ ___ I could not sit in Court to
heare any Case ___ ____ this very day I have mett
___ such a fall that ____ ___ ___ ___ of moveing this day.
If I may be capable of moveing ___ Countrey To-morrow, I
purpose to come, ___ ___ ___ I know I must, & some
will say can't but ___ ___ ___ I'll ___ in ye morning.

Gentlemen. ___ I ___ ___ if in any Case there
wants a Cypher to ___ ___ to ___ number (as soon as I can)
you shal have ___

I ___ ___ ___ ___ ___ tired for any thing
more but ___ ___ you gentlemen, I am
your Servant,

N. Saltonstall

To
ye Essex County Court now
sitting,
at Ipswich,

p Doctor Woodland

wants a Cypher to be added to yor number (as soon as I can) you shall have me.

I cannot compliment, I have not time for anything more but to tell you, Gentlemen, I am,

your Servant,
NATH. SALTONSTALL

To ye Hon^d County Court now sittin in Ipswich, per Edwd Newland.

Extracts from the Watertown Records (1894 reprint), p. 172 : —

"Nathaniel Saltonstall. At a General Meeting of the Proprietors of the Common and undivided Land in Watertown regularly Notifyed And Assembled on the 23 Day of April 1731. . . .

"Mr. Nathl. Saltonstall Appeared and Claimed A right in propriety which he made Appear by showing a Copy of a Deed wherein he had reserved the right of Commonage to himself. And it was put to Vote whether the Proprietors Do Allow Mr. Saltonstall to a Vote among them. And the Vote Past in the Affirmative."

87 A. JOHN WARD

Rev. Nathaniel Ward, whose name is found in the pedigree of Ward (Harleian MSS. 1476), came to New England, as did also his sons John and James, and his daughter Susan and her husband Giles Firmin. All of this family but John returned to England. John was the first minister of Haverhill, Mass. Though he left no posterity bearing his own surname, his descendants, through his daughters Elizabeth and Mary, are numerous, and many of them are distinguished in the literature and history of England. Among his descendants may be named Gov. Gurdon Saltonstall of Connecticut, Hon. Dudley Woodbridge of Barbadoes, Gen. Gurdon Saltonstall, Hon. Leverett Saltonstall, M. C., Rev. Thomas W. Coit, D. D., Rev. Edward B. Hall, D. D., and

Rev. Nathaniel Hall, Rev. Phillips Brooks, D. D., Francis
Parkman, LL. D., Donald G. Mitchell, LL. D., William
Everett, Ph. D., Charles Francis Adams, Hon. Stephen H.
Phillips, Rev. Edward H. Hall, Daniel C. Gilman, LL. D.,
Rev. O. B. Frothingham, and Leverett Saltonstall.[1]

87 B. HAVERHILL, MASSACHUSETTS

The town of Haverhill, the home of the family for five
generations, and where during four generations they occupied
the old " Seat " on the bend of the lovely Merrimac, possessed
such natural charms of location and scenery that even Washington on his visit was enchanted by it, then a sweet, quiet,
rural country town.   It is now a large, busy, active manufacturing city; the banks of its beautiful river hidden from view
by great shoe-factories, its streets full of electric cars and
bustling life.   In the year 1880 its population was 18,472;
in 1890, 27,812, and it is still fast growing.

In July, 1890, a three days' festival was held there, com-
memorative of the 250th anniversary of the settlement of the
town.   Nothing was left undone which could in any way add
to the interest of the occasion.   It was celebrated by religious
exercises, by games, sports, oration, poems, hymns, parades,
processions, a ball, and a great banquet.   Every feature of
the celebration was attended to with an earnest and heartfelt
zeal such as rarely is equalled.   All citizens, old and young,
men and women, gave themselves up to it, and seemed to vie
the one with another in making it successful.   All the old
houses and spots of historic interest were marked and pointed
out to the visitor, and those who felt themselves bound to the
place by successive generations of their ancestors who lived
there were filled with the spirit of the occasion.

At the great banquet, where were assembled a host of the
inhabitants, with visitors from every direction, including a
delegation from old Haverhill in England, the presiding officer proposed a toast in these words: —

[1] *The New England Bibliophilist*, July, 1887.

"No feature of New England life starts out more prominently than that of the home. The family life of New England is the rock out of which have been hewn the men and women of this country. I propose 'The Colonial Families of Haverhill; their best monument is the virtue of their children and the prosperity of their town.' We feel ourselves greatly honored in having with us a most worthy descendant of one of these families, which, to quote from our latest historian, 'was in prestige, official station, and education the most distinguished family of the town.' You will gladly welcome the Hon. Leverett Saltonstall of Boston."

In the course of his speech, Mr. Saltonstall said: —

"I am greatly honored in being called upon to respond to the toast for the old colonial homes and families, and feel deep emotion in so doing, for, though not a Haverhill boy, yet I am next to it, and have more of old Haverhill in me than most of those here present, being, as I am, directly descended from the Rev. John Ward, William White, and Simon Wainwright, as well as from the long line of good men whose name I bear, original settlers and townsmen of Haverhill.

"Two hundred and fifty years carries us away back to the very beginning of things, to a day which was only twenty years after the landing of the Pilgrims, twelve after the arrival of Governor Endicott, and ten from the lovely June day when Governor Winthrop and Sir Richard Saltonstall sailed into Salem harbor, after their long, tempestuous voyage of many weeks in the Arbella with their company, from whom so many of us are descended.

"Can we ever cease to wonder that any amount of religious persecution could have driven those people, many of them cultivated and refined men and tender women, unused to labor, from the comforts and luxuries of their homes in Old England which they so dearly loved, across the stormy ocean, in small overcrowded vessels, such as a sailor would nowadays laugh to look at, and consider it a huge joke to be asked to navigate, — that they might settle in a howling wilderness with its endless tracts of dark forest inhabited by the wild beast and savage Indian? But what always seems to me so inexplicable is why, with so much land about them, they should have always been pushing farther and farther into the wilderness,—why, for instance, John Ward, William White, and that brave handful of men should have gone so far away from Ipswich for a settlement. It was, however, all a part of the design of that great 'wonder-working Providence' which impelled devout men to achieve so much without themselves foreseeing the best results of their sacrifices.

"The minister in those days was a sure attendant upon a new settlement, though not a pioneer; but the Rev. John Ward was a natural leader of men, son of that Nathaniel Ward, first minister of Ipswich, who was author of 'The Simple Cobbler of Agawam,' which excited so much attention in its day, both here and in England, but better known as the author of 'The Body of Liberties,' a work now considered to have been the foundation of our whole system of colonial laws. John Ward inherited his father's fine intellect and stalwart character and was a rare man. Brave, adventurous, and highly educated, with his Bible, his axe, and his gun, he brought his young wife, and led his little company into the forest, settled this beautiful site on the banks of the lovely Merrimac, and never took a step backward, but continued to the end of his long and eventful life to be the guide, protector, and religious teacher of the little band who accompanied him with trusting love and deep respect."

After referring to his ancestors who lived in Haverhill, and to his father, who was born there, he continued:—

"It has been the fashion in this country to ridicule and to speak slightingly of those who love to dwell upon the virtues of their ancestry, and it is to be much regretted. Do not the brave, good men who ventured so much, who experienced the horrors of savage warfare and of every kind of deprivation, who were the heroes of tales of suffering which seem as we read them to be fabulous, who in the fear of God performed their various and trying duties with such faithfulness and with so little reward, — should not such men be honored and praised by their descendants? And should we not all feel their example an incentive to do something in life worthy of them, and to hand down to our sons the same obligation?

" May my right hand forget her cunning and my tongue cleave to the roof of my mouth ere I forget my forefathers, and all they endured in their simple prayerful lives, in their cold houses and churches, with few comforts and fewer luxuries : for many long years never going into the field nor visiting a neighbor, nor to church, without the danger of being shot by the skulking savage; aye, who never went to bed without the dread of being wakened by the terrific war-whoop, and of seeing their wives and children slaughtered before their eyes, or, worse still, dragged off to horrible captivity and torture : while we, even those least blessed with worldly goods, are enjoying comforts which would have been to the richest of them undreamed-of luxuries.

" Should not the thought of this and of their great sacrifices and sufferings take us out of the rut of mere money-making and selfishness, and excite in our breasts a noble ambition to do our part individually and collectively to secure and hand down to posterity, ' without a spot or wrinkle,' the priceless heritage which we have received from the noble men and women who lived in those sternly simple old colonial homes ? "

---

91. ELIZABETH SALTONSTALL (VI.)

Elizabeth Saltonstall, b. 17 Sep., 1668, m. 1st, Rev. John Denison, grad. Harv. Coll. 1684, d. 1689, leaving one child, John Denison; m. 2d, 1690, Rev. Roland Cotton, b. 27 Dec., 1667 (son of Rev. John J. and Joanna (Rossiter) Cotton of Plymouth), grad. Harv. Coll. 1685, ordained in Sandwich 2 Nov., 1694, d. 22 March, 172½. She d. in Boston, 8 July, 1726.

In the "New England Genealogical Reg." vol. vii. p. 307, article "Cotton," we find the following notice of this excellent woman, which it is supposed was written by Cotton Mather: —

"Ecclesiæ Monilia. The peculiar Treasure of the Almighty King opened, and the jewels that are made up in it exposed, at Boston Lecture, July 14, 1726, whereof one is more particularly exhibited in the character of Mrs. Elizabeth Cotton, who was laid up a few days before, and certain Instruments and Memorials of Piety written by that valuable and honorable gentlewoman, Boston 12 m. 1726."

Notice of her death: "Boston, Saturday, July 9, 1726. Yesterday morning deceased here, after a short fever, and is decently interred, Mrs. Elizabeth Cotton, only daughter of the late Colonel Nathaniel Saltonstall, Esq., of Haverhill, and sister of the late Hon. Gurdon Saltonstall of Connecticut. [Dates of birth, marriage, and death are then given.] She was known to be a person of very superior wit, knowledge and virtue, from her youth up."

Child by first husband, Rev. John Denison: —
1. John.

Children by second husband, Rev. Roland Cotton:[1] —

2. John, b. 15 July, 1693; grad. Harv. Coll. 1710; ordained in Newton, 3 Nov., 1714; m. 9 Feb. 1719, Mary, dau. of Robert Gibbs of Boston. He d. 25 May, 1757. Children: —

    1a. Mary, b. 7 Dec., 1719; m. May, 1746, Rev. Thomas Cheeney of Brookfield.

    2a. Elizabeth, b. 21 Jan., 1722; m. Oct., 1750, John Hastings, Jr., Esq., of Cambridge, grad. Harvard Coll. 1730; d. 1783.

    3a. Anna, b. 9 Oct., 1723; m. 1742, Rev. Samuel Cook of Menotomy.

[1] Roland Cotton of Sandwich "refused an invitation from New London, after their minister, Mr. Saltonstall, H. U. 1684, was made governor, and it was thought he might have had an invitation to the Old Church in Boston if he would have encouraged it.

"He had an excellent gift in prayer, had a good faculty in making and delivering his sermons, so that he was a celebrated and admired preacher." — Sibley's *Harvard Graduates*, vol. iii. p. 325.

4a. Rebecca, b. 3 Nov., 1725; m. 1762, Captain Samuel Baldwin of Weston.

5a. Martha, b. 28 Sep., 1727; d. young.

6a. John, b. 22 Dec., 1729; grad. Harv. Coll. 1747; a physician; m. 8 July, 1750, Mary Clark; d. 1758, *s. p.*

7a. Nathaniel, b. 6 July, 1731, grad. Harv. Coll. 1750; d. 1771.

8a. Samuel Gibbs, b. 7 Feb., 1734; d. 1734.

9a. Henry, b. 28 Oct., 1735; d. 1736.

10a. Samuel, b. 24 Jan., 1738; grad. Harv. Coll. 1759; d. 1819.

11a. Martha, b. 30 Nov., 1739; m. Oct., 1766, Rev. Ebenezer Thayer of Cambridge.

3. Nathaniel, b. 1694; grad. Harv. Coll. 1717; ordained at Bristol 30 Aug., 1721; d. 3 July, 1729.

4. Sarah.

5. Abigail, m. 1725, Rev. Shearjashub Bourne, grad. Harv. Coll. 1720, ordained at Scituate, Dec., 1724. She d. 1732, and he m. in 1738, Sarah Brooks of Medford. He d. in 1768.

6. Meriell, b. about 1698.

7. Roland, grad. Harv. Coll. 1719; m. 3 Oct., 1760, Deborah Mason.

8. Josiah, grad. Harv. Coll. 1722; ordained at Providence, R. I., 23 Oct., 1728; installed at Woburn 15 July, 1747, and at Sandown, N. H., 28 Nov., 1759; d. 27 May, 1780, aged about 77.

9. Ward, grad. Harv. Coll. 1729; ordained at Hampton, N. H.; d. at Plymouth 27 Nov., 1768, aged 57.

10. Joanna, m. Rev. John Brown of Haverhill, b. in Cambridge 1696, grad. Harv. Coll. 1714, ordained in Haverhill 3 May, 1719, d. 2 Dec., 1742, aged 46, "greatly esteemed for his learning, piety, and prudence." Children : —

1a. Elizabeth, b. 26 Oct., 1721; m. July, 1744, Hon. John Chipman, b. 23 Oct., 1722, grad. Harv. Coll. 1738, d. July, 1768. Child : —

1b. Elizabeth, b. 9 June, 1756; m. 28 March, 1782, Hon. William Gray of Salem, b. 27 June, 1750, d. 3 Nov., 1825. She d. 29 Sep., 1823. Children: —

  1c. William R., b. 23 June, 1783; grad. Harv. Coll. 1800; m. 19 Oct., 1809, Mary Clay of Georgia. He d. 29 July, 1831. Children: —

    1d. William, b. 20 Dec., 1810; grad. Harv. Coll. 1829; m. 18 Oct., 1834, Sarah F. Loring. He d. 11 Feb., 1892. Children: —

      1e. William, b. 2 July, 1837; m. 3 May, 1859, Katherine H. Cunningham; d. 16 Aug., 1886.

      2e. Francis.

      3e. Ira E.

      4e. Frances L., m. M. A. W. Stewart of New York.

      5e. Anna G.

      6e. Florence.

      7e. Edward, m. Elizabeth G. Story.

      8e. Ellen.

    2d. Joseph Clay.

    3d. Francis H., grad. Harv. Coll. 1831; m. 10 July, 1844, H. Regina Shober of Philadelphia. Children: —

      1e. Francis C., grad. Harv. Coll. 1866.

      2e. Mary Clay, b. 18 Aug., 1848.

      3e. Samuel S., b. 30 Dec., 1849; m. 15 Jan., 1879, Caroline B. Weld.

      4e. Reginald, b. 19 March, 1853; grad. Harv. Coll., 1875; m. 2 April, 1892, Rose Lee.

      5e. Morris, b. 7 March, 1856; grad. Harv. Coll. 1877; m. 15 Sep., 1883, Flora Grant.

    4d. Frederick, b. 1815; d. 1877.

    5d. Mary, b. 1817; d. 1843.

6d. Anne E., b. 1819; d. 1884.

7d. Horace, b. 1821.

8d. George, b. 1825; grad. Harv. Coll. 1845; d. 1850.

9d. Ellen, b. 1830.

2c. Henry, b. 1784; m. 1810, Frances Pierce; d. 1854. Children:—

id. Elizabeth, b. 1811; d. 1894.

2d. William H., b. 1812; d. 1871.

3d. John, b. 1813; d. 1871.

4d. Henry, b. 1815; d. 1851.

5d. Francis, b. 1816; d. 1817.

6d. Caroline, b. 1818; m. 1863, John Harkins.

7d. Charles Russel, b. 1819.

8d. Lydia F., b. 1820; m. 1845, E. Cornelius.

9d. Mary Codman, b. 1821; m. 1854, Charles A. Winthrop.

10d. Frederick W., b. 1823.

11d. Arthur, b. 1824.

12d. Francis, b. 1826.

13d. Francis, b. and d. 1828.

14d. Horatio, b. 1828.

15d. Ellen Cordis, b. 1830; m. 1852, Rev. William H. Brooks, D. D. Children:—

1e. William Gray, b. 1853.

2e. Grace E., b. and d. 1860.

3c. Lucia, b. 1788; m. 1807, Samuel Swett; d. 1844. Children:—

id. William Gray, b. 1808; grad. Harv. Coll. 1828; m. 1842, Charlotte B. Phinney. Child:—

Charlotte B. W., b. 1843; m. 1869, Edw. N. Hallowell.

2d. Samuel B., b. 1810; m. 1845, Mary S. Lord of New Hampshire; d. 1890. Children:—

1e. Samuel, b. 1846.

    2e. Elizabeth Hale, b. 1849.
    3e. Lucia Gray, b. 1851.
    4e. Mary Coolidge, b. 1853.
    5e. William Low, b. 1854.
  3d. Lucia Gray, b. 1814; m. Francis Alexander. Child: Francis.
  4d. Eliza Charlotte, b. 1815; d. 1832.
  5d. John B., b. 1821; m. 1849, Annie Cecilia de Wolf; d. 1867. Child: —
  Elizabeth Gray, b. 1852.
4c. Francis C., b. 1790; grad. Harv. Coll. 1809; LL. D. 1841; d. 1856.
5c. John C., b. 1793; grad. Harv. Coll. 1811; LL. D. 1856; m. 1820, Elizabeth Gardner; d. 1881.
6c. Ward, d. in infancy.
7c. Horace, b. 1800; grad. Harv. Coll. 1819; m. 1st, 1827, Harriet Upham; m. 2d, Sarah R. Gardner; d. 1873. Children by first wife, Harriet: —
  1d. Horace, b. 1828; grad. Harv. Coll. 1845; LL. D. 1871; Justice Supreme Court U. S.; m. Jeannette Mather.
  2d. Elizabeth Chipman, b. 1830.
  3d. Harriet, b. 1832.
  Children by second wife, Sarah: —
  4d. John Chipman, b. 1839; grad. Harv. Coll. 1859; m. 1873, Anna Sophia Lyman Mason. Children : —
    1e. Roland, b. 1874.
    2e. Eleanor Lyman, b. 1876.
  5d. Russell, b. 1850; grad. Harv. Coll. 1869; m. Amy Heard. Children: —
    1e. Horace, b. 1887.
    2e. Augustine Heard, b. 1888.
2a. John, 2d child of Joanna and John Brown, grad. Harv. Coll. 1741; minister at Cohasset 45 years; d. 1792, aged 67.

3a. Cotton, grad. Harv. Coll. 1743; ordained in Brookline, 26 Oct., 1748; d. 13 April, 1751.

4a. Ward, grad. Harv. Coll. 1748; d. same year.

5a. Merriel, b. 5 July, 1730; m. 1st, —— Dane of Brookline; m. 2d, —— Cutting of Brookline; d. 1795. Children of Merriel by second husband, Nathaniel, John Brown, Joanna Cotton, Nancy, and Silent.

6a. Thomas, grad. Harv. Coll. 1752; ordained in Marshfield; afterwards, 1765, at Stroudwater, in Falmouth, Me. He d. there in 1797.

7a. Abigail, m. Edward Brooks, Sep., 1764. He was b. at Medford, and grad. Harv. Coll. 1757, ordained at North Yarmouth, Me., 4 July, 1764, dismissed in 1769 on account of liberality of his opinions. In 1777 he was Chaplain of Frigate Hancock (Bond's Hist. Watertown, p. 726; Smith's Journal, pp. 199, 214, 320, 324). She d. 29 Nov., 1800, aged 69. He d. 6 May, 1781, aged 48. Children:—

　1b. Cotton Brown, b. 20 July, 1765; m. 1st, 17 Dec. 1794, Jane Williams[1] of Salem; m. 2d, Jan., 1831, Ann Noyes of Portland; lived in Medford, Haverhill, and Portland; d. 12 May, 1834. Children:—

　　1c. Charles, b. 3 Sep., 1795; m. 29 Aug., 1824, Nancy Dicks of Portland. Had 5 children.

　　2c. George, b. 5 Aug., 1797; m. 16 Nov., 1825, Henrietta Tracy of Newburyport. Had 5 children.

　　3c. Jane, b. 15 Nov., 1799; m. 21 May, 1822, Franklin Tinkham of Belfast and Portland. Had 3 children. She d. 6 Jan., 1827.

　　4c. Thomas Brown, b. 22 May, 1802; m. 29 June, 1827, Elizabeth A. Gordon of Belfast. Had 5 children.

[1] Daughter of Benjamin and Jane (Gray) Williams, the same a sister of William Gray who m. Elizabeth Chipman, and Samuel who m. Mary Brooks.

5c. William Gray, b. 12 Oct., 1805; m. 9 Sep., 1833, Ann Phillips, dau. of John Phillips of Andover. Children: —

1d. William Gray, b. 2 July, 1834.

2d. Phillips, b. 13 Dec., 1835; grad. Harv. Coll. 1855; Bishop of Massachusetts; d. 23 Jan., 1893.

3d. George, b. 13 Dec., 1838; d. Feb., 1863.

4d. Frederick, b. 5 Aug., 1842; grad. Harv. Coll. 1863; Rector St. Paul's Church; d. Sep., 1874.

5d. Arthur, b. 11 June, 1845; grad. Harv. Coll. 1867; Rector Church of the Incarnation, New York.

6d. John Cotton, b. 29 Aug., 1849; grad. Harv. Coll. 1872; Rector Christ Church, Springfield.

6c. Edward Cotton, b. 20 Oct., 1806; d. 12 Oct., 1807.

7c. John Cotton, b. 1 July, 1809.

8c. Joanna Hall, b. 21 Aug., 1811; m. William Swasey, M. D., of Limerick. Had 7 children.

2b. Peter Chardon, distinguished merchant, 2d child of Rev. Edward and Abigail (Brown) Brooks, b. 6 Jan., 1767; m. 1792, Ann, dau. of Nathaniel Gorham. She d. 21 Feb., 1830. He d. 1 Jan., 1849. Children: —

1c. Edward, b. 22 Dec., 1793; grad. Harv. Coll. 1812; m. 3 May, 1821, Elizabeth Boott; d. 1 April, 1878. Children: —

1d. Edward, b. 14 Feb., 1822; M. D. Harv. Univ. 1843; d. 22 June, 1855.

2d. Francis, b. 1 Nov., 1824; LL. B. Harv. Univ. 1846; m. 1st, Mary Jones Chadwick, 6 May, 1850, d. 14 March, 1851; m. 2d, Louise Winsor, 29 Nov., 1854, d. 31 Oct., 1893. He d. 28 Oct., 1891. Children: —

1e. Fanny, b. 22 Aug., 1855.

2e. Edward, b. 19 Oct., 1856; m. 1885, Mary C. Hammond. Had 2 children.

3e. Henry, b. 16 Oct., 1857.

4e. Frederick, b. 20 Nov., 1858; m. 3 June, 1890, Grace Oakes. Had 2 children.

5e. Elizabeth Boott, b. 20 June, 1860; m. 18 June, 1887, Edward M. Wheelwright. Had 2 children.

6e. Louise Winsor, b. 9 Sep., 1874.

2c. Gorham, 2d son of Peter Chardon and Ann (Gorham) Brooks, b. 10 Sep., 1795; grad. Harv. Coll. 1814; m. 20 April, 1829, Ellen, dau. of R. D. Shepherd of Virginia, b. 22 Aug., 1809; d. 11 Aug., 1884. He d. 1 Jan., 1849. Children:—

1d. Lucy, b. 8 Feb., 1830; d. 10 Sep., 1830.

2d. Peter Chardon, b. 8 May, 1831; grad. Harv. Coll. 1852; m. 4 Oct., 1866, Sarah, dau. of Amos A. Lawrence, b. 5 July, 1845. Children:—

1e. Eleanor, b. 18 Sep., 1867; m. 17 Oct., 1891, Richard Middlecott Saltonstall (129). Children: 1. Leverett, b. 1 Sep., 1892 (143); 2. Eleanor, b. 19 Oct., 1894; 3. Muriel Gurdon, b. 26 March, 1896.

2e. Lawrence, b. 9 Nov., 1868; grad. Harv. Coll. 1891.

3d. Shepherd, b. 23 July, 1837; grad. Harv. Coll. 1857; m. 10 Dec., 1872, Clara, dau. of George Gardner, b. 8 Feb., 1845. Children:

1e. Helen, b. 3 Dec., 1875.

2e. Gorham, b. 19 June, 1881.

3e. Rachel, b. 5 Jan., 1883.

3c. Peter Chardon, b. 4 July, 1796; d. young.

4c. Ann Gorham, b. 2 June, 1797; m. 2 March, 1818, Rev. N. L. Frothingham, grad. Harv. Coll. 1811, S. T. D. 1836, mem. Mass. Hist. Soc. Children:—

1d. Thomas Bumstead, b. 2 Feb., 1819.

2d. Francis Greenwood, b. 16 Nov., 1820.

3d. Octavius Brooks, b. 26 Nov., 1822; grad. Harv. Coll. 1843; Div. S. 1846; mem. Mass. Hist. Soc.; m. Caroline Curtis.

4d. Edward, b. 17 Feb., 1825; m. Eugenia Mifflin. Had 3 children.

5d. Ward Brooks, b. 29 Aug., 1828.

6d. Ellen, b. 25 March, 1835.

5c. Peter Chardon, b. 26 Aug., 1798; m. Susan Oliver Heard, *s. p.*; d. June, 1880.

6c. Sidney, b. 7 Oct., 1799; grad. Harv. Coll. 1819; m. Frances Dehon, *s. p.*; d. March, 1878.

7c. Charlotte Gray, b. 4 Nov., 1800; m. 8 May, 1822, Hon. Edward Everett, b. 11 April, 1794, grad. Harv. Coll. 1811, LL. D., President Harv. Coll., etc., d. 15 Jan., 1865. She d. 2 July, 1859. Children: —

1d. Ann Gorham, b. 3 March, 1823; d. 1844.

2d. Charlotte Brooks, b. 13 Aug., 1825; m. 20 Aug., 1850, Henry Augustus Wise, b. 24 May, 1819, d. 2 April, 1869. She d. 15 Dec., 1879. Had 4 children.

3d. Grace Webster, b. 1828; d. 8 Jan., 1836.

4d. Edward Brooks, b. 6 May, 1830; grad. Harv. Coll. 1850; m. 1853, Helen, dau. of Benjamin Adams. He d. Nov., 1861. Had 2 children.

5d. A daughter, b. and d. 1832.

6d. Henry Sidney, b. 31 Dec., 1835; m. 1866, Katharine, dau. of Richard Sullivan Fay. Children: —

1e. Sidney Brooks, b. 3 Nov., 1868.

2e. Alexander Leo, b. 24 July, 1871.

3e. Lilian, b. 30 June, 1873; m. 30 June, 1892, Captain Charles Harry Fenwick of England. Children: 1. Elma Lilian,

b. 13 May, 1893; 2. Audrey Ethel, b. 15 June, 1894.

4e. Hildegarde Clotilde Louisa, 30 Nov., 1877.

5e. Sybil Anna Pélagie, b. 10 Nov., 1884.

7d. William, 7th child of Charlotte and Edward Everett, b. 10 Oct., 1839; grad. Harv. Coll. 1859, LL. D., mem. Mass. Hist. Soc., Ph. D., M. C., etc.

8c. Ward Chipman, 8th child of Peter Chardon and Ann (Gorham) Brooks, b. 21 April, 1804; grad. Harv. Coll. 1822; d. 19 March, 1828.

9c. Abigail Brown, b. 22 Jan., 1806; d. young.

10c. Henry, b. 2 Feb., 1807; d. 2 Sep., 1833.

11c. Abigail Brown, b. 25 April, 1808; m. Hon. Charles Francis Adams, grad. Harv. Coll. 1825, LL. D., M. C., U. S. Minister to Great Britain. Children:—

1d. Louisa Catherine, b. 13 Aug., 1831; m. 13 April, 1854, Charles Kuhn; d. 13 July, 1870.

2d. John Quincy, b. 22 Sep., 1833; grad. Harv. Coll. 1853; m. 29 April, 1861, Fanny Crowninshield. Children:—

1e. John Quincy, b. 23 Feb., 1862; d. 12 April, 1876.

2e. George Caspar, b. 24 April, 1863.

3e. Charles Francis, b. 2 Aug., 1866.

4e. Fanny, b. 19 Aug., 1873; d. 11 April, 1876.

5e. Arthur, b. 20 May, 1877.

6e. Abigail, b. 6 Sep., 1879.

3d. Charles Francis, b. 27 May, 1835; grad. Harv. Coll. 1856; m. 8 Nov., 1865, Mary Ogden. Children:—

1e. Mary, b. 27 July, 1867.

2e. Louise Catherine, b. 28 Dec., 1871.

3e. Elizabeth Ogden, b. 3 Dec., 1873.
4e. John and Henry, twins, b. 17 July, 1875.
4d. Henry Brooks, b. 16 Feb., 1838; m. 27
June, 1872, Marian Hooper.
5d. Arthur, b. 23 July, 1841; d. 9 Feb., 1846.
6d. Mary, b. 19 Feb., 1845; m. Henry P.
Quincy. Children: —
　ie. Dorothea, b. 4 Dec., 1885.
　2e. Eleanor, b. 11 March, 1888.
7d. P. C. Brooks, b. 24 June, 1848; grad.
Harv. Coll. 1870; m. 7 Sep., 1889, Evelyn
Davis.
12c. Horatio, 12th child of Peter Chardon and
Ann (Gorham) Brooks, b. 20 Sep., 1809; d.
24 May, 1843.
13c. Octavius, b. 27 Oct., 1813; d. young.
3b. Mary, 3d child of Edward and Abigail (Brown)
Brooks, m. 25 April, 1799, Samuel Gray of
Salem and Medford, b. 1760, d. 1816, who m.
1st, 1787, Anna Orne, and who was brother of
Hon. William Gray, who m. Elizabeth, dau. of
Hon. John Chipman and Elizabeth (Brown)
Chipman (supra). Children: —
1c. Elizabeth Gorham, b. 4 March, 1800; m.
2 Dec., 1822, Franklin H. Story of Salem.
Children: —
　id. Franklin H., b. 12 Feb., 1825; m. 7 Dec.,
　1854, Adeline Wainwright of New York.
　Children: —
　　ie. Elizabeth Gray, b. 16 Oct., 1855; m. 21
　　Sep., 1874, Edward Gray, great-grandson
　　of William and Elizabeth Chipman Gray.
　　Children : Edward, Marguerite, and
　　Howard Story.
　　2e. Marion, b. 30 Jan., 1858, m. 22 May,
　　1887, Marie Louise Hunt of New York.
2c. Winthrop, d. unmarried.

3c. Sarah Charlotte, b. 7 April, 1809; m. 23 Dec., 1828, Ignatius Sargent of Boston. Child: —
Sarah Ellery, b. 19 Oct., 1829; m. 22 April, 1854, Winthrop Sargent of Philadelphia. Child: —
    Ignatius, b. 18 April, 1852; m. 30 April, 1885, Annie Childs of Waquoit. Child: William Winthrop, b. 16 Oct., 1887.
4c. Henrietta, b. 1 Oct., 1811; m. 6 May, 1834, Ignatius Sargent of Boston as his second wife. Children: —
    1d. Henrietta Gray, b. 14 June, 1838; m. 19 Oct., 1858, James M. Codman, grad. Harv. Coll. 1851. Children: —
        1e. Francis, b. 4 Aug., 1859; d. 11 Nov., 1885.
        2e. James M., b. 20 April, 1862; grad. Harv. Coll. 1884.
        3e. Henry Sargent, b. 19 June, 1864; d. 13 Jan., 1893.
        4e. Philip, b. 6 Oct., 1867; grad. Harv. Coll. 1889.
        5e. Cora, b. 12 July, 1874; m. 24 July, 1894, William Ely.
    2d. Charles Sprague, b. 24 April, 1841; grad. Harv. Coll. 1862; Director of Arnold Arboretum, Fellow Am. Acad., mem. Am. Philos. Soc., Nat. Agricultural Soc. of France, etc.; m. 26 Nov., 1873, Mary Allen Robeson. Children: —
        1e. Henrietta, b. 28 Aug., 1874.
        2e. Andrew Robeson, b. 2 Dec., 1876.
        3e. Mary, b. 8 April, 1878.
        4e. Charles Sprague, b. 7 March, 1880.
        5e. Alice, b. 26 March, 1882.
5c. Francis A., b. 5 Oct., 1813; m. 2 June, 1857, Helen W. Wainwright of New York. Children: —

1d. Mary, b. 17 March, 1858; m. 10 Dec.,
1885, George Audenried.
2d. Francis A., b. 28 May, 1867.
4b. Joanna Cotton, 4th child of Edward and Abigail (Brown) Brooks, m. 1793, Nathaniel Hall.
Children: —
1c. Caroline, m. Rev. Francis Parkman, grad.
Harv. Coll. 1807, S. T. D.; d. 1852. Children: —
1d. Francis, m. Catherine Scollay Bigelow.
He d. 1893. Children: —
1e. Grace, m. Charles Pratt Coffin. Children: 1. Francis Parkman. 2. Miriam.
3. Mary Bigelow.
2e. Francis.
3e. Katharine Scollay, m. John Templeman
Coolidge. Children: 1. Mary. 2. Katharine. 3. Louisa Riche. 4. John Templeman.
2d. Caroline H., m. Rev. John Cordner. Children: —
1e. Mary Agnes.
2e. Elizabeth Parkman.
3e. Caroline Parkman.
3d. Mary Agnes.
4d. Mary Brooks.
5d. Eliza Willard Shaw.
6d. John Eliot.
2c. Mary Brooks.
3c. Nathaniel, d. young.
4c. Edward Brooks, m. 1st, Harriet Ware; m.
2d, Louisa Jane Park. Children: —
1d. Edward, d. young.
2d. John, d. young.
3d. Edward Henry.
4d. Robert, d. young.
5d. Francis Parkman.

6d. William Ware.

7d. Harriet Ware.

5c. Nathaniel, m. Sarah Coffin.   Children: —

  1d. Henry Ware.

  2d. Nathaniel.

  3d. Caroline, m. Nathaniel Washburn.

  4d. Mary Louisa.

6c. Peter Chardon, m. Ann Rose Swann.   Children: —

  1d. Jane Webb.

  2d. Anna, m. Edward L. Zalinski, U. S. A. Child: —

  Edward Robins.

  3d. Louisa.

  4d. Fanny Maria, m. Frederic Knapp.   Children: —

    1e. Frederic.

    2e. Lucia Bradford.

  5d. Francis Parkman.

The only child of Elizabeth by her first husband, Rev. John Denison, grandson of Major-General Daniel Denison, was John, grad. Harv. Coll. 1710, m. 9 April, 1719, Mary Leverett, b. 29 Oct., 1701, dau. of Hon. John Leverett, President of Harvard College, and his wife Margaret (Rogers). He was Librarian of Harvard College 1713–14; studied divinity and preached one year, but was never ordained; afterwards settled in Ipswich as a lawyer and attained the rank of Colonel.   He d. 25 Nov., 1724, leaving a widow, one son, and one daughter.[1]   His widow, Mary, married 25 Dec., 1728, Rev. Nathaniel Rogers, b. 4 March, 170½, son of Rev. John and Martha (Whittingham) Rogers, grad. Harv. Coll. 1721, ordained in Ipswich 18 Oct., 1727; she d. at Ipswich

---

[1] " John Denison was a Young Gentleman of Uncommon Accomplishments and Expectations; of whom the Church of Ipswich hoped ' *Under his shadow we shall sit many years !* ' and he was a Pastor to them, of whose Fruit they tasted with an Uncommon satisfaction." — Cotton Mather's Lecture on Elizabeth Cotton, 1726, p. 28.

27 June, 1756; and he d. 10 May, 1775. A monument to
the memory of Col. John Denison, son of Elizabeth (Saltonstall) Denison in the cemetery at Ipswich, has the following inscription : —

[Coat of Arms of Denison.]

Huic Tumulo mandatur quod erat mortale
Johannis Denison, Armigeri,
Tribuni Militum Vicarii,
Et de Comitatu Essexiæ Vice-comitis,
Illustrissimi Danielis Denison, Armig.
Militaris quondam Præfecti Provincialis,
Et non minus Illustris Richardi Saltonstall, Armig.
Gubernatori olim a Consiliis,
(Quorum utroque gaudebat Nova-Anglia
Patre ac Patrono semper memorando)
Pronepotis non Indigni :
Quippe qui
In Collegio Harvardino liberaliter educatus,
Judicii acumine Singulari dotatus,
Jurisprudentiam non vulgarem adeptus,
Æquanimitate haud æquiparanda præditus,
Moribus Socialibus et Christianis Pollens,
Reipublicæ Ornamento fuit,
Et Fulcimento,
Dumque viveret bonis omnibus
Non immerito Dilectus
Et cum Animam efflaret, 25 Nov., 1724.
Ætat 35°
Non mediocriter deflectus
Famam reliquit Unguento optimo meliorem.

(TRANSLATION.)

" Here rests the mortal part of Lieut. Colonel Mr. John Denison, Esq., Sheriff
of Essex County; great-grandson of the most illustrious Daniel Denison, Esq.,
late Major-General in the Province ; and also of the not less illustrious Richard
Saltonstall, Esq., formerly one of the Governor's Council (in each of whom, as in
a father and champion ever to be remembered, New England used to delight), a
descendant not unworthy of his ancestry; having been liberally educated in Harvard College, endowed with extraordinary acuteness of judgment, remarkably
skilled in jurisprudence, gifted with unequalled steadiness of mind, mighty by his
social and Christian character; an ornament and pillar to the state; while he lived
deservedly beloved by all good men, and at his death Nov. 25, 1724, in the 34th
year of his age, lamented in no common degree. He left a memory more precious
than the most fragment ointment." [1]

[1] *Denison Memorial*, Ipswich, Mass., Sep. 20, 1882, two hundredth anniversary
of the death of Major-General Denison.

93. NATHANIEL SALTONSTALL (VI.)

Nathaniel, son of Nathaniel (87), is mentioned in letter of Robert Livingston to Fitz John Winthrop, 7 April, 1705, as in England,[1] and in consultation with him about the affairs the colony. Judge Sewall in his Diary, 26 Dec., 1728, says : " Mr. Nathaniel Saltonstall, brother of Gurdon, was at lecture to-day. He came lately from England, after a long and cold voyage."

Dorothy Saltonstall, wife of Nathaniel Saltonstall (93), who died in 1733, made a liberal bequest to Harvard College for the benefit of poor students.[2] This fund, hitherto known as the Dorothy Saltonstall Scholarship Fund, has been recently increased by a liberal gift of three thousand dollars from Henry Saltonstall, Esq. (124), on condition that the name of that fund shall be changed to Saltonstall Scholarship Fund.[3]

---

95. JUDGE RICHARD SALTONSTALL (VII.)

Judge Richard Saltonstall was born on the beautiful estate in Haverhill which was the marriage gift to his father by the Rev. John Ward, his maternal grandfather. The old mansion was in a commanding position on the bend of the Merrimac, with an extensive view of the river. Two rows of noble buttonwood trees were planted by him in 1736, and until they were destroyed by the blight which so sadly destroyed this beautiful tree throughout New England, about the middle of this century, they formed a prominent feature in the landscape, and were very dear to the judge's descendants for more than half a century after the place had passed from the possession of the family.

The place was known as the " Saltonstall Seat," and was sometimes called the " Buttonwoods."

[1] *Mass. Hist. Coll.* 6th series, vol. iii. pp. 286–288.
[2] Quincy's *History of Harvard University*, vol. i. p. 421.
[3] Treasurer's Statement, 1893, p. 9.

Judge Saltonstall was a man of talents and learning, was distinguished for generous and elegant hospitality, and for bountiful liberality to the poor. His address was polished, affable, and winning, his temper was gentle, his disposition benevolent, and he enjoyed the love and esteem of all. In 1741, while the court was in session at York, the celebrated Samuel Moody wrote the following lines on the court: —

> "Lynde, Dudley, Remington, and Saltonstall,
> With Sewall, meeting in the Judgment Hall,
> Make up a learned, wise, and faithful set
> Of Godlike judges by God's Counsel met."

He died 20 Oct., 1756.[1]

Judge Lynde in his diary, under date of 20 Oct., 1756, says: —

"Died ye Hon. Richard Saltonstall, one of ye Judges of our Superior Court, after an illness which took him off. From February, 1755, till this sickness he had been of so hale and strong a constitution as not to have missed attending one Court from his first appointment in 1736."

95 A. JOHN LEVERETT

John Leverett, only son of Thomas Leverett, the ruling elder, descended from one of the most ancient and honorable families of England,[2] came to New England in the Griffin with his father, Elder Thomas Leverett, in 1633, in company with Rev. John Cotton, late Vicar of the Borough of Boston, and other noted men. He was then 17 years of age, having been baptized at the famous old St. Botolph's Church, 17 July, 1616. His father had been alderman of the borough, resigning that office on the 23d day of July, 1633, and on arriving here was made a "ruling elder," and continued in that and other offices of trust for seventeen years, till his death.

---

[1] Notice of the life of Hon. Leverett Saltonstall, by Benj. Merrill *Mass. Hist. Coll.* 3d series, vol. ix. p. 124.

[2] Heralds' Visitation of Lincolnshire, 1564.

John Leverett 98.

"When Boston's streets were first named, in 1808, Congress Street extended from State (then King Street) to Water Street, and was named Leverett Lane, but more frequently called Quaker Lane.

It was named in honor of Elder Thomas Leverett, whose residence stood on the southeast corner of State Street, where the Exchange Building is now; he owned the land through which the lane passed. He was one of the earliest colonial settlers, and came from Boston, Eng., where he had been an alderman. He was a man of property and distinction.

His son, John Leverett, was governor of the colony at the time of King Philip's War. For him the present Leverett Street, which passed through his pasture, was named."

The following is a letter from Robert Atkyn to Elder Thomas Leverett : —

WORTHY S^r

my respected friend & ould acquaintance & schoole fellow, &c. I am very hartily joyfull to heare of you — and from you & that God is pleased to lengthen out y^r dayes to stand up in the roome of good old Xtians gone into another better habitation   I hope it is for the best good both to yor selfe & to the place you are in, we here are full of loosenes & debauchery & what not cryinge synns aboundinge & little restraint the mouths of good men restrained chariotts & horsemen laide aside malligned & dispised for the good they have done or would continue to doe lycentiousnes much more pleasing to ye generallity of people than a strict holy course of Livinge. I doe not question but greatly hope but yor acquaintance with God is much & that yor Lives is very holy & pleasing to him,   I suppose you may have heard of the death of Doctor Tuckney some time of o^r towne wth m^r Cotton but blessed be God we have good teachinge had we hearts to make a right improvement by holy meditation & practis   I have inclosed sent a regester of all y^r fathers children. the Clerk thinks he has omitted none, there is

one m'' Thomas Underwood sometimes wollen dray' in London, who I think lives in Boston & has been there 10 or 12
years that marryed old m'' Tilson's daughter one of them but
she is dead and since he went to New England has marryed
againe.   I would desire the fovo' of you to convey this inclosed tre to him & soe desireing from my heart if God
bestow place of choise or choisest trust upon you consider
yo' rule not for man but for y° lord who wilbe with yo" &
assist you & its the reall desire of him that he may soe be
who with his true respects to you subscribes himselfe
Yo' cordiall frend & humble servant
ROBERT : ATKYN
BOSTON, March 18ᵗʰ, 1672.

March 18, 1672.   A true coppy of the regester of the Borough of Boston in the Countty of Lincoln to certify whom
it may concern.

John, y° son of m'' Thomas Leveret was baptized the 16
day of August 1612.

Jaine y° daughter of m'' Tho. Leveret was baptized August
y° 9, 1613.

Jaine y° daughter of the same was baptized December y°
6 1614.

John, y° son of the same baptized July 7, 1616.

Thomas y° son of the same baptized July 30, 1618.

Ann y° daughter of y° same baptized January 8, 1619.

James y° sonne of y° same baptized June 28, 1621.

Sarah, y° daughter of y° same baptized Septemb' 26, 1622.

Mary, y° daughter of y° same baptized ffeb. 5, 1623.

Jabes, y° son of y° same baptized Septemb' 6, 1627.

Israel y° son of y° same baptized Septemb' 25, 1628.

Elisha, y° son of y° same baptized July 3, 1630.

Nathaniel, y° son of y° same baptized April 12, 1632.[1]
Witness Dan. Jenkinson.

" No man in our country ever filled more important offices,

---

[1] These papers in the original are in the possession of the author.

nor with happier repute, than John Leverett. He was Representative in 1651, and several succeeding years; Speaker in 1663 and 1664; Assistant 1665 to 1671; Major-General in 1663; Deputy Governor 1671 to 1673; and, on the death of Governor Bellingham, Governor 1673 to his own death, 16th March, 1679, aged 62."[1] In 1644-5 he was in England and was appointed to a command in Rainsborrow's regiment, and in several actions during the civil war then raging between the unfortunate Charles and the iron legions of the Protector, he is said to have distinguished himself. He was at this time about 28 years of age, and acquired invaluable training and experience in military affairs under Cromwell, who it is said greatly esteemed him.

In 1652 he was commissioned to visit the eastern settlements in Maine, and to declare them under the jurisdiction of Massachusetts, and several times afterwards to arrange terms of submission; Massachusetts, being required to assign these rights to the Crown, declined to yield what she considered her rightful claims, — manifesting afterwards the same high spirit against the claims made by Randolph in behalf of the Crown. Leverett was then Governor, and refused to take the oaths demanded.

In 1653 he was appointed one of the commissioners to the government at New Netherlands, and made commander of the forces to be raised in the event of hostilities; and in 1654 he had a commission under General Sedgwick to expel the French from Penobscot, and was successful.

LETTERS FROM OLIVER CROMWELL TO CAPT. JOHN LEVERETT

OLIVER, PR.

Wee have received an Account from Major Sedgwick of his having taken several Forts from the French in America, and that he hath left you to command and secure them for Us, and this Commonwealth; and although Wee make no doubt of your fidelitie and diligence in the performance of

[1] Savage's *Gen. Dic.* vol. iii. p. 83.

your trust, yet Wee have thought it necessary to let you
know of how great consequence it is, that you use your utmost care and circumspection as well to defend and keep the
Forts above said, as also to improve the regayning of them
into Our hands to the advantage of Us and the State, by
such wayes and meanes, as you shall judge conducible thereunto.   And as Wee shall understand from you the state and
condition of those places, we shall from time to time give
such directions as shall be necessarie.

Given at Whitehall, this third day of April, 1655.

To Captain John Leverett, Commander of the Fort, lately
taken from the French in America.

OLIVER P.

Whereas Wee have committed vnto our Trusty and welbeloved Colonell Thomas Temple the charge custody and
government of our Forts of Sᵗ John, Port Royall, and Pentacoet in Acadia commonly called Noua Scotia in America,
and the Martiall stores and provisions there being or thereunto belonging ; Our will and pleasure therefore is, That you
deliver or cause to bee deliuered vnto the said Thomas
Temple ymediatly upon his arrivall there, the full and peaceable possession of the said Forts, and of all the Ordnance,
Gunnes, Amunicon, and martiall stores, and other provisions of Victualls, Clothes, Barkes, Boates, Shipps and other
thinges whatsoeuer in the said Forts, or any of them being
or of right belonging to this Commonwealth by a true and
iust Inventary and Appraisement at indifferent and iust rates
and values, and that the said Inventary and Appraisement
you doe with all convenient speed send vnto Us, or our
Councell to the end the same may bee entred of Record, and
brought to Accompt in our Exchequer; For which this
shalbee a sufficient warrant; Given under our Signet at
Whitehall the six and twentyeth day of September 1656.

To Captⁿ John Leveret Governoʳ in chiefe of our Forts of
St John, Port Royall, and Pentacoet in Acadia comonly
called Nova Scotia in America, and to his Lieutenant and
other the officers there, or any of them.

Whereas Wee haue now committed vnto our Trusty and welbeloved Colonell Thomas Temple the charge custody and government of our Forts of St John, Port Royall and Pentacoet in Acadia commonly called Noua Scotia in America, and the Martiall stores and provisions there being or thereunto belonging; Our will and pleasure therefore is, That you deliver or cause to bee delivered vnto the said Thomas Temple ymediatly upon his arrivall there, the full and peaceable possession of the said Forts, and of all the Ordnances, Gunnes, Amunicon, and martiall stores, and other provisions of Virtualls, Clothes, Barkes, Boates, Shipps and other thinges whatsoever in the said Forts, or any of them being or of right belonging to this Commonwealth on a true and iust Inventary and Apprisement at indifferent and iust rates and values, and that the said Inventary and Apprisement you doe with all convenient speed send vnto Us, or our Councell to the end the same may bee entred of Record and brought to Accompt in our Exchequer, for which this shalbee a sufficient warrant; Given under our signet at Whitehall the six and twentyeth day of September 1656.

To Captn John Leveret Governor in cheife
of our Forts of St John Port Royall and
Pentacoet in Acadia comonly called Noua
Scotia in America and to his Lieutennt
and other the officers there, or any of them—

Cap: Jhon Ext
& Ja: Nurley.

In 1655 he received an appointment as Agent for the Colony at the Court of the Lord Protector and remained till 1662, two years after the restoration.

It was undoubtedly owing to the intimacy known to exist between Leverett and the Protector, and to his influence, that Cromwell's displeasure at the proceedings of the colony in its aggressions against certain sectarians was softened. Leverett, to his credit, was opposed to the persecutions which so sadly disfigure the escutcheons of the early Puritans.

His administration of the affairs of the colony at a time when men of the very purest character, clearest judgment, and firmness of purpose were demanded, was such that he was reëlected with unanimous acclaim for five successive terms till his death.

He was respected for his vigorous and stalwart character, trusted and beloved for his many virtues and attainments. It is said by most writers that no chief magistrate, before or since, has been held in higher estimation by the people, and few ever received more grateful testimonials of reverence and affection.

" His modesty, notwithstanding his superior talents, elevated rank and fortune, was equal to his merit. This was a beautiful feature of his character, and added no little to his renown."

Washburn, in his Judicial History of Massachusetts, says: " He was so much respected in his office and so popular as a man, that his election was never contested."

Hutchinson says: " The weighty affairs of the war,[1] and the agency during his administration conducted with prudence and steadiness, caused him to be greatly respected." Hon. James Savage tells us that " his great military talents fitted him for the place of major-general, held many years, and in the higher station of governor, in the most perilous period Massachusetts ever knew,— King Philip's War,— they were fully exerted." [2]

[1] King Philip's War.
[2] Report of Heraldic Committee, *New England Historical and Genealogical Register*, July and October, 1881.

Whether Governor Leverett was knighted or not seems to be a matter of very trivial importance, but has of late been a mooted question. The fact that he was agent for the colony for a year or more after the Restoration, and that he probably produced upon the mind of the King the same favorable impression that he invariably made upon those who knew him, coupled with the letter of the King,[1] addressed, " To our trusty and well beloved Sir John Leverett, Knt., Governor of Massachusetts Bay in New England," with the signature of the King and the Secretary, would seem strongly to favor the affirmative of the question. It is asked, why did not the Governor acknowledge the honor and wear the title? We agree with Mr. Savage that he showed his excellent judgment in not doing so. This unusual and exceptional honor at that time would have perhaps excited the jealousy of his friends and interfered with his usefulness.

On the other hand, the argument presented by the learned and able committee of the New England Historic Genealogical Society assumes to settle the question in the negative. It is unnecessary here to review at length the reasons pro and con, as we repeat that the question is of small importance.

The letter above referred to is as follows: —

CHARLES R.

Trusty & welbeloved, wee greet you well. Whereas wee have been humbly informed by the petiĉon of John Wampas als. White, that he was about six months since put into prison here for a small debt, where he hath since remained to his utter ruine, & that he hath a certain parcell of land in Massachusetts bay, the which he hath held for many years, having taken the Oaths of Allegiance & Supremacy as our subject; and having humbly besought us to interpose with you that he may bee restored to his s^d lands, or have liberty to sell the same for his present reliefe & the payment of his debts, wee taking into our gracious consideraĉon the miserable con-

---

[1] In the possession of the author, and here reproduced in heliotype.

Charles R

Trusty & Welbeloved Wee greet you
well: Whereas Wee have been humbly
informed by the peticon of John Wampas
alɪ. White, that he Was about six months
since put into prison here for a small debt
where he hath since remained to his utter
ruine, & that he hath a certain parcell
of land in Massachusetts bay, the which
he hath held for many years, having
taken the Oaths of Allegiance & Supremacy
as our subject; and having humbly
besought us to interpose With you
that he may bee restored to his lands,
or have liberty to sell the same for his
present reliefe & the payment of his
debts. Wee taking into our gracious
consideracon the miserable condition
of the petɪ. have thought fitt to
recomend him to you, that he may
have Justice done him & What favour
the matter will fairly beare. And soe
Wee bid you farewell. Given at our
Court att Whitehall the 22th day of
August 1676 in the 28th yeare of our
reigne.

By his Maɪ. ties comand
William ——

To our Trusty and Welbeloved
Sr John Leverett Knt: Governour
of Massachusetts bay in new
England   Kensington 2 junij 1677

dition of the pet[r] have thought fitt to recõmend him to you, that he may have Justice done him & what favour the matter will fairly beare. And soe wee bid you farewell. Given att our Court att Whitehall, the 22d day of August 1676 in the 28th yeare of our reigne.

By his Maties comand   WILLIAMSON.

To Our Trusty and welbeloved Sr John Leverett Kn[t]. governour of Massachusetts Bay in new England.

Governor Leverett died on the 16th March, 167$\frac{8}{9}$, and his interment on the 25th was attended with unusual parade and ceremony. His funeral sermon was preached by the Rev. Samuel Willard, and his remains were placed in the King's Chapel Cemetery.

In the papers of his son-in-law, Elisha Cooke, was found one giving part of the order of march, as follows: —

M[r] John Joyliffe
M[r] James Whitcombe } to carry each a Banner Roll at the 4 corners of the
M[r] Ric[d] Middlecott [1]   Herse.
M[r] W[m] Tailer

  To march next before the Herse as followeth :
{ M[r] Sam. Shrimpton, or in his absence
{ Capt. Clap to carry the helmet.
{ M[r] John Fairweather to carry the Gorget.
{ M[r] E[m] Hutchinson to carry the Brest
{ M[r] Charles Lidgett   Back
{ M[r] Samp[n] Sheafe   one tace
{ M[r] John Pincheon   one tace
{ Captain Nich[o] Paige, M[r] Dummer in case one Gauntlet
{ Capt.   Jona Curwin   one Gauntlet
{ Lieut. Edw. Willys the Target
{ Capt. Edw[d] Tyng the Sword
{ M[r] Hez. Usher   One Spur
{ M[r] Peter Sargent One Spur
  Capt. Wm. Gerrish to lead the Horse per the Rein.
  And Return Waite, as Groom per the Head stall.
M[r] Lynde
M[r] Saffin } To carry Banners mixt in the Banner Rolls above.
M[r] Rock
M[r] Green

[1] Father of Jane Middlecott, wife of Elisha Cooke, Jr.

The epitaph on his grave is recorded to have been as follows : —

To y* sacred memory of
N. E's Heroe, Mars his Generall
Vertue's Standard Bearer, and Learning's Glory
y* faithfully pious and piously faithful
subject to y* great
Majesty of Heaven & Earth
Y* Experienced Souldier in y* Church Militant
Lately listed in y* Invincible Triumphant
Army of y* Lord of Hosts,
y* deservedly worshipful
Jn° Leverett, Esq'.,
y* Just, Prudent & Impartial
Governo' of ye Mattachusetts Colony in N. E.
Who surrendered to y* all conquering command of Death
March 16. Anno Dom : 167⅜.
Et Ætatis suæ 63.

Governor Leverett's family Bible is in the author's possession. It is one of the edition of 1599, known as the
" Breeches Bible," owing to the peculiar translation given
the seventh verse of the third chapter of Genesis, " Then the
eyes of both of them were opened, and they sewed figge tree
leaves together and made themselves breeches ; " but it is of
more interest as it contains in Leverett's writing the record
of his two marriages and of his children's birth and death.[1]

John Leverett his booke Anno Dom̃ 1639
In Boston New Engld
He marryed Hanna the Daughter of m'. Ralph Hudson June 18 1639
Hudson my first sonn ⎰ My sonn was maryed to Sarah Payton ye 20
borne May 3 1640　　⎱ August 1661 at bostõ in New Engld
John : my seccond sonn borne 1 July 1641 : departed this life Jũ 1642
buryed in bostõ
Hanna : my first daughter borne 16 April : 1643 : departed this life Dec' :
9 1657 : buryed in ye parish church olivs Southwark.
John. my third sõ : Borne March : 1645 : departed August : 1646 and
buryed in bostõ New Engld these foure childrē I had by Hanna my first
wife who departed this life the 7th day of july 1646 & was buryede in Boston in New Engld :
9th Septemb' 1647 marryed Sarah daughter to m" Elizabeth Sedgwicke

[1] The original is here reproduced in heliotype.
The portrait of Governor Leverett is from an excellent miniature set in a gold
locket, and represents him when he was a young man. The miniature is in the
author's possession, and is of undoubted authenticity.

John Lewis: his booke in Anno 1639

[...] in Boston in New England

[...] marryed Hanna the daughter of [...] Ralph Mason June: 28 : 1639
Hudson my first borne may: 3: 1640 & ye: 20 August 1661 at Boston in New England
John: my second sonne borne [...] July [...] 1642 buryed in Boston
Hanna: my first daughter borne in Aprill 1643 departed this life this wer: 9 : 1647 buryed
John: my third son borne March: 1644 departed August: 1646 } in ye parish church [...]
and buryed in Boston New England these fower children [...]
I had by Hanna my first wife [...] departed this
life the 7th: day of July 1646 & was buryed
in Boston in New England

9th: September: 1647 : marryed Sarah daughter to mrs Elizabeth Sedgwicke
ye widdow of mr: william Sedgwicke marryed at Tuisham in Kent at ye house
of her brother mr Robert Houghton ————

August: 4: 1648 Sarah my first by her was borne in Boston New England
departed the 18 of same month & buried there

August 18: 1649 Sarah my 2d daughter by her was borne at Boston
departed in december same yeare & buryed at Boston

April 26: 1651 Elizabeth my 3d daughter was borne in Boston maryed: 9 : ju: 1668
to Elisha Cooke: physicke.

November: 15: 1652 Ann my fourth daughter was borne in Boston maryed: 12: noo[...]
1671 [...] Rudlard son to ye Revered mr [...] pastor to ye church
at [...]

August: 1: 1654 Sarah my fifth daughter was borne in Boston as her; v / s:
departed this life 14 August & buried there

feb: 13: 1655 mary my sixth daughter was borne at Boston in New England
maryed 19: 10 : 7[...] to Paul Dudley Esqr.

July: 31: 1658 Thomas my first sonne & first child by her about 11: or 12 oclock
at night was borne at Richam in ye County of Surry in England: departed
the 20th of August [...] & [...] buryed in olaves church in
Southwark ye 22 the day.

August 21: 1659 Sarah my [...] daughter & [...] child by Sarah was borne
in Criple gate parish in whytecrose street Londō: Sarah
departed this life ye 19 octob: 1661 buryed ye: 19 day in ye church
of olaver south wark

August: 19: 1661 Hanna: was borne in Londo at ye house of brother mr 15th
Barrell at ye George in breed street at 4 clock afternoone:
it was maryed to Elizabeth [...] 14 June 1661

December: 5: 1664 [...] Rebekah Leverett was borne at 4 clock after noone
at Boston in New England

August 23: 1667 John Leverett was Borne between five & six a clock
in ye afternoone in Boston N: E: dyed a yeare & buryed
in Boston

August: 10: 1669 James Leverett Borne in Boston in New England ye
[...] 10: [...] at three a clock in [...]
the [...] morning [...]

jᵉ: 1670 Sarah Leverett

Daughter by her was born ... baptⁱᵈ 10 oclock
in the ...ing at low water, Baptized 3 july, dⁱʳⁿᵉˡⁱᵉ
16 day july. ... was a clock afternoon, ... filled.

June 1673. Sarah Leverett yᵉ ... by Sarah & 12ᵗʰ. Daughter
by her was born the 18ᵗʰ Day being Sabath day at two
of the clocke in the afternoon one hower before low water
... bapti... she was marry'd to the Honᵇˡᵉ Colᵒ Nathᵗˡ Byfield Eſqˢ
of Bristol N.E. Apⁿ 17. 1718. at the Hour of 4 Revᵈ Mʳ B. Wadsworth.
Boston.

ye widdow of m^r William Sedgwicke marryed at Lvishā in Kent at ye house of hir brother m^r Robert Houghton.

August 4 : 1648   Sarah my first by hir was Borne in bostō New Engld departed the 18 of same month & buried there.

August 18 : 1649.   Sarah my 2d daughter by hir was borne at boston departed in Decembr : same yeare & buryed at bostō

April 26 : 1651   Elizabeth my 3d daughter was borne in Bostō maryed 9 jū : 1668 to Elisha Cooke, phesitiā.

Novemb^r : 15 : 1652.   Ann my ffowrth daughter was borne in bostō maryed 12 Novr 1672 to m^r John Hubbard, sonn to ye Reverend Wm Hubbard Pastor to ye church at ipswitch

August 1 : 1654   Sarah : my fifth daughter was borne in bostō departed this life 14 August & buried there.

ffeb^r : 13 : 1655   Mary my sixt daughter was borne at bostō in New Engld married 15 : 10 : 75 to Paul Dudley

July : 31 : 1658   Thomas my first sonn & seventh chyld by hir about 11 : or 12 clocke at night : was borne at Peckhā in ye County of Surry in Engld. departed the 20th of August & buryed in olaves church in Southwarke ye 22th day.

August 21 : 1659   Sarah my seveth daughter & eight chyld by Sarah was borne in Criplegate parish in whytecrose street Londō : Sarah departed this life ye 15 Octobr. 1661 buryed ye 17 day in ye church of olaves south-warke[1]

August : 29 : 1661.   Hanna : was borne in Londō at ye house of brother m^r Wm Barret at ye George in breedstreet at 4 clock afternoone : & was married to Eleazar Allin 14 June 1691.

Decemb^r : 5 : 1664   Rebekah Leverett was borne at 4 clock afternoone at Boston in New Engld

August 23 : 1667   John Leverett was Borne between five & six a clock in ye afternoone : in bostō N. E : dyed 2 Sept. & buryed 3d in bostō

August 20 : 1668, Janne Leverett Borne in bostō in New Engld at three a clocke in the morning being thursday, these twoe children we baptised at ye new Church.   Jane departed 15 : 7br 68 at three clock morning being (illegible)

jū : 1670.   Sarah Leverett ye 13 birth by Sarah & eleventh Daughter by hir was borne 30th Day at 10 clock in the evening at Low water bap-tized 3 july departed 16 day july at 2 a clock afternoone, halfe flood.

june 1673.   Sarah Leverett ye 14 birth by Sarah & 12th Daughter by her was borne the 15th day being Saboth day at twoe of the clock in the after-noone one hower before Low water at bostō : She was marry'd to the Honble Col^o Nathl Byfield Esqr of Bristol N. E. Apr. 17 1718 at the House of ye Rev^d m^r B. Wadsworth Boston

It will be seen that by his first wife, Hannah Hudson, b. in

[1] St. Olave's Church, Southwark.   The Governor carefully omits the "St." before Olave in the three burials there of his children.

England 1621, m. 1639, d. 1643, he had four children, one of whom only survived, Hudson, whose son John was for seventeen years the distinguished President of Harvard College.

By his second wife, Sarah Sedgwick, daughter to Mrs. Elizabeth Sedgwick, widow of William and sister of the distinguished soldier, Major-General Robert Sedgwick,[1] b. 1629, m. 1647, d. 1704, he had fourteen children. The eldest surviving daughter m. Elisha Cooke of Boston. (See below.)

95 B. ELISHA COOKE, SENIOR AND JUNIOR

" The history of the two Elisha Cookes is interwoven with that of the colony at the period in which they lived." [2]

Elisha, senior, son of Richard Cooke, a physician, was born 6 Nov., 1637; grad. Harv. Coll. 1657; m. Elizabeth, dau. of Governor Leverett, June, 1668; d. 31 Oct., 1715, aged 78. She d. 21 July, 1715. He early in life took a deep interest in public affairs, and at the time of the charter dispute in 1680 was the leader of the popular party in the General Court in opposing sending agents to England or submitting to acts restricting trade, and stoutly stood for the old charter.

" The ill-concealed joy of the people of Massachusetts at the fate of Charles I. was not forgotten by his son, and in 1676 Edward Randolph was sent over with ' Enquiries ' concerning the state of the colonies. This man was an active and implacable enemy of New England. Cooke resisted his demands from the first, and was prominently named by him in a letter to the Bishop of London as one of the chief opponents of the Crown."

He was one of those who were held to answer for high misdemeanors. The question whether it was advisable to

---

[1] Major-General Robert Sedgwick was one of the most distinguished of the early settlers. Carlyle says in his life of Cromwell that Sedgwick was a " very brave, zealous, and pious man, whose 'letters in Thurloe' are of all others the best worth reading on this subject."

[2] *Biographical Sketches of Lawyers, Statesmen, and Men of Letters*, by Samuel L. Knapp, p. 273.

Elisha Cooke, Senior.
(From a portrait in the possession of the Author.)

submit and surrender the charter at once greatly agitated the people. The General Court resolved not to surrender, thinking it better " to die by the hands of others than by their own," and the agents were instructed " to make no concessions of any privileges conferred by the charter."

The Governor and majority of Assistants, however, upon the issuance of a *quo warranto* against the charter, passed a vote of submission. This was acted upon by the house under the leadership of Cooke as follows : —

" Nov. 30, 1683. The Deputies consent not, but adhere to their former bills."

In 1685 and 1686, Cooke was chosen Assistant in place of one who had voted for submission.

We cannot, however, follow Cooke in his courageous opposition to the Royal Government in its various attempts to enforce its arbitrary acts against the colony. Oppressive measures culminated in the appointment of Andros in 1686. James II. vested him and his Council with all powers executive and legislative. " Randolph was prime minister, licenser of the press, secretary, etc. They laid what taxes they pleased, and punished with severity such as refused obedience." " He declared all titles and estates to be forfeited, and that the soil had reverted to the Crown."

The people, hitherto free, were now subjected to the rigor of desperation, and, upon hearing the rumor of the landing of the Prince of Orange, the smothered flame burst forth. The Governor with the most active of his Council and other obnoxious persons were seized, and the old magistrates restored. A bold act, and one of the most stirring events in the history of the colony. Had the rumor proved false, or the revolution in England failed, it would have proved fatal to the principal persons engaged, among whom was Cooke.

Cooke and Thomas Oakes, both Assistants, were chosen to support the charges in England against Andros. Hutchinson, vol. i. p. 349, says: " Mr. Cooke had always stiffly adhered to the old charter, and when all the rest of the Assistants declined reassuming it, he alone was in favor of it."

Elisha Cooke, Junior.

(From a portrait in the possession of the Author.)

ley had been of his father. The Governor's rejection of Cooke as a member of the Council created such a feeling of strong opposition in the House that the Governor dissolved the Assembly. Governor Hutchinson says that the contests and dissensions were greater in 1720 than they had been since the religious feuds of 1636. Cooke was chosen Speaker, the Governor negatived him, and requested the House to choose another Speaker; but, after debate, the House voted unanimously to adhere to their first selection. After several messages between them, the Governor again dissolved the House. Articles of complaint were exhibited by Governor Shute against the House for encroaching on his Majesty's prerogative in seven instances; and after much altercation between the Council and the House, it was agreed to send over an agent, and Dr. Cooke was chosen by joint vote.

After divers hearings before the Privy Council, the decision was unfavorable to the House, and ended in the charter of 1724; but the House, appreciating Cooke's conduct and his stout defence before the Privy Council, again chose him into the Council, and Lieut.-Governor Dummer approved of the choice.

The famous contest between the House and the Governor concerning a fixed salary for the Governor, which had continued nearly half a century, and been maintained with unyielding constancy by the House against the instructions of the King, at last terminated in 1733; and thus ended that famous controversy, perhaps the most memorable and important in our colonial history; for the people thus became accustomed to support their rights, however unequal the contest, and were trained for the great controversies that succeeded.

" These early contests were the germ of the Revolution." While, then, we value our civil liberty, we should hold in grateful remembrance the early patriots of the country,— such men as the first Cooke, who would have this infant colony " make no ' concession of any privileges conferred by the charter,' and who would say, even in the royal presence, ' the old charter or none.' "

Eliot, in his "Biographical Dictionary," remarks that "Hutchinson, though the great friend to Dudley, Burnet, and other governors on the side of prerogative, uniformly gives praise to the Cookes. He says they were both fair, honest men, open in their conduct, and acted from a love to their country. It is some credit to him as a historian, that he should delineate so fairly the characters of men who certainly were the most zealous republicans that ever acted their parts in Massachusetts Bay."

"They were men of strong, inflexible character, of great energy of mind, and consistent in their political conduct, and should hold a high rank among American patriots."

Elisha Cooke, the younger, was born 20 Dec., 1678, and grad. Harv. Coll. 1697. He m. 7 Jan., 1703, Jane, dau. of Richard Middlecott, Esq., of Boston (Part II. 95 C), who m. 1672, a niece of Governor Edward Winslow. He d. Aug., 1737.

Elisha Cooke, Jr., was a prominent citizen, representative of Boston, served as Councillor 1717, 1724, 1725, 1726, 1728, negatived in 1718. Chosen Speaker 1720, negatived, and the House thereon dissolved. His father, Dr. Elisha Cooke, was even more prominent in our local politics. Hutchinson, ii. 211, speaks highly of him, and thanks his grandson Middlecott for the use of valuable papers.

The Cookes were said to have been the wealthiest men in Boston. They resided in a stone mansion which stood where now stands the City Hall, and owned much land in School Street and what is now Beacon Street, as well as on Cornhill (Washington) and King (State) streets. "The frequent political meetings at that house have by some (says the late Dr. Bentley) been supposed to be the origin of the word 'caucus,' corruption of *Cook's house*."

The portraits of the two Elisha Cookes and of Jane (Middlecott), wife of the younger Cooke, are in the author's possession, and are at present at his house at Chestnut Hill. Heliotype copies of them are in this volume.

Jane Middlecott, Wife of Elisha Cooke, Junior.
(From a portrait in the possession of the Author.)

95 C. RICHARD MIDDLECOTT

Richard Middlecott of Boston (father of Jane, who married Elisha Cooke, Jr.) came from Warminster, Co. Wilts; m. here Sarah, widow of Tobias Paine, who had been widow of 2d Miles Standish, and dau. of John Winslow[1] of Boston, merchant (and his wife Mary Chilton), brother of Edward Winslow of Plymouth, governor; was freeman 1690; one of Council under the new charter; d. 1704. His widow d. 1728. Children:—

1. Mary, b. 1 July, 1673 (Savage says 1674); m. 1st, Henry Gibbs, and 2d, Othniel Haggett of Barbadoes.
2. Sarah, born 2d June, 1678; m. 26 March, 1702, Louis Boucher.
3. Edward, b. 1680; lived with his father for a time and then went to England, where he purchased his father's life interest in an estate at Warminster for £300 per annum, which was entailed to him by his uncle. He married and had one child, Jane, b. at Warminster 26 Sep., 1682, m. 7 Jan., 1703, Elisha Cooke, Jr. (Part II. 95 B), and had children:—
    1. Middlecott Cooke, grad. Harv. Coll. 1723; d. Aug., 1737.
    2. Mary Cooke, m. Richard Saltonstall (95), Judge of the Superior Court.

See "Mass. Hist. Soc. Proceedings," vol. xvii. pp. 410–412 and note; Savage, "Genealogical Dict. of New England," vol. iv. p. 601. Portraits of Richard Middlecott and of his son Edward (taken when he was young) are in the possession of the author, and are here reproduced in heliotype.

[1] Generally said to have been son of the Governor. This is an error, according to Hon. James Savage.

99. ABIGAIL SALTONSTALL (VIII.)

Abigail Saltonstall m. Colonel George Watson of Plymouth (his first wife), and had George, b. 1749, d. young; and son unnamed, 1751. Colonel Watson m. 2d, Elizabeth, dau. of Peter Oliver, and had Mary, b. 1754, m. Elisha Hutchinson, son of Governor Hutchinson; George, b. 1757; Sarah, m. Martin Brimmer; and Elizabeth, b. 1764, m. 1st, Thomas Russell, 2d, Sir Grenville Temple, whose son, Sir Grenville Temple Temple, b. 1799, m. 1829, Mary, dau. of George Baring, brother of Lord Ashburton. Colonel Watson m. 3d, Mrs. Phœbe Scott, and d. 1800, aged 83.[1]

---

101. COLONEL RICHARD SALTONSTALL (VIII.)

Colonel Richard Saltonstall, eldest son of Judge Richard Saltonstall (95), was commissioned Colonel of the regiment in Haverhill and vicinity in 1754, at the age of 22, and was the fourth of the family in succession who held that office. He graduated from Harvard College with high rank, and delivered the Latin oration at Commencement. The oration, written in elegant Latin, is in the possession of the author, and shows him to have been an accomplished scholar.

His acceptance from Governor Shirley of the commission of colonel, so soon after leaving college, evinced a spirit which was not long after to be tried in arduous service for his country. In the French War in 1756 he was Major in the army, and in 1757 (August 9) was one of the unfortunate prisoners at the capitulation of Fort William Henry. When the Indians fell upon the unarmed prisoners, he escaped that dreadful massacre by concealing himself in the woods, where he lay through the day while they constantly passed and repassed in search of him, and a day or two later he reached Fort Edward, nearly exhausted with hunger and fatigue. He commanded a regiment and was in active service until the

[1] See Sabine's *Loyalists of the American Revolution*, vol. ii. p. 403.

Richard Middlecott, Father of Jane (Middlecott) Cooke.

(From a portrait in the possession of the Author.)

close of the war. He was soon after appointed Sheriff of the County of Essex.

Colonel Saltonstall was a steady loyalist in principle, and never for a moment wavered in his devotion to the flag under which he had so bravely fought, and which he had so often sworn to support. Like nearly all officials of all grades at that time, he adhered to the Crown.

He was uniformly opposed to the measures taken in opposition to the Government. "The proceedings [of the Government] were in his opinion extremely inexpedient, but he never doubted their right to tax these colonies."

"He was much beloved by the people of Haverhill and its vicinity, and it was long before he lost his popularity; but, in 1774, a mob from the West Parish of Haverhill and Salem, N. H., assembled for the purpose of proving themselves true *Sons of Liberty* by attacking him. By a word he could have collected a great part of the inhabitants of the village to his defence, but he would not, though urged by some of his friends. The rioters marched to his house and paraded before it, armed with clubs and other offensive instruments, when he came to the door and addressed them with great firmness and dignity. He told them he was under the oath of allegiance to the King, that he was bound to discharge the duties of the office he held under him, that he did not think the people were pursuing a wise or prudent course, but that he was as great a friend to the country as any of them, and had exposed his life in its cause, etc. He then ordered some refreshment for the *gentlemen*, who soon began to relent, when he requested them to go to the tavern and call for entertainment at his expense. They then huzzaed to the praise of Colonel Saltonstall, and never attempted to mob him again."

"In the autumn of 1774 he left Haverhill, and soon after embarked for England. He refused to enter the British service, saying, if he could not conscientiously engage on the side of his native country he never would take up arms against her. He was an excellent officer, and, it was supposed, might have had a high command in the American army had he embraced the popular cause."

" The King granted a pension to Colonel Saltonstall, and he passed the remainder of his days in England.   In his letters he expressed great affection for the 'delightful place, of his nativity,' but had no desire to return to this country unless he could be received into the office he formerly held. In one of his last letters he says, ' I have no remorse of con- science for my past conduct.   I have had more satisfaction in a private life here than I should have had in being next in command to General Washington, where I must have acted in conformity to the dictates of others, regardless of my own feelings.'

" Colonel Saltonstall was never married.   In Haverhill he resided upon the family estate in a liberal and hospitable manner, was much beloved, and had great influence from his integrity, frankness, and benevolence of disposition, politeness of manners, his superior understanding, and knowledge of the world.   He died in Kensington, G. B., October 6, 1785."

" Colonel Saltonstall was hospitably received in England by his remote family connections, who paid him every kind and generous attention while living, and erected a monument to his memory by Kensington Church, with the following inscription : —

" ' Near this place are interred the remains of RICHARD SALTONSTALL, Esq., who died Oct. 1st, 1785, aged 52.   He was an *American Loyalist* from Haverhill, in the Massachu- setts ; where he was descended from a first family, both for the principal share it had in the early erecting, as well as in rank and authority in governing the Province.   And wherein he himself sustained, with unshaken loyalty and universal applause, various important trusts and commands under the crown, both civil and military, from his youth till its revolt, and throughout life maintained such an amiable private Character, as engaged him the esteem and regard of many friends. As a memorial of his merits this stone is erected.' "[1]

[1] *Mass. Hist. Coll.* 2d series, vol. iv. pp. 164, 165. See, also, Sabine's *Ameri- can Loyalists,* vol. ii. pp. 252, 253.

Edward, Son of Richard Middlecott.
(From a portrait in the possession of the Author.)

Several interesting papers of Colonel Saltonstall's are in the author's possession : —

Plan of Crown Point, drawn by him.

Epic composed by him after the capitulation of Fort William Henry and his marvellous escape.

Muster Rolls of Troops under his command as Captain, at Capitulation of Fort William Henry, August 9, 1757.

Commission by Governor Pownall as " Lieutenant Colonel, 1759, of the first Battalion of a Regiment of Foot, whereof Brigadier General Timothy Ruggles is Colonel, and by me to be employed in his Majesty's service in the ensuing campaign."

Commission by Governor Bernard, in 1761, as " Colonel of a Regiment of Foot, raised by me, to be employed in his Majesty's service, under the Commander in Chief of his Majesty's Forces in North America."

---

105. DR. NATHANIEL SALTONSTALL (VIII.)

Nathaniel Saltonstall, first son of Judge Richard Saltonstall by his third wife, Mary Cooke, at the age of ten years, upon the decease of his father, was received into the family of his uncle, Middlecott Cooke, Esq., of Boston, and, after graduating from Harvard College in 1766, pursued the study of medicine and returned to his native town, Haverhill, and devoted his life to the practice of his profession.

" His classical education and general intelligence, his eminent professional skill and conscientious discharge of duty, his gentle manners and kind disposition, and his strong attachment to the liberty and independence of his country, acquired for him great respect in the community, and the affection and entire confidence of his patients. He was remarkable for his humane and assiduous attention to the poor, consoling them by his friendly, cheerful demeanor, and by the medicines and other necessaries which he freely supplied without the prospect of any pecuniary remuneration." [1]

[1] *Mass. Hist. Coll.* 2d series, vol. iv. p. 166.

"At a time when all his brothers and brothers-in-law adhered to those principles of loyalty in which they had been
educated, Dr. Saltonstall remained true to those principles of
civil liberty and humanity which he inherited from his worthy
ancestor, Sir Richard Saltonstall, and his not less worthy
son, Richard of Ipswich.

"This conscientious adherence to his principles separated
him forever from those he most loved. It was to him a
severe trial, and gave the strongest proof of his sincerity
and the strength of his principles. These had probably
been much invigorated by his training in the patriotic Cooke
family." [1]

"He was a sincere, liberal, and humble Christian. He
felt an ardent attachment to those venerable religious and
literary institutions in the establishment of which his ancestors had an important influence, particularly to Harvard College, in whose growing prosperity he rejoiced, and was ever
ready to promote such objects as in his opinion would have
a beneficial influence on society."

The "Merrimack Intelligencer" contained the following:
"Died on the morning of the 15th [May], very suddenly, universally respected and deeply lamented, Dr. Nathaniel Saltonstall of this town, Æ. 69.

"This gentleman was descended from some of the most
ancient and respectable families in this country. His father,
Richard Saltonstall, Esq., was for many years a Judge of the
Supreme Court. [2]

"Dr. Saltonstall was graduated at Harvard University in
1766, and, like his ancestors, cherished a warm attachment
to that venerable seat of learning. Highly respectable and
useful in his profession, he was remarkable for his liberal and
humane attention to the poor. . . .

"He was distinguished for public spirit, and was a firm
supporter of literary, civil, and religious institutions. His

---

[1] Bond's *Genealogies and History of Watertown*, vol. ii. p. 928.
[2] The Superior Court was then the highest court; the word "Supreme" is evidently an error.

house was the abode of hospitality. Social and benevolent himself, he inspired his guests with the same generous feelings. He was exemplary in all the relations of life. A Christian in principle and practice, no man was his enemy. An affectionate husband and father, he was tenderly beloved by his family and friends. His fellow-citizens have to lament the loss of a most valuable member of society. He preserved his social disposition to the last; and although he labored under a combination of bodily infirmities, his friends were sure to find their visits to him cheerful and agreeable."

Then follow " Lines occasioned by the death of the highly respected and greatly lamented Nathaniel Saltonstall, M. D."

> "Sorrow, mute silence through the village reign!
> Hush'd is the din of industry and mirth,
> The sable throng, slow breathing o'er the plain,
> Swells full our sadness, and gives anguish birth.
>
> "Yes, 't is no shame that anguish fills the breast,
> That woe has clouded every face with gloom,
> His country's friend, who succoured the distressed,
> The husband, father, summoned to the tomb.
>
> " If worth, distinguished birth, or e'en conspicuous wealth,
> Could save a mortal from the shades of death,
> Thou, Salt'nstall, hadst not died, unwaning health
> These gifts had purchased, and immortal breath.
>
> " Ye poor and needy, born to pinching want,
> To him no longer you prefer your prayer;
> But know the blessings that he once did grant
> Brighten the glory that he 's gone to share."

As a mark of respect to his virtues and character, the citizens of Haverhill, spontaneously, and without any previous concert, all closed their stores and suspended business to attend the obsequies.

In " Bentley's Notes," by Stanley Waters, "Salem Gazette," December 17, 1880, we find the following: " July 25th, 1804. At Dr. Saltonstall's I saw for the first time the portraits of the two Elisha Cookes, very celebrated as agents and active magistrates of Massachusetts." And again: "May 28, 1815. The death of Hon. N. Saltonstall of Haverhill, æt. 69, regards a very distinguished family in the history of New England. His father Richard was a judge of the Supreme Court. His mother was dau. of Elisha Cooke, Jr., and great-granddaughter of Governor Leverett, all of whom must rank among the first men of New England. The Cookes were the greatest and best of men. Leverett was the best governor of the second generation. Dr. N. S., grad. at Camb. 1766, was a physician. He was a gentleman of polite and very easy manners, very hospitable. . . . At his house I saw the best collection of his ancestors, and, in the way of family pride laudably displayed, that I ever witnessed. . . . The son of Hon. N. S. is settled in Salem, and is at present a representative of Salem. He has the manners of the family, and probably will succeed to many of its civic honors."

105 A. Anna (White) Saltonstall

Anna White, wife of Nathaniel (105), was the "daughter of Samuel White, Esq., whose ancestor was one of the first settlers of Haverhill in 1640. Through life she was distinguished for the gifts of her mind and the virtues of her heart."[1]

William White, b. 1610, landed at Ipswich 1635. In 1640 he removed to Haverhill, of which he was one of the first settlers, and was one of the grantees of the Indian deed of Haverhill, dated Nov. 15, 1642; which instrument was, it was said, both written and witnessed by him. The Haverhill town records show that he held a good social position among the first settlers. He d. 28 Sep., 1690. His only child, John, b. 1639 or 1640, m. in Salem 25 Nov. 1662, Hannah French. He d. in Haverhill 1 Jan., 166⅞, aged 29 years, leaving an only child, John, born 8 March, 166¾. He m. 24 Oct., 1687, Lydia Gilman, dau. of Hon. John Gilman of Exeter, N. H. He had 14 children, the fourth being William, b. 18 Jan., 169¾.

---

[1] *Mass. Hist. Coll.* 3d series, vol. ix. p. 125.

Deacon William White (great-grandson of the first William White), Captain and Justice of the Peace of Haverhill, m. 12 June, 1716, Sarah Phillips,[1] b. 28 Jan. 169½, dau. of Samuel and Mary (Emerson) Phillips of Salem, a granddaughter of Rev. Samuel Phillips of Rowley and a great-granddaughter of Rev. George Phillips of Watertown. He d. 11 Dec., 1737. He had 11 children.

Samuel White, second child of Deacon Samuel White, b. 15 Sep., 1718, lived in Haverhill, where he acquired a large estate; was Justice of the Peace, Representative to the General Court, etc. He m. Sarah, dau. of Rev. Richard Brown, minister of Reading. She d. 9 March, 1773, and he d. 21 Aug., 1801. They had 8 children. Their fourth child, Anna White, b. 12 April, 1752, m. Nathaniel Saltonstall. She was therefore a granddaughter of Sarah (Phillips) White, who was a great-granddaughter of Rev. George Phillips of Watertown, and her descendants look back with satisfaction to that good man as an ancestor.

---

108. LEVERETT SALTONSTALL (VIII.)

" Leverett, youngest son of Judge Saltonstall, received his name from his mother's connection with the family of that name. [Part II. 95 A and B.] He was born December 25, 1754, and at the commencement of the war had nearly completed his term of service with a merchant of Boston, when Colonel Saltonstall (his brother) came to that place for protection. Being in the habit of looking up to him for advice and direction, he embraced the same political opinions, and, becoming acquainted with the British officers, he was fascinated with their profession, and entered the British service. He was in many battles and commanded a company in the

---

[1] Sarah Phillips, who was grandmother of Anna (White) Saltonstall, was a daughter of Samuel Phillips and Mary Emerson his wife. She was a daughter of Rev. John and Ruth (Symonds) Emerson. The latter was a daughter of Lieut.- Governor Symonds, who married a sister-in-law of Governor Winthrop.

army of Lord Cornwallis. He d. at New York December 20th, 1782.

" His brother-in-law, Rev. Moses Badger, who was also a loyalist, in a letter to Dr. Nathaniel Saltonstall concerning his illness (consumption) and death, which he attributed to the fatigues he endured in Lord Cornwallis's campaign, which, he says, ' I believe to be as many and as great as any army ever met with in any country, at any period since the creation,' adds, ' It may be some consolation to you and his mother to hear that his behavior in the regiment endeared him to every officer ; and the soldiers, who had so frequent opportunity to see his intrepidity, coolness, and gallantry in action, absolutely revered him. He was agreeable to people of all ranks. He was exceedingly cautious in speaking, seldom uttering a word without reflection, and was never heard to speak ill of any one, and reprobated the man or woman who indulged themselves in this infirmity. He never fell into the scandalous and fashionable vice of profaneness ; in short, I looked upon him to be as innocent a young man as any I have known since I have been capable of making observations on mankind.' " [1]

110. LEVERETT SALTONSTALL (IX.)

Leverett Saltonstall, son of Dr. Nathaniel Saltonstall (105), was born in Haverhill at the " Buttonwoods " in the old house which belonged to his uncle, Colonel Richard Saltonstall, and which had for four generations been the home of his ancestors. He was the last of his family to occupy it, as it soon afterwards went out of their possession.[2]

His boyhood was passed most happily, and he always recurred with fondest recollections to his happy home in what was then a pretty rural town, nestling between its hills on

[1] *Mass. Hist. Coll.* 2d series, vol. iv. p. 167.
[2] His portrait, painted by Chester Harding, in the possession of the author, is here reproduced in heliotype.

Leverett Saltonstall

the lovely banks of the Merrimac, with his brother and sisters and kindest of parents. (Part II. 105.)

At an early age he was sent to Exeter Academy to fit for college. The excellent Benjamin Abbot was chief preceptor, and endeared himself to his pupils by his considerate treatment of them. Mr. Saltonstall always loved Exeter, making frequent visits to refresh the associations of his boyhood, and to see the venerable preceptor who for fifty years presided over the Academy. He always spoke of it most tenderly, and made a bequest to it in his will.

Among his schoolmates were Daniel Webster and Lewis Cass, for whom he maintained a warm friendship through life.

On entering college he was at once a favorite with students and professors. One of his classmates says: "We found him so frank and amiable in his manners, with so little reserve and no disguise, that his character was soon understood, and he won immediately that confidence which is commonly the growth of long acquaintance. Every one admired his good-fellowship, his generous temper and warm heart."

Leverett Saltonstall was among the few who appreciate at the time they enter it the happiness of a college life. His ancestors for many generations had been educated at Cambridge, which created in his mind a peculiar respect for the University, and made the college grounds sacred soil to him. He regarded it as truly his *Alma Mater*, and left it with regret. He never ceased to the end of his life to feel the warmest affection for it, and to manifest on all occasions his zeal for its welfare and progressive improvement. One of the last efforts of his life was, as an Overseer of the College, to write a carefully considered report covering the requirements for admission to the University. When remonstrance was made by his wife that he was too ill to do this work, he replied, "I would most cheerfully lay down my life for my *Alma Mater.*"

A classmate says: " The love of truth which he manifested at college then and ever after secured for him the undoubting and implicit trust of his friends; he never said what he did not believe, or promised what he did not intend to perform; and his fine candid countenance and manly deportment soon gained for him the same credit with strangers. His rank as a scholar was high, and he had an earnest and fervent manner in his declamation which made him an interesting and agreeable speaker."

"He had been piously educated, and brought from home impressions of his religious duties which were not effaced by the gayety and frivolity by which he was surrounded; for he obeyed the paternal injunction of searching the Scriptures and revering the Sabbath."

And again he says: "With many of his classmates he contracted friendships which were continued without intermission through his life. No man was ever truer to his friends than Leverett Saltonstall, or stood by them more steadily in distress and adversity. Many of them were less fortunate than he was in the distribution of the prizes of life. He never forgot the claims of these or turned from them in coldness. On the contrary, his counsel, his countenance, and his purse he gave freely, and of the latter bountifully. Prosperity and success did not change his manner or harden his heart. He never calculated the hazard of assisting a friend in need, but committed himself generously in the cause of those in whose integrity he confided."

The Class of 1802 was celebrated, not only for the character of the men composing it, but for the exceptional class feeling, — *the esprit de corps* which united them as brothers through life. Social meetings of the Class occurred invariably at Commencement and at frequent intervals throughout the year. No member of the Class who could do so ever failed to attend these meetings, where they renewed their youth together. The Class Fund for aiding the families of those of their number who needed assistance, and was given to the college after the decease of its members, was the model of many other class funds which have since been raised for a similar purpose.

Among such men as Governor Lincoln, Rev. John Codman, Samuel Hoar, Rev. James Flint, William Minot, James T. Austin, and others, Mr. Saltonstall was in his element; his presence was always earnestly looked for, he so added to the life of the occasion.

He failed to be present at Commencement only twice after his graduation: once when he was ill, and again when a long session of Congress kept him in Washington. He always seemed to give himself, heart and soul, on that day to the beloved University and to his cherished classmates. His face was radiant, the grasp of his hand was earnest, his voice was gladsome at Cambridge on Commencement day.

After leaving college Mr. Saltonstall studied law in Salem with the Hon. William Prescott, and, on entering the bar in 1805, he commenced the practice of his profession in Haverhill, but soon removed to Salem, which was then the seat of an extensive commerce. Her ships, owned by the Derbys, Grays, Crowninshields, Peabodys, and Pickmans, were known the world over, and the names of their owners were identified with all the great commercial enterprises of the day. Salem was as renowned for its social and literary circles as for its merchants and business life. No place could boast of a bar comprising so many eminent men as the famous Essex bar of that day. There were Prescott, Dane, Parsons, Putnam, Pickering, Story, and others distinguished for their ability and learning. It was a hard ordeal for a young man to meet such accomplished scholars at the bar; but with his bright, enthusiastic nature and attractive bearing he entered into the social life, and soon won the cordial regard of all, both old and young. He devoted himself to his profession, and at once took an honorable stand with the eminent men of the bench and bar. Respectful mention of his name has invariably been accompanied with loving words. He made no enemies, and no one knew him but to love him. His life in Salem for forty years was one of hard intense application to the practice of his profession. He rose with the birds, walked an hour before breakfast to hear them (for their song brought joy to his heart), and gave the entire day to his work in court or in the office, seldom passing even the evening with his family. With his ardent nature, quick and sensitive feelings, he never allowed himself to utter a quick word or to show any irritation, even when most oppressed by the many cares which weighed upon him. His presence at home was eagerly looked for by his wife and children.

Lawyers then had to do their own work; there were no stenographers in their offices, no typewriters, telegraph and telephone; and, in Essex County, courts were holden in three towns. There were no railroads, and long hours had to be occupied in crowded stage-coaches between Salem, Boston, Newburyport, and Ipswich, on bad roads, with all the discomfort of dust, heat, and cold.

Mr. Saltonstall was for many years President of the Essex bar, and appeared in almost every case of any importance at that bar as well as in Suffolk and other counties. He gave himself no rest till every step had been taken for his clients' interests. He rarely if ever appeared in court for a client in the right and justice of whose cause he did not believe, and therefore had great influence with judge and jury. But whatever his weight of care, even with a term of court opening the next day and retained in every case before the court, he never on Sunday looked at a paper or law book, nor visited his office. Sunday was ever to him a day of holy rest, a day for communion with his Maker, a day at home with his family, with his books, and at church, where in the choir he lifted his fine voice and joined in the songs of praise. Sunday evenings he always passed with his most cherished friends. He was a great lover of books, and eagerly read everything that came out which was worth reading. He frequently said to his children, " Always have a good book with a mark in it; if you have but five minutes, take it up and read, and you will be amazed at what you can accomplish."

The late Hon. Daniel Appleton White of Salem, Judge of Probate, was a lifelong friend of Leverett Saltonstall; a connection of the family, the tutor of his class in college; they maintained for each other sentiments of deep respect and affection. Judge White nine years after his death wrote a memoir of him, which he presented to his children, but which was never printed. It gives a glowing picture of the youth as he first presented himself in college, with touching reminiscences of his life there; his early life at the bar, with many of his early letters; and sketches of his association with him to the close of his life. It is full of interest, and a touching tribute to his memory. A few extracts from it are here given : —

"In 1813, the first year after his removal to Salem that the Federalists succeeded in the election, he was chosen a Representative of Salem to the General Court. He had been a candidate of the Federalists several years before. He was also chosen in 1814 and in 1816, having declined to be a candidate in 1815. In 1817, 1818, 1819 he was successively elected a Senator of the Commonwealth from the County of Essex, and in 1820, declining to be a candidate, he received the cordial thanks of a public meeting of the Federalists of the county for his able and faithful services in the Senate.

"In 1820, however, he consented to be a delegate from Salem to the convention for revising the Constitution of Massachusetts, and he distinguished himself among the eminent members of that body, especially in the important debate upon the "third article." In 1827 he was again prevailed upon to be a Representative of Salem in the Legislature of the Commonwealth. In 1831 he was renewedly chosen a Senator from the County of Essex, and became President of the Senate. In 1836, upon the town being constituted a city, he was elected the first Mayor of Salem, and was reëlected in 1837. In 1838 he was elected one of the Representatives of Massachusetts in the Twenty-sixth Congress of the United States. In 1840 he was reëlected to the Twenty-seventh Congress, which terminated in March, 1843. It is well known that he was among the most able, influential, and useful members of Congress. In 1816 Mr. Saltonstall was chosen a member of the Massachusetts

Historical Society, and his History of Haverhill, written about the same time, shows how well entitled he was to that honor.[1]

"He was among the founders of the Essex Historical Society in 1821, and was Vice-President of it at the time of his decease. He was President of the Salem Bible Society. In 1841 he was elected President of the Essex Agricultural Society, and soon after delivered an excellent address before the society. He was appointed to deliver the address before the Society of the Harvard Alumni in 1845, the year of his death. He was a member of various other literary, religious, and philanthrophic societies. About the year 1822 he was elected a Fellow of the American Academy of Arts and Sciences. In 1835 he was elected a member of the Board of Overseers of Harvard College, and held the office during his life. In 1838 the University, his *Alma Mater*, conferred upon him the honorary degree of Doctor of Laws. I am tempted to add to these facts and dates relating to Mr. Saltonstall my own impressions and feelings as recorded at the time, though no eye but my own has ever yet seen the record. In 1845, May 8, ' Mr. Sheriff Sprague calls before breakfast to give us the melancholy news of Mr. Saltonstall's decease this morning at four o'clock. Immediately after breakfast I went to the study, and after indulging the emotions irresistibly excited, — for I could not restrain my tears, — I wrote a few lines to accompany Mr. F.'s [2] communication of the sad event in his to-morrow's "Salem Gazette." "Died in the city yesterday, in the 62d year of his age, the Hon. Leverett Saltonstall, LL. D. Eminent as a counsellor, an orator, and a civilian, he was yet more remarkable as the warm-hearted friend, the high-souled patriot, the ardent, enlightened Christian, and the true man, noble, generous, faithful, and beloved in all the relations of life. An honor to an honored race,

[1] It was in this History of Haverhill that Mr. Saltonstall gave an account of the family of Saltonstall. He was the first to do this, and we are greatly indebted to him for gathering together valuable fragments which would otherwise have been lost. *Mass. Hist. Coll.* 2d series, vol. iv. p. 154.

[2] Caleb Foote editor of *Salem Gazette*, Judge White's son-in-law.

and the idol of an idolized Harvard class, his memory will receive its full tribute of respect, and some abler pen will portray his character and worth for the instruction of youthful genius, the encouragement of active virtue, and the consolation of bereaved friendship and love."

" ' I called soon after ten o'clock at Mrs. N. Saltonstall's who gave me full particulars of her brother's dying hours, which shed a delightful influence over his family, leaving such endearing and elevating associations as serve to strengthen and console them. On Tuesday he called his wife and children around him, knowing his time was short, talked to them all delightfully, and then proposed to them to kneel by his bedside and join in prayer once more. His wife asked who should pray. " I will," he replied, and then proceeded in a clear and full voice, which seemed given him for the purpose, to utter one of the most impressive and sublime prayers ever listened to, remembering particularly his only son Leverett, now abroad, and invoking for him the protection, guidance, and blessing of God.

" ' We shall all feel the bereavement while we live, but we cannot but admire the goodness of Providence to him, — giving him just the portion of sickness necessary to enable him to exhibit his character in this trying relation, and to leave an example more complete than would otherwise have been in his power, and taking him from suffering and pain to a happier world before his powers had become dimmed or his infirmities developed. His sun has set full-orbed and radiant.'

" In 1846, in my eulogy on his friend, the late John Pickering, delivered before the American Academy of Arts and Sciences, speaking of Mr. Pickering's miscellaneous labors and writings, I introduced the following passage : ' In some of these various professional and benevolent efforts he found a cordial helper and admiring friend, whose genius and learning were as practical as his feelings were generous and Christian. I mean our late eloquent associate, that warm-hearted and noble-minded gentleman, Leverett Saltonstall, whose delightful image mingles sweetly with the memory of the friend whom he so honored and loved.'

" I have observed among some reflections written by me at the close of the year 1845, the following passage, introduced after the allusions to the more intimate family circle : ' In the circle of friends we have shared in severe bereave- ments. Mr. Saltonstall and Judge Story, whose deaths were public calamities, will be long held in affectionate remem- brance by us.

" ' The former, both a friend and relative, was dear as a fellow-townsman and neighbor, and his death was a heavy loss to Salem.   His noble and generous virtues, his diffusive benevolence and public spirit, shed over our population and society the very sort of influence which Salem, so occupied in commerce and money-getting, most needs.' " [1]

Another writer says: " Leverett Saltonstall of Salem, Massachusetts, was one of Nature's noblemen.   His high an- cestral blood was ennobled by the generous, manly, estima- ble qualities of his heart and his superior mental powers. Of a nervo-sanguine temperament, he had the delicacy and sentiment of a woman, combined with the intellectual vigor of a man.   The soul of honor, he scorned and despised every- thing low, mean, hypocritical, and false.   He loved his friends with unusual warmth, respected an open manly opponent, but loathed a treacherous friend or a cowardly enemy. When excited by any of these feelings, as he was greatly by Mr. Tyler's third veto, he carried the House by his impas- sioned and scorching eloquence.   Mr. Saltonstall was as refined in his manners as in his feelings and sentiments; a warmer heart than his never beat in human bosom.   No wonder, then, that he was a universal favorite." [2]

The Rev. Dr. Brazer of Salem, in a " Discourse on the Life and Character of the late Hon. Leverett Saltonstall," after dwelling at length upon the strength and completeness of his character and the beauty of his nature, says: " I come

---

[1] *Memoir of Leverett Saltonstall*, by Hon. Daniel Appleton White, MS.
[2] *Public Men and Events*, by Nathan Sargent, vol. ii. p. 173.

now to speak of what I have ever considered the most distinctive, as well as crowning grace, in the character of Mr. Saltonstall. This was the sentiment of reverence. He was eminently and thoroughly a reverential man. This principle was deeply implanted in the natural constitution of his mind, and to cultivate and improve it was his constant care. Superior to pride, that is ever looking downward for contrasts favorable to its own glorification, and despising vanity, which is too full of its own emptiness to look beyond itself, he delighted to look reverentially upward. He loved to recognize and to honor all that was approvable, great, and excellent, wherever found. This fair and grand universe, considered as the work of God and the earliest revelation of his power and goodness; rank, influence, and high condition worthily won and worthily used; distinction of all kinds, honorably achieved and meekly borne; legitimate authority; established usages; time-honored institutions; monuments of antiquity; places where great and stirring deeds have been done; the sepulchres of the departed; great names and recognized authorities, that gleam forth like beacons in the long track of the past; eminent worth among his associates and contemporaries, — all these, and all things else which bear the mark of rightful superiority, received his ready and deferential homage."[1]

Rev. Dr. Flint, his classmate, in a discourse full of deep feeling, at the East Church in Salem, holding before his hearers a most striking picture of Mr. Saltonstall's life and character, from which only a single quotation can be made, said: "When I first met him in his fresh and blooming boyhood at the University, his person and deportment were strikingly beautiful and engaging, indicative of the purity of his untainted soul, of the truthfulness and trust, the social and joyous heartiness, with which he met and reciprocated the love and cordial companionship of his classmates of congenial warmth of feeling, — a trait which marked his character in after years."

[1] *Discourse delivered in the North Church, Salem*, by the Rev. Dr. Brazer, May, 1845.

" His collegiate course was without stain or reproach ; be-loved alike by his fellow-students and instructors, evincing the justice of the old Latin adage, 'Virtue is more lovely emanating from a beautiful form.' " [1]

" Mr. Saltonstall regarded his descent from illustrious ances-tors, distinguished through a long line for talents and worth and high standing in the community, not as a subject for self-complacent and insolent pride, but as a call and incentive to emulate their virtues, their public services and generous deeds, which proved them to be Nature's noblemen ; and thus to add another shining link to the chain that had been lengthening and kept bright through successive generations from the first of the name in New England down to himself, who has now been gathered to his progenitors with honors equal to those of the most honored of his race, and as universally beloved as he was known and honored." [2]

One of his nearest neighbors and friends [3] wrote of him : " In the discharge of his duties as a Representative in Con-gress, Mr. Saltonstall fully sustained the reputation he had previously acquired, and made the most favorable impression upon all who there observed his official course,' and became personally acquainted with him. He spoke with evident effect upon many important occasions; he discussed consti-tutional questions as one familiar with the principles and ne-cessary rules of construction to be applied to them; he op-posed rash and hasty legislation with the instinctive caution which always characterized him ; and he addressed himself with assiduity and intelligence to the promotion of measures which the welfare of the people demanded.

" At the commencement of the administration of General Harrison he was appointed to the responsible station of Chair-man of the Committee on Manufactures, and upon him con-sequently developed the burdensome duty of digesting a new

[1] " Virtus pulchrior est eveniens e corpore pulchro."
[2] *Discourse delivered in the East Church, Salem*, by Rev. James Flint, D. D., May, 1845.
[3] Late Hon. Stephen C. Phillips of Salem, grad. Harv. Coll. 1819, Mayor of Sa-lem and M. C.

and entire tariff, having reference alike to the supply of the ascertained deficiency of the revenue, and to the protection and development of the vital interest of domestic industry. Few can estimate the magnitude and difficulty of this task; but being required to undertake it, he entered upon the work with resolute determination, and prosecuted it to its completion with persevering energy. For months he gave the greater part of every day to severe intellectual labor upon the subject. He engaged in an extensive correspondence for the purpose of obtaining desirable information from all sources; and by his patience and industry in collecting facts, and his judgment and skill in collating them, he was enabled to understand the actual condition and the wants of the country, and to exhibit a result which might prove the basis of wise and safe legislation.

" The report and bill which he presented in behalf of the committee are memorials of the value of his services as a practical statesman, and, although the system which he prepared was not formally accredited as it came from his hands, it was substantially adopted to such an extent that none will hesitate to ascribe to him a large share of the honor which is due for the passage of the tariff of 1842."

In the year 1882, nearly forty years after Mr. Saltonstall's death, a lady who had not resided in Salem after her marriage wrote his son a letter, which so illustrates the deep and lasting impression left by him upon those who had ever known him, as well as the tenderness and depth of his religious nature, that extracts from it cannot but be appropriate : —

" My nephew sent me, a few weeks since, at my request, some extracts which he made, years ago, from his mother's earliest journals, but which I had never seen. This one of them I am sure will be of interest to you.

" How vividly it brings before me your father's look and manners, his delightful presence and charming discourse ! For some years just previous to my marriage, which occurred in 1830, Mary and I were teachers in the Sunday-school of the North Church, of which your father was then the super-

intendent. Teachers' meetings were held during some months
of each year, once a fortnight, at Mr. Brazer's house.   I shall
never forget the glow of enthusiasm with which, on those occasions, your father used to talk of the Scriptures and kindred
subjects.   I remember, with special distinctness, one evening
when your father talked with delight, at great length, of the
book of Acts.   It was as if he had just found a new volume
of wondrous interest, which he would have us share with him
and enjoy as he did.   I felt ashamed at the time that my
acquaintance with it was so imperfect, and the book has been
associated with him in my mind from that hour to the
present."

    " Extract from my sister's journal of July 8, 1829: ' After
tea, as cousin . . . and I were strolling about in Chestnut
Street, Mr. Saltonstall joined us and proposed extending our
walk into Broad Street.   We entered there just as the sun
was setting, and, the gate of the graveyard being open, we all
entered it.   We found the names of many there who, last
year at this time, were as full of health and vigor and happiness as we — and now!

    " ' We directed our steps to the plain but beautiful monu-
ment to Col. Pickering's memory, where he and his wife lie
together.   Just as we reached there the sun threw his latest
beams upon the tomb where are deposited the remains of this
noble being.   There seemed a touching appropriateness in
the time and place, and our own emotions which accorded so
well with the associations they called up.   We had a distinct
view of the sunset heavens ; everything seemed calm and
tranquil ; but yet the brightness of the sky and the beauty of
the earth were shaded by our own recollections, so that everything looked serious and solemnly at rest.   I can never forget the feelings of the hour.   As we left the scene which
called up so much interest, Mr. Saltonstall broke the silence
by saying : " How well has it been called the mighty congregation of the dead !   How many are here, forgotten and at
rest, who once thought the affairs of their little hour of more
importance than the world beside, and who would go into a

passion at a trifle which did not outlive the hour! How many hearts have ached as they have followed those they loved to this spot, that now are gathered here themselves and at rest! And yet people live on as if they had never had an intimation that this were not their continuing city, and that the interests of the present day were not of supreme importance." ' "

Resolutions were adopted on the day of his death expressing the respect and affection felt by the members of the Essex bar for him who had been for so many years their president. In presenting these resolutions to the Supreme Court on the same day, his lifelong friend, Hon. Benjamin Merrill, addressed the Court, and in the course of his remarks he said : —

" A familiar acquaintance with him for nearly fifty years, through his academic, collegiate, and professional life, authorizes me to bear testimony in which all will concur, that the qualities of his heart and the faculties of his mind formed a combination that attracted, in an uncommon degree, respect, attachment, and love.

" His warmth of heart, cordiality of feeling, disinterested kindness, sincerity, and frankness ever cheered and gladdened the circles in which he moved ; the purity and firmness of his moral principles, the independence of his conduct, and the soundness and vigor of his intellectual powers secured the respect and consideration of his fellow-citizens.

" His preparatory legal studies he prosecuted under the tuition of the learned William Prescott, an intimate friendship and mutual high regard existing between them until the decease of the latter. At the time Mr. Saltonstall was admitted to the Essex bar he found in practice there an extraordinary assemblage of eminent lawyers : Theophilus Parsons, Nathan Dane, William Prescott, Samuel Putnam, Charles Jackson, Joseph Story, John Pickering, Daniel A. White,[1] —

---

[1] The learning and worth of each of these lawyers, as well as of Mr. Saltonstall, were so distinguished that the honorable degree of Doctor of Laws was at various periods conferred on each of them.

all of them celebrated in the history of our jurisprudence, and many of them elevated to high judicial dignities in the State and nation. By the side of all these eminent men Mr. Saltonstall soon acquired high rank by his ability, learning, and integrity. His eloquence at the bar and in legislative bodies was powerful, persuasive, and brilliant; it was the eloquence of the heart, the sincere and cordial impression of the ardent feelings, and the deep emotions of a generous and noble nature. He has died, not of an advanced age, but his life has been long, for it has been filled with deeds of benevolence and acts of usefulness."

Judge Wilde, in replying, said: " I have known Mr. Saltonstall forty years or more. I first met him in the State of Maine, when first released from collegiate life, with all those charms of manner, grace, and frankness so peculiarly attractive in youth. Mr. Saltonstall was a most useful member of society. His integrity of character, his open, ingenuous conduct, attracted the attention of all with whom he had intercourse. Not a stain rested upon his good name. A perfect integrity of character, never more entirely unsullied, attracted and secured the highest confidence and respect."[1]

A writer, after recounting the various offices filled by Mr. Saltonstall, adds : " But for his stern integrity and patriotism he would have held yet higher offices, but he always acted from principle and never truckled to arrogance or selfishness. Office could add no honor to him, but he adorned every office he held. By the most faithful and devoted attention to every duty he fully illustrated the character of the faithful steward. His lamp was always trimmed and burning, and all his talents faithfully employed.

" With a fine person and most musical voice, his eloquence was peculiarly attractive and persuasive; and he was so strongly marked by honesty and sincerity that he was a most successful advocate. . . .

" But it was not in public life, nor in his most successful professional career, that we are to look for those character-

---

[1] Proceedings of the Supreme Court, May 8, 1845.

istics which made him the truly great man. His greatness
was to be found in the qualities of the heart, in private life,
in the domestic circle, by his own fireside, in the church of
which he was the ornament, and in all the incidents of every-
day life. Generous, kind-hearted, and benevolent, who could
be his enemy? As the humble superintendent of the Sunday-school, he evinced the same qualities that were so conspicuous and powerful in public life. Ask all who were
honored by his acquaintance where they can find a husband,
a father, a friend, so faithful, so heart-surrendering to all their
wishes. His humblest client found him as faithful, and could
secure as devoted services, as the most opulent could purchase. When he was at the bar, he breathed around him
the atmosphere of honor and truth. He never drilled a
witness, promoted a quarrel, or gave way to an angry feeling.
Where he prosecuted one suit he discouraged ten. He
was the deadly enemy to litigation. It was his pleasure
to heal breaches, not to make them; and to promote peace
and harmony, for he was the son of peace. His presence
was the sunshine of all his friends and associates; it scattered every cloud and diffused pleasure and happiness. His
benevolent heart could never find pleasure in selfish pursuits."

A communication to the " Boston Journal," after referring
to his many striking characteristics, his hostility to litigation,
his unusual efforts to reconcile difficulties and to keep those
who applied to him for professional services "out of the law,"
his enlarged and patriotic views as a statesman, continues:
" Mr. Saltonstall was a patriot of the John Winthrop school,
and gloried in the principles of the ' old charter ' which that
distinguished man brought with him to Salem,[1] and which
for fifty-five years secured to the colonists of Massachusetts
Bay ' the privilege of complete independence.' "

" His warm and generous spirit," said an eloquent orator,
" will respond to every patriotic appeal, but mention in his
hearing the old charter, and his Puritan blood will glow with
additional warmth, his New England heart will beat with a

[1] In company with his own ancestor, Sir Richard Saltonstall.

quicker and fuller pulse, and his frank and manly eloquence will rise to a loftier level in the defence of your rights, and of the rights and glory of independent America."

As Mr. Saltonstall lived, so he died, a Unitarian Christian. A few hours before his death he sent this message to some of his dearest friends who were not of that persuasion. " Tell them," he said, "that as I have lived, so I die, a Unitarian Christian, and that I have found my faith sufficient to sustain and comfort me in this trying hour."

Resolutions regarding Mr. Saltonstall were adopted by the Essex Agricultural Society, the City Council of Salem, the American Bible Society, and a memoir of him was written by Hon. Benjamin Merrill for the Massachusetts Historical Society.[1]

It would be an agreeable task to make extracts from the numerous sketches of Mr. Saltonstall's exceptional life and character, as well as to let his own letters to his classmates, his family, and his many friends here express better than all else his fresh, ardent, loving, and trusting nature ; but space does not admit. I conclude this very brief and imperfect account of this admirable man with a letter recently written me by the late venerable and much-honored Robert C. Winthrop.[2]

BOSTON, 26th Nov., 1892.
90 Marlborough St.

DEAR SALTONSTALL,— Yours of the 20th inst. was duly welcomed. I entered Congress in 1840. Of the fourteen Massachusetts members with whom I was then associated, I believe that I am the sole survivor. Webster and John Davis were our Senators; John Quincy Adams, Levi Lincoln, Caleb Cushing, Geo. N. Briggs, William B. Calhoun,

---

[1] *Mass. Hist. Coll.* 3d series, vol. ix. p. 117.

[2] Mr. Saltonstall had been in Congress one term before Mr. Winthrop was elected, and, as a much older man, he welcomed to Washington the young Representative bearing the grand old surname of the chief founder of the Commonwealth. He took the deepest interest in him, and often spoke with much feeling of the striking coincidence that they, whose ancestors had crossed the ocean together in the Arbella in 1630, and had been so intimately connected in the earliest settlement of the colony, should now be so closely associated as representatives of that Commonwealth in Congress, and occupying rooms together.

and your honored father were with me in the House, with others of hardly inferior grade. For no one of them all had I a greater respect or a warmer regard than for your father. I was in the same mess with him for two successive sessions, one of them a very long one, when we occupied chambers opening into each other, and were in the way of communication with each other by night and by day, on week days and on Sundays.

Agreeing as we did in politics, our intercourse was of the most intimate and confidential character. He had as large a heart as ever beat in human bosom. He had a ready, natural, charming eloquence, and poured out clear and wise and honest counsels, whether in private conversation or in public debate, in a most impressive and captivating strain.

He had thought enough, and had studied enough, to know what he was talking about, and was an accomplished lawyer and scholar. But he was no delver, and never spoke merely for effect or popular applause. His ambition was chastened and regulated. He would follow principle to the death, but he was not a follower of men. Yet he commanded the respect and won the admiration and affection of the greatest and best of the men in Congress; Henry Clay was one of his warmest and most appreciating friends, and was in frequent consultation with him on public affairs.

Meantime he had an earnest faith in things higher than human. I recall the concluding passage of a letter, written to me on a Sunday when I was absent from Washington : —

"And now (wrote he) I must close this letter to go to our little church, to forget for one hour the cares and exciting turmoils of this bustling world, and to direct my thoughts to that world which is soon to be our home, our final home, and to that all-gracious Being, — the source of all our blessings, the foundation of all our hopes. We cannot be sufficiently grateful for this blessed day. We should forget that there was an existence beyond this narrow life without it."

He was much older than myself, a full quarter of a century; a schoolmate for a time with Daniel Webster, and a classmate of Levi Lincoln at Harvard. But although these contemporaries, from whom he sometimes differed on public questions, never lost their warm attachment to him, he had the faculty of winning younger men to his confidence and affection, and no member of Congress, Northern or Southern, of whatever age, had more attached and intimate friends than Leverett Saltonstall. To myself he was like a brother.

I cannot forget the last letter he ever wrote to me: " Do you know that it is my present intention to go to Europe,— to England in April ? I have written to my son at Fayal to join me there. I have always felt a desire to see the old world, but never expected to visit it until recently. Why should I not go ? It is easily done. I shall return probably in October. Now, my dear sir, of all things I want you to go. Let us visit together the home of our fathers which they left together. You can go as well as not, and be back a month before the meeting of Congress. Go, — you will always be glad of it. It will be gratifying to you for the rest of your life. We could travel over the world together as agreeably as we used to stroll along Pennsylvania Avenue. We should jump in judgment and in taste. I am serious in my proposal and my wishes. Think of it and decide affirma-tively, and the difficulty is over. If the session passes off without serious difficulties with England, I shall be glad to be off from these scenes of turmoil for six months."

This letter was written at the end of January, 1845. Alas, he never saw England! He was seized with a fatal malady soon afterwards, and I attended his funeral at Salem before the middle of May of the same year.

Believe me ever, with the greatest regards, yours sincerely,
ROBT. C. WINTHROP.

HON. LEVERETT SALTONSTALL.

110 A. THOMAS SANDERS

Thomas Sanders of Salem, father of Mary Elizabeth, wife of Leverett (110), and of Caroline, wife of Nathaniel Saltonstall (111), was a successful merchant of Salem, born in 1759 and died in 1844, aged 85.

He was born in Gloucester, and his ancestors on the paternal side were worthy citizens of that old town, the first of the name being Thomas Sanders who was one of the first and most respected of those who settled at Cape Ann about 1640. His son Thomas, born about 1648, sustained the reputation of his father as a good and respected townsman. His son Thomas, born in 1675, commanded the Massachusetts sloop of war appointed to guard the coasts of this Province. In 1704 he married Abigail Curney, who died at the age of 94, and whose funeral Thomas Sanders of Salem distinctly remembered having attended, she being his great-grandmother.

Thomas Sanders, their son, born in 1705, succeeded his father in command of the Massachusetts sloop. He was present at the siege and capture of Louisburg, where he was commissioned by the British admiral to take charge of all the transport ships and prisoners. After the capture of the place he received from the admiral a letter thanking him for his vigilance and good conduct. He was remarkable for his personal appearance as well for his polished and dignified manners, and was always represented by those who knew him as one of the bravest and most benevolent of men.

Thomas Sanders, his son, born in 1729, graduated at Harvard College 1748. He was for many years Representative from Gloucester to the General Court, and afterwards Councillor. He took an active part in opposition to the encroachment of the British government, and his election as councillor was several times negatived by the royal governor. He died in 1774.

His son, the sixth Thomas Sanders, born in 1759, was sent to Byfield Academy to be fitted for college; but upon the death of his father he went to Salem and entered the

counting-room of Elias Hasket Derby, the celebrated East
Indian merchant, who became his warm friend, and so continued during Mr. Derby's life.   He married in 1782 Elizabeth Elkins, a relative of Mr. Derby, and died in 1844, leaving four children, — Charles Sanders, his eldest son, who was
born May 2, 1783, grad. Harv. Coll. 1802, lived to the age
of 80, and was a refined and cultivated gentleman.   He left
a large fortune in trust for charitable purposes.   Besides be-
queathing ten thousand dollars to Cambridge, and the same
sum to Gloucester, to promote the cause of temperance, he
founded the beautiful and useful Sanders Theatre at Harvard
University.   Catherine, the eldest daughter, married Dudley
L. Pickman, a distinguished merchant of Salem, and died
many years before her father.   The two other daughters, as
above stated, married respectively Leverett and Nathaniel
Saltonstall.

Thomas Sanders acted successfully and well his part
through a long life.   He was grandson of Rev. Thomas
Smith of Portland, who preached there seventy years and
died at the age of 95,[1] and he had a distinct recollection of
seven generations of his own family.

Elizabeth (Elkins), wife of the sixth Thomas Sanders, and
mother of Mary E. and Caroline Saltonstall, lived to the
great age of 89 years and 6 months.

"By the virtues of her heart and the strength of her intellect, her long life was made a constant blessing to her family
and to the public.   Originally endowed with a noble nature,
it had become refined and sanctified by a true philosophy,
resting upon Christian faith, and carried out into the constant practice of daily life.   The sweetness of her disposition,
the generosity and magnanimity of her spirit, and the com-
prehensiveness of her benevolence, with the advantage of her
social position, mental endowments, and personal address,
gave her an influence such as few individuals of either sex
reach; and that influence was uniformly exerted in the cause
of philanthropy, justice, and the truth.   By several elaborate

[1] Smith's Journal, by Willis.

and valuable publications, her frequent communications through the newspaper press, by letters addressed to prominent characters, and by zealous and eloquent appeals and arguments, in conversation with her friends and acquaintances, she was known and appreciated as the friend and advocate of the aboriginal races of America. She was deeply interested in all the great movements of the times having the interests of liberty and humanity in view. She lamented the wrongs of the oppressed and the suffering of the poor. Few persons have given such subjects more attention, and her views were worthy of the consideration of legislators and statesmen. Her philanthropy did not rest within the limits of speculations or writings, but went out into the actual conditions of life, in works of compassion and liberality. The means of relieving want and conferring benefits, with which a bountiful Providence had blessed her, were employed, with a wise discrimination, to make others happier and better. . . .

" Her religious sentiments were truly catholic, embracing in an enlightened sympathy all sects. The infinite benevolence of the universal Father was adored by her in its application to all races and all beings, in all ages and all worlds. In the service of the sanctuary and in domestic retirement, in public worship or the communion of private converse, prayer and pious meditation were ever seen to be her refuge in sorrow, and the chief delight of her soul in its happiest hours. . . .

" Her heart never grew old, but participated to the last in the happiness which it was her constant study to spread around her. Her principles and her spirit made her life beautiful, and her death serene and full of faith and hope.

" Her children and children's children ever called her blessed, and her friends regarded her as one of the noblest and best specimens of our nature, and among the first of women and the best of Christians." [1]

[1] From an obituary of Mrs. Sanders, supposed to have been written by Rev. Charles W. Upham, minister of the First Church, Salem.

111. NATHANIEL SALTONSTALL (IX.)

Nathaniel Saltonstall, son of Dr. Nathaniel (105), received a mercantile education in one of the first houses in Boston, and afterwards for twelve years pursued with great success the business of a commission merchant in Baltimore. He then removed to Salem, where he married Caroline Sanders, the sister of his brother Leverett's wife, and lived in the house adjoining his; and the brothers, between whom there had always existed a close tie, were again brought together to enjoy to the full a delightful intercourse which was terminated only by his sad and sudden death.

Mr. Saltonstall, retiring and unobtrusive, never seeking nor accepting public office, was distinguished for his good sense, kind feelings, and excellent judgment. Wholly free from ostentation, he did nothing for show or effect. Numerous were those who testified to the faithfulness of his friendship, or who had experienced the readiness of his kind advice and generous assistance. None ever knew him but to respect him, and even to feel for him a much stronger and more tender regard. He was fond of reading, and his mind was well stored with information. Few were better acquainted with the political questions of the day, or felt deeper interest in the success of wise measures.

When a young man, he was one of the gallant band of volunteers who repelled the assault of the British army on the city of Baltimore.

He was faithful to the whole circle of duties; a most excellent son and husband, a devoted brother and father, his presence was the sunshine of his home.

In his business career he was singularly punctilious and exact, and ever stood firm and unmoved on the solid basis of his own sound principles.

116 and 117. ANNE ELIZABETH AND CAROLINE
SALTONSTALL (X.)

Anne Elizabeth and Caroline Saltonstall were both women
of strong character, and were much beloved by a large circle
of friends. Their kind hearts and charitable deeds endeared
them to the people among whom they passed their lives.
They lived with their mother in the house in Chestnut Street,
Salem, which was built for her by her father, Thomas Sanders, on her marriage, and, after the death of their venerable
grandmother, they occupied the adjacent house built by Mr.
Sanders in the beginning of the century for himself, and
occupied by him and his wife.

This house, so endeared to the family by its precious associations, became the home of their mother till her death, and
afterwards of these two ladies while they lived.[1]

There they endeavored to keep up those hospitalities
which had always made the house so beloved by the numerous children and grandchildren who had gathered around its
hearthstone.

They travelled much in this country and in Europe, and
their minds were enriched by stores of information gathered
during these journeyings, through varied intercourse with
the best and most cultivated people whom they met here and
abroad. Their conversation was always of a character to
render them attractive. They were eminently worthy descendants of a long line of distinguished ancestors, in whose
history they were always interested, encouraging the younger
members of the family to emulate their virtues.[2]

[1] These houses with that of Mrs. Nathaniel Saltonstall were the three adjacent
houses with gardens connected standing at the head of that beautiful street.
[2] It was owing to Miss Caroline Saltonstall's zeal, in connection with her
brother, that Mr. Somerby was employed in Europe, and Mr. Phippen in Salem,
to collect the materials and arrange the chart which accompanies Drake's *History
and Antiquities of Boston* (folio edition, 1857), and from them much valuable
information was obtained by Dr. Bond in collecting material for his account of the
family of Saltonstall in his *Genealogies and History of Watertown.*

119. LUCY SANDERS SALTONSTALL (X.)

Lucy (Saltonstall) Tuckerman was equally remarkable for her noble traits of character. She inherited all the virtues which distinguished her parents, and, as a daughter, sister, wife, and mother, no lovelier or more attractive woman ever lived. She was faithful in every relation of life. She possessed a singular intelligence; her mind was cultivated by much and varied reading; she was brilliant in conversation, generous, and charitable. These characteristics, with her strong religious faith, made her beloved and respected by all who knew her, while to her husband and children she was endeared by every virtue that can adorn the wife and mother.

Dr. John Francis Tuckerman, her husband, was born 13 June, 1817; grad. Harv. Coll. 1837; was assistant surgeon in the United States Navy for ten years after taking his degree at Harvard University as M. D., 1841, and afterwards took charge of important trusts. His sudden death in 1885 was deeply lamented, and called forth many beautiful tributes to his character.

The late venerable Henry K. Oliver wrote of him to the " Salem Gazette " as follows : —

" The sudden death of Dr. J. Francis Tuckerman filled this community with inexpressible grief, it being an irreparable loss to all whose hearts he won by his daily innate kindness, by the unaffected and uniform manifestation of a cheerful and cheering disposition. His face was a benediction, his smile a blessing, and his words were gladness and sunshine.

" No man can we recall from the long memories of a long life whose ways were so winning, whose personal presence was so attractive and assuring; his integrity and truthfulness of character vying with the charms of his appearance, and begetting a confidence that never was broken ; a business wisdom, guided by a strong common-sense, putting wholly at ease those who intrusted their affairs to his management. His probity of conscience paralelled his probity of heart and charm of manners, an unvarying gentleness and the winning way of his ordinary salutation illustrating his character and ingratiating all into friendship and earnest love. One kind act will never be forgotten by its recipient, an invalid, who had been housed for many months. Knowing this invalid's love of church music, Dr. Tuckerman brought his choir (of Grace Church) to his friend's house, and treated him to a repetition of the recent Easter music, adding some compositions of his friend, which his friend had never before heard.

" Let me add something concerning a talent which he possessed to an exceptional and eminent degree. He had an exquisite sense of music, and the rare power of expressing that sense both in composition and in vocal utterance. His voice was a perfect tenor of wide range, and his management of it of that uncommon accuracy of tone, tune, and expression that at once claimed attention, not by a loudness that overmastered other voices, but by a certain indescribable quality that won the ear by its peculiar attractiveness. There might be a score of voices on the same part, but this voice was clear, and could only come from high cultivation and from surpassing taste. So, too, of high order were his compositions. They were mostly for the church, being hymn tunes, chants, and Te Deums. He had an exquisite sense of what constituted truth and beauty in melody as indicated in the leading part or air of a composition.

" In his ordinary thoughts there must have been germinating an unfailing brain growth of melodies, all these expressive and beautiful. . . .

" He was for a time conductor of the music at the North Church, and afterwards (and until his death) of that at Grace Church. When the History of Music in Salem shall be written (and no place more merits such history), the name of Dr. Tuckerman will be among the most eminent. This from one who loved him with a brother's love."

120. LEVERETT SALTONSTALL (X.)

Leverett Saltonstall, son of Leverett and Mary Elizabeth (Sanders) Saltonstall, was born in Salem March 16, 1825.

Having been fitted for college in the Salem Latin School, he entered Harvard University, and was graduated therefrom in the Class of 1844.

After graduating he went to Fayal with his classmate Dabney, and passed a most delightful winter in that lovely island, where for many years Mr. Dabney's father and grandfather had been consuls. In April, 1845, he went to England, expecting to meet his father and to travel with him for a year; but on reaching London he heard of his extreme illness, and immediately returned home, arriving too late to see his father.

Choosing the profession of law, he continued his legal studies in the Harvard Law School, and was graduated A. M. and LL. B. in 1847. After an extended tour in Europe and the East, he was admitted to Suffolk bar in 1850, where he continued in active practice until 1862, when he retired from the bar and devoted himself to agriculture and to the care of various trusts. From December, 1885, to 28 Feb., 1890, he was Collector of Customs for the Port of Boston, to which office he was appointed by President Cleveland.[1]

Mr. Saltonstall was first marshal of his class in 1844; marshal of the University in 1869, at the inauguration of President Eliot; marshal of the Alumni at Commencement, 1870, and again at Commencement, 1872, on the reception of General Grant, President of the United States. He was a member of the Board of Overseers of Harvard College from 1876 to 1888, and was elected again in 1889 for another term of six years.

He is a member of the Massachusetts Historical Society, the New England Historic Genealogical Society, the Colonial Society of Massachusetts, and of other societies. He is

---

[1] The portrait of Mr. Saltonstall in this volume is from a painting by D. Huntington, now in the Custom House in Boston.

President of the Massachusetts Society for Promoting Agriculture, and a member of the Board of Trustees of the Perkins Institution and Massachusetts School for the Blind, and of the Sailors' Snug Harbor.

He was for two years President of the Unitarian Club. In 1854 he was appointed on the staff of Gov. Emory Washburn, with the rank of Lieutenant-Colonel. In 1876 he was the Commissioner from Massachusetts to the Centennial Exhibition at Philadelphia. He was married in Salem 19 Oct., 1854, to Rose S., daughter of John Clarke and Harriet (Rose) Lee.[1] Of this union were six children: (128) Leverett Saltonstall, Jr. (deceased 1863), (129) Richard Middlecott, (130) Rose Lee (Mrs. George West, deceased), (131) Mary Elizabeth (Mrs. Louis Agassiz Shaw), (132) Philip Leverett, and (133) Endicott Peabody Saltonstall.

His residence is at Chestnut Hill, Newton, where he has lived since his marriage.

120 A. JOHN CLARKE LEE

John Clarke Lee, father of Rose S. and Josephine Rose Lee, wives of Leverett and William G. Saltonstall (125), was born in Boston 9 April 1804, grad. Harv. Coll. in the Class of 1823, but received his degree in 1842. He married 29 July, 1826, Harriet Paine Rose. She was born in Antigua 5 Feb., 1804, her father being of English descent, her mother a daughter of William Paine, M. D., of Worcester, Mass., and was a woman of singular refinement, intelligence, and loveliness of person and of character. Of this marriage ten children were born, all but one of whom survived their parents.

Mr. Lee went into business as a merchant in Boston, and at first resided there, but soon removed to Salem, where he lived the rest of his life.

[1] See 120 A, above. Rev. John Pierce, D. D., in his Diary gives a somewhat flattering account of the disquisition on " Clarendon as a Statesman," by Leverett Saltonstall. *Mass. Hist. Soc. Proceedings*, new series, vol. ii. p. 304.

In 1848, in connection with Mr. George Higginson, he founded the well-known banking house of Lee & Higginson in Boston, going daily from Salem to his office, but finally retired from active business in 1862.

He was an active horticulturist, especially before the year 1848, when he devoted most of his time and attention to the cultivation of trees, plants, and fruit on his farm in North Salem.

He was a man of clear, strong sense, and, while he had special tastes, he had a large curiosity for general knowledge, and his conversation showed that he had gathered it in many fields. He read much, and with his mind stored with reading and observation, his conversation was entertaining and intelligent.

In person he was tall, of large frame, of self-reliant expression and bearing; his look open, manly, and free from self-consciousness. In the words of his cousin, Henry Lee, "The features of Mr. John C. Lee were strongly marked; he was 'like a study in two crayons,' as the French would say; there was not much shading in his character. The trait by which he was distinguished was his honesty and sturdy independence. This flavored his speech and gave character to his opinions and actions."

Some of his strongest and most individual traits, if mainly derived from Lee ancestors, were singularly reinforced by powerful tributaries. The most casual acquaintance with the Pickerings and the Cabots leads up by an open path to the discovery that John Lee's worship of truth, sincerity of speech, squareness of integrity, independence of public opinion, sensitiveness of honor, were the reappearance of what had been deemed characteristic traits in those sturdy men and women whose blood he bore in his veins.

He died on the 19th Nov., 1877, in the seventy-fourth year of his age.[1]

---

[1] The above is taken in great measure from the memorial of John Clarke Lee by Rev. E. B. Willson, printed in the *Essex Institute Historical Collections*, vol. xv. Nos. 1, 2.

Leverett Saltonstall

PEDIGREE OF JOHN CLARKE LEE

ROSE S. LEE, b. 24 Jan., 1851; d. 24 Oct., 1851; Laurens Silbennill, b. 10 March, 1855.

John Clarke Lee, b. 9 April, 1804, d. 19 Nov., 1877.

m. 29 July, 1826,

Harriet Paine Rose, b. 3 Feb., 1804, d. 14 Aug., 1885.

Nathaniel Cabot Lee, b. 30 May, 1772, d. 14 Jan., 1806; m. 11 April, 1803, Mary Ann Cabot, d. 25 July, 1809, æt. 25.

Joseph Lee, b. 22 May, 1744, d. 6 Feb., 1831; m. Elizabeth Cabot, 1760, b. 24 Feb., 1748, d. 20 Sept., 1804.

Francis Cabot, b. 19 June, 1757; m. 28 June, 1780, Ann Clarke.

Joseph Warner Rose, b. 5 May, 1753, d. 1806; m. 27 March, 1802, Harriet Paine, b. 21 Nov., 1779.

Thomas Lee, b. 1702, d. 14 July, 1747; m. 29 Dec., 1737, Lois Orne, b. 16 March, 1711-12.

Joseph Cabot, b. 29 July, 1720, d. 8 Dec., 1767; m. 30 March, 1744, Elizabeth Higginson, d. Nov., 1781, æt. 60 years.

Joseph Cabot, b. 29 July, 1720, d. 8 Dec., 1767; m. 30 March, 1744, Elizabeth Higginson, d. Nov., 1781, æt. 60 years.

John Clarke, d. 7 Jan., 1800; m. Sarah Pickering, b. 28 Jan., 1730, d. 31 Nov., 1826.

Thomas Rose, m. Ann ——.

John Rose, b. 25 Dec., 1738; m. Alice Bacon, b. 23 July, 1735, d. 14 Feb., 1760.

Samuel Bacon, m. Rebecca Elliott.

William Paine, b. 5 June, 1750, d. 19 April, 1833; m. 23 Sept., 1773, Lois Orne, b. 18 Feb., 1756.

Thomas Lee, b. 1673, d. 16 July, 1766; m. Deborah Flint, d. 3 April, 1763.

Timothy Orne, d. April, 1751; m. 7 April, 1709, Lois Pickering.

John Cabot, d. 7 June, 1742; m. 29 Oct., 1700, Anna Orne.

John Higginson, b. 10 Jan., 1697-98, d. 15 July, 1744; m. 4 Dec., 1719, Ruth Boardman, d. 14 June, 1727.

John Cabot, d. 7 June, 1742; m. 29 Oct., 1700, Anna Orne.

John Higginson, b. 10 Jan., 1697-98, d. 15 July, 1744; m. 4 Dec., 1719, Ruth Boardman, d. 14 June, 1727.

Josiah Clarke, m. Mary Wingate.

Timothy Pickering, b. 10 Feb., 1703, d. 7 June, 1778; m. Mary Wingate.

John Elliott, m. Ann ——.

Nathaniel Paine, d. 1741; m. Sarah Clarke.

John Chandler, m. Hannah Gardiner.

Timothy Orne, d. April, 1751; m. 7 April, 1709, Lois Pickering.

William Taylor, m. Sarah Burrill.

— **Lee**, m. Martha Mellowes.

Edward Flint, m. Elizabeth Hart.

Joseph Orne, m. Ann Thompson.

John Pickering, m. Sarah Burrill.

Francis Cabot, m. Susanna Gruchy.

Joseph Orne, m. Ann Thompson.

John Higginson, b. 30 Aug., 1675; d. 26 April, 1718; m. 13 Sept., 1695, Hannah Gardner, b. 1675, d. 24 June, 1713.

Andrew Boardman, m. Elizabeth Truesdell.

Francis Cabot, m. Susanna Gruchy.

Joseph Orne, m. Ann Thompson.

John Higginson, b. 30 Aug., 1675, d. 26 April, 1718; m. 13 Sept., 1695, Hannah Gardner, b. 1675, d. 24 June, 1713.

Andrew Boardman, m. Elizabeth Truesdell.

John Wingate, m. Ann Hodgdon.

John Pickering, b. 10 Sept., 1658, d. 19 June, 1722; m. 14 June, 1683, Sarah Burrill, d. 16 Dec., 1747.

Joshua Wingate, m. Mary Lunt.

Nathaniel Paine, b. 20 Nov., 1677, m. Dorothy Rainsford.

Timothy Clarke, m. ——.

John Chandler, m. Mary Raymond.

John Gardiner, m. Mary King.

Joseph Orne, m. Ann Thompson.

John Pickering, m. Sarah Burrill.

James Taylor, m. Rebecca ——.

Samuel Burrill, m. Margaret Jarvis.

Mrs. Lee survived her husband eight years, and died 14 Aug., 1885.

_____

124. HENRY SALTONSTALL (X.)

Henry Saltonstall was born at Salem 2 March, 1828, and was fitted for college at Salem and at Phillips Academy, Exeter, N. H. He entered Harvard College in 1843, but by reason of poor health was obliged to leave at the end of his Freshman year and take a sea voyage. He passed nearly a year away from home, of which eight months were in sailing ships on a voyage to and from the East Indies. Returning, he entered college again, in a class below that in which he entered, graduating in 1848, seventh scholar in rank. He was a member of the Phi Beta Kappa Society and the second marshal of his class.

After a year's absence in Europe, in 1851 he began business with the East Indies, continuing therein, with a constantly enlarging and very profitable trade, for several years; but at the beginning of the civil war, this business having become unremunerative, he gave it up, and in 1862 accepted the treasurership of the Chicopee Manufacturing Company, a small mill of 31,000 spindles, which he ran to its fullest capacity throughout the war, often by night as well as by day, with a double force of operatives, while most mills were closed. When he left this mill, in 1880, its capacity had increased to 62,000 spindles, with abundant working capital, and the shares had advanced to five times as much as they were sold for when he took charge. In seventeen and a half years the net profits had amounted to three and a quarter millions of dollars, or nearly eight times the original capital stock.

In 1876 the Atlantic Mill of Lawrence, Mass., had by various reverses been compelled to stop work, and was lying idle and in a condition which called for very prompt and skillful treatment to save it from ruin. Mr. Saltonstall accepted the task, was chosen treasurer, and in six months reported to the owners that the mill was running with a full force, and that in spite of the most unfavorable conditions a good profit had already been made, with a promising outlook for the future. The stockholders unanimously voted " that the sincere thanks of this corporation be given to Mr. Saltonstall, who declines a reëlection as treasurer, for the masterly manner in which he has effected the reorganization of the company."

In 1880 his success as manager of the above two mills procured him the offer of the treasurership of the Pacific Mills at Lawrence, the largest and most important mills in the country, which he accepted. These mills, which had been supposed to be in thoroughly good order, he found in a very disorganized state, and for many years it required anxious thought, great knowledge and firmness, with a large but judicious expenditure of money, to put the property into the condition necessary to enable it to compete with other first-class mills, and to adapt it to the changed requirements of trade. That he succeeded is partly demonstrated by the very complimentary remarks made by the president of the company at a meeting of the stockholders only three years after the commencement of his labors, and before the final and greatest success of his administration had begun to be shown.

In addition to the offices mentioned above, Mr. Saltonstall was president and for many years manager of the New England Mortgage Security Company, director of the Boston Manufacturers' Factory Mutual Insurance Company, treasurer and trustee of the Massachusetts Society for Promoting Agriculture, and one of the Executive Committee of the Massachusetts Institute of Technology. Nor was he solely a business man, but enjoyed to the utmost social intercourse with his friends, by whom he was greatly respected and beloved for his genuine manner and great intelligence. He was greatly interested in the care and improvement of his farm, woodlands, and pleasure grounds.

In 1862 he left Salem to occupy his house in Commonwealth Avenue, Boston, which was one of the very first built in that district, where he resided at the time of his death,

which occurred 3 Dec., 1894. But all the summer months were passed at his beautiful residence on the shore of Suntaug Lake, in Peabody and Lynnfield, of which one of the best judges of landscape effects in America wrote that it possessed "all the charms of the best New England sylvan scenery, unspoiled with a single inharmonious note."

This short sketch of the life of Henry Saltonstall cannot be closed without referring to his liberal donations to Harvard University, and his constant numerous gifts to charitable objects during his life, which entitled him to the credit of having been a liberal giver.

In addition to these large donations during his life, he made by his will the following bequests: To Harvard College, $59,000; to the Boston Society of Natural History, $15,000; to the Massachusetts Institute of Technology, $50,000; to the Massachusetts General Hospital, $10,000; to the Massachusetts Charitable Eye and Ear Infirmary, $10,000; and to such charities as may be selected by the trustees under his will, $20,000.

124 A. NATHANIEL SILSBEE

Hon. Nathaniel Silsbee of Salem, father of Mrs. Henry Saltonstall, was a distinguished merchant of Salem, Mass. Born in 1773, he commenced his mercantile career in the house of "Elias Hasket Derby, the leader of the vanguard of India adventure," and sailed for him as commander of one of his ships before he had attained the age of twenty-one. After retiring from active business with a handsome fortune, he was elected to Congress from the Essex District in 1816 for two terms, was President of the Senate of Massachusetts 1823–25, and in 1826 was elected to the United States Senate to fill a vacancy, and, being reëlected, he served until 1835. He ever enjoyed the highest confidence of his constitutents and of his colleagues. "He did honor to the pioneer class of merchant princes reared and nurtured in the early days of the republic." "No man was more respected. Hospitable and liberal, he lived beloved and honored," and died on the 14th day of July, 1850.

---

125. WILLIAM GURDON SALTONSTALL (X.)

William Gurdon Saltonstall, second son of Nathaniel (111), was born in Salem, and lived there the greater part of his life.

Owing to weakness of the eyes, he had to abandon his studies and prepare himself for a mercantile career. Though Salem had then lost her prestige as a shipping port, yet Salem merchants owned many ships commanded by Salem captains, and Salem boys who did not go to college learned to be navigators in them. It was thus that in his youth William Saltonstall took to the sea, doing duty first as a common sailor, and afterwards in high positions, acquiring an education and experience which proved later on of great value to him, and enabled him to play an active and heroic part in the great War of the Rebellion.

Our merchant marine was then unexcelled, and afforded a branch of industry very tempting to lads of active and adventurous disposition. It gave them a knowledge of the world which prepared them for a useful life and made them men.

On giving up the sea he became an East India merchant; but in 1855, at the age of 24, he made an extended and most interesting and adventurous tour through Europe and the East, visiting India, going through the interior to the Himalayas, before there were any railroads in India, to St. Petersburg and Moscow, to witness the coronation of the Czar Alexander II. at the Kremlin, after the Crimean War; and thence to the great fair at Nizhnee-Novgorod.

In May, 1861, he was one of the first to offer his services to the government as a volunteer in the naval service, and received at once a commission as acting-master, serving a year as flag lieutenant on the staffs of Rear Admirals Goldsborough and Lee, and while on the frigate Minnesota was thrown violently from the gangway onto the rail of a tug eighteen feet below, sustaining serious injury which threatened his life and laid him up in hospital for several months.

In the autumn of 1862 he was ordered to New York to fit out and command the Commodore Hull, a large ferry-boat which was hastily converted into a gunboat. In this unseaworthy craft he had to make his way in the month of December round Hatteras to Washington on Pamlico River, North Carolina, arriving just in time to play a most important part in the defence of that place against the overwhelming force of General D. H. Hill, consisting of 14,000 men, whereas our own troops amounted in all to only 1,139 men after the arrival of reinforcements under Major-general J. G. Foster, — very insufficient to man the long lines of defence around the town.

Mr. Saltonstall in an interesting sketch of his adventurous life thus tells the story of this siege and of his own part in the defence of Washington : —

" General Foster, having undoubted information of the enemy's approach, ordered me on the evening of the 30th of March to drop down the river and shell the woods in the rear of the town until ordered to stop, about midnight, by which time I had expended much of my ammunition for the large guns. During the night a company of our North Carolina regiment, which had been stationed at Rodman's Point, abreast of where I was, were driven to their boats by the enemy, and the next morning I ascertained that Hill's Point below, commanding the obstructions, had been reoccupied by them, and the buoys marking the channel removed, thus rendering any attempt to pass through extremely hazardous under their plunging fire.

" At dawn on the 1st of April, a shell whistled over my vessel, quickly followed by others, which I observed proceeded from Rodman's Point, where an earthwork had been erected during the night, mounting several Whitworth rifled guns. The crew were mostly asleep at the time and had never before been under fire, but, after a few moments of confusion, obeyed their officers, stowed their hammocks, and went to quarters, returning the fire effectively. The wind for the previous twenty-four hours had been blowing hard down the river, forcing the water into the sound, and the consequence was, that when, finding the enemy had our exact range and was hitting us every time, I tried to change the position of my vessel, we very soon ran helplessly aground, heading up stream, at short range from the battery, and there remained partly careened throughout the day and until the water came up on the subsidence of the wind after dark. We here returned the fire of Rodman's Point battery with our after pivot, and that of another earthwork in a cornfield with our forward one until our ammunition gave out, about twelve o'clock, when, as the crew could no longer be of use on deck, I sent them as far below as possible, remaining on deck with one or two adventurous spirits to watch the progress of affairs, which had become very decidedly lively.

" At least six or seven guns, from half to three quarters of a mile distant, blazed away at us all day, and, as nearly as we could tell, hit the hull and light upper works over ninety times, tearing the latter pretty thoroughly to pieces, riddling the smokestacks, and doing all sorts of damage except to life and boilers, both of which miraculously escaped. Some men were wounded by splinters, but subsequently recovered, and it was to the infinite surprise of all outside the vessel who witnessed the affair, and who thought that when we stopped firing it was because of great loss of life, that we appeared at our old anchorage next morning, a sorry-looking craft to be sure, and very deficient in sleeping accommodations, but nevertheless with the majority of the crew intact and ready to do further fighting as soon as we could get ammunition. Of course all had most wonderful escapes. In one instance a shrapnel shell entered and exploded in the little fire-room in front of the boilers, where six men were standing, and none were harmed; while another, which I have in my possession, passing through the oak sides of the vessel and the outer and inner casings of the magazine, dropped on its floor with its

W. G. Saltonstall.

fuse-hole so tightly corked with oak, on its passage through, as to have extinguished the fuse, and prevented our sudden exaltation. My mess-room was strewn with the fragments of my furniture and crockery, while my little cabin, through which many shot passed, looked like a rat's nest, from the remnants of clothing, bedding, and uniforms scattered about. The attentions of the enemy that day were all directed to my vessel, and hundreds of various missiles, but mostly solid shot, — they believing us an ironclad, — were fired at her. My report says that from 5 to 5.30 P. M. I counted twenty-five shot and shell thrown at us, twelve of which took effect. . . .

"Soon a large fleet of gunboats and transports collected in the river below Hill's Point, and in plain sight, but considered the risk of getting through the obstructions and running the gauntlet for seven miles of artillery and sharp-shooters too great to venture, the channel running close to the shore occupied by the enemy's batteries all the way. . . .

"In the mean time the enemy in large force had erected to the north and west of the town eight batteries with ten rifled and six smooth-bore guns, from which at frequent intervals during the day that followed they poured a converging fire, ploughing the face of our works and going into the houses in town. . . .

"In addition to the river batteries I have mentioned, a very disagreeable one with two guns, constructed of bags and cotton-bales at night just opposite where I lay, 650 yards off in a swamp, opened on me at dawn of April 3d, the shot and shell going through us in a lively manner for a while, until we knocked it over and dismounted their guns. They were replaced once or twice with similar results, and loss of some life, until they found it too dangerous to pay. . . .

"It certainly was very wearing, and after a time the men had to be put on decreasing allowance. And so the anxious days went by, no one knowing at what moment one of the many shot that filled the air might end his career, until we got in a measure used to the life, but never to like it. It was odd after a while how nearly we could tell where a shot from the Rodman's Point or cornfield batteries would strike ; with the noise of the report the projectile could be seen, and, if its arc seemed to end on board, there was naturally more anxiety felt than if it did not. . . .

" A heavy storm now set in, making it extremely uncomfortable for all, and apparently dampening the enemy's ardor ; for on the morning of the 16th of April our pickets discovered that they were in full retreat from both sides of the river, and our troops soon occupied their works with great rejoicing.

" Thus ended one of the most remarkable experiences of the war, and, so far as I am aware, quite unlike any other. Had it not occurred when public attention was absorbed by other much more important events, it would have attracted considerable interest.   At it was, only those there and those at home specially interested were aware how tight a place we had been in.   Certainly I know no other instance where a little vessel was struck over one hundred times by cannon-shot, — mostly from rifled Whitworth field-pieces, but many of them thirty-two pound shot and shell.

" We seemed to be under special protection, — the sailors claiming because the captain had complied with the navy regulations and read service on Sundays.

" For eighteen days the town had been closely besieged. All attempts to raise the siege had been unsuccessful.   We were so largely outnumbered, it seemed to all that a determined assault against our thinly manned lines could not fail of success, though attended with much loss of life, as the garrison were always alert, brave, and determined.   Once in possession of our lines and of the town, the prospect of the gunboats, with musketry and artillery pouring in on them from all sides, seemed hopeless, and surrender or destruction unavoidable.   It was understood by my officers that in the last emergency the vessel would be blown up rather than surrendered."

Mr. Saltonstall was soon afterwards promoted to be lieutenant, "for gallantry displayed in action at Washington, North Carolina," and was ordered to command the Buckingham — then fitting out at New York for blockading service off Wilmington, — a large new sea-going steamer with powerful armament. He sailed in her in October, 1863, and passed the winter on that stormy coast, engaged in the tedious but at times exciting work of trying to seize or destroy the swift blockade-runners. In the spring of 1864 he was ordered North for repairs, and was assigned to the command of the steamer Kensington, dispatch boat to the different squadrons, and first sailed for Mobile Bay, just after its capture by Admiral Farragut, who described to him the details of that famous naval achievement, the scene lying spread out before them.

In December, 1864, at the request of Admiral Lee, he was ordered to join him in Western waters, and commanded several gunboats, and later the large flagship Black Hawk, going to New Orleans with Admiral Lee on board. In February, 1865, he was ordered to Cincinnati to superintend the construction of gunboats, and, taking command of the last one built, on its completion, he saved the lives of the admiral and three hundred men from the flagship Black Hawk, which took fire and blew up just after the last man had been taken off.

Mr. Saltonstall was promoted to be lieutenant-commander, the highest grade attainable for volunteer naval officers, " in consequence of the very favorable report of the admiral commanding the squadron in which you are serving." He resigned in September, 1865, leaving a record for gallantry and manly devotion to the cause of his country second to none.

After leaving the service he again entered the field of commerce, finally accepting the treasurership of the York Manufacturing Company, and later of the Everett Mills.

The death of his lovely wife in February, 1889, after a most painful illness, had a most serious effect upon his health, and during the summer he went to Europe, hoping that rest and change of scene might in a measure reëstablish his health.

He never returned, dying suddenly a few days after his arrival, while passing through the Alps with a few intimate friends. He was an honorable, whole-souled, large-hearted man, much respected and beloved by all who knew him.

---

128. LEVERETT SALTONSTALL (XI.)

Leverett Saltonstall, born at Chestnut Hill 3 Nov., 1855, died there 14 Feb., 1863, son of Leverett (120). "Rarely does the death of one so young occasion such deep and widespread grief as the death of this lovely boy. It is in part because he bore a name which in this community is so universally revered, and we fondly hoped that he would bear it down to another generation, with its honor worthily sustained. But it is yet more because of the singular beauty of his character.

"There was in this something very remarkable, so much so as to deserve a notice even aside from any personal interest in him. His entire unselfishness, — notwithstanding he was long in the relation, so unfavorable to this quality, of an only and a darling child, — his winning playfulness, his quickness of intellect, and his warmth of affection, all combined to make him what might be called a perfect child.

"But what was most remarkable was the wonderful development of his devotional feeling and his conception of spiritual things. Many a parent has been led to wonder at the deep spiritual insight of his child. It often seems as though, heaven lying ' close about us in our infancy,' there were some peculiar communications of its truth to the child's pure mind, — as though the angels were whispering in its ear. But we know of no more remarkable illustration of this than we find in the remembered sayings of this little one who is thus called away."[1]

[1] From the *Salem Gazette*, February, 1863.

134. GURDON SALTONSTALL (XI.)

Gurdon Saltonstall was born in Salem 15 Aug., 1856; but his parents removing to Boston, he resided there until he entered college in 1874. He showed great interest and ability in all his studies, in which he took high rank, but especially in natural history. At the age of fourteen he became connected with the Natural History Society, helping to arrange and classify the collections, and for three summers before he was eighteen, either alone or with others, represented the Society in the work of the United States Fish Commission. While he was devoted to his studies, he did not neglect his pleasures, but rejoiced in the society of his friends, and was enthusiastically fond of riding, in which he excelled, and of other out-of-door sports and exercises. He was six feet tall, handsome, with singularly attractive manners, spirited, and a great favorite with all who knew him of every age and class. His abilities were uncommon, his ambition great, his industry unfailing, and his life was full of promise, of happiness, and of help to others in a measure far beyond his years. But in the vacation of his first college year he attempted a long and difficult canoe voyage, in which he was greatly exposed, and in which he contracted the disease which cost him his life. He returned to college in 1875, but was soon obliged to leave it and go to the South of France, where he spent his winters, and where he died in his twenty-second year. His three years of illness and disappointment were borne with a patience, fortitude, and sweetness which could not be surpassed. Few young men of his age have left a better name.

His teacher wrote, " Of all my pupils Gurdon was the one in whom I took the most pride and loved the most, for his splendid qualities of mind and character won my admiration and affection, as they did of every one he met."

His classmates resolved " That, while he reflected high credit on himself and his class by the excellence of his scholarship, he endeared himself still more to them by his upright character, his generous disposition, and his genial manners." One of his college professors wrote, " From the first of Gurdon's all too brief connection with my class, I formed a very high estimate of his mind, character, and spirit. He was better prepared for the work of the class than any other member of it; and the serious, earnest, manly but modest purpose that he showed was very striking and delightful. Of all the young men I ever had as pupils, during an experience of twenty-three years with college classes, I can say confidently that I remember no other who so fully as he seconded every effort made in his behalf, nor did any other ever so gain my affectionate regard. When he left, though a good share of excellent men remained, I felt and said that the *jewel* of my class was gone."

The President of Harvard University wrote, " He had a face and bearing which expressed with rare clearness his beautiful character. He has left behind him sweet memories and an honorable name. He made the achievements suited to his years; was universally liked and respected; and succeeded in what he undertook. His short course in Cambridge was highly honorable to him in all respects. When he went away, everybody regretted it, — teachers, students, and servants, even, with whom his relations seemed of the slightest description. The sweetness and nobility of his nature had impressed them all."

His pastor wrote, " He was a most gracious boy, or better man, for manliness compassed him about like a robe of righteousness and beauty. Many a man has lived out his threescore or four-score years, and decently too, and yet his many days were only as a mere fragment and shred of a life compared with this short span."

Upon the memorial window erected to his memory in the chapel of the First Church of Christ in Boston is this appropriate inscription: " Honorable life consisteth not in length of years, but wisdom is gray hair unto a man, and an unspotted life is old age."

149. GOVERNOR GURDON SALTONSTALL OF CONNECTICUT (VI.)

Gurdon Saltonstall received the name of Gurdon in remembrance of his grandmother, Muriel Gurdon.[1]

After graduating at Harvard College in 1684, with much distinction as a scholar, he studied for the ministry, was called to New London as a candidate for the pulpit, and was ordained 19 Nov., 1691.[2]

At Cambridge he had been a distinguished scholar, and he soon acquired the reputation of an eloquent preacher and a discriminating theologian.

He was noted for sound judgment in cases of law and jurisprudence, and in general for a penetrating mind and great fluency of expression. In the pulpit he was imposing and impressive. His fame spread rapidly, and so prominent was he that upon the death of Governor Fitz John Winthrop[3] he was at once regarded as the proper person to succeed him.

It was an unprecedented circumstance that the pastor of a church should be summoned to relinquish the sacred office, but so strong was the conviction of his fitness that a committee of eight persons, four of them Assistants, with three deputies and the Speaker of the House, were sent to New London to solicit his acceptance of the office and break the force of all objections against it.

The Legislature also addressed a letter to the church and

[1] His portrait is in the Trumbull Gallery, and the heliotype reproduction in this volume is from a copy in the possession of the author.

[2] Of his eloquence and power as a minister there are many evidences in the recorded impressions of the time. Miss Caulkins, in her *History of New London*, says: "The high encomiums pronounced upon Governor Saltonstall render it a matter of regret that none of his sermons have been preserved. It is probable that none are extant." This, however, is a mistake, two being now in the author's possession.

[3] Governor Winthrop had long been in poor health, and went to Boston in the hope of receiving benefit from prominent physicians. In the "Boston News Letter" appeared the following notice of his death: "Boston Nov. 27, 1707. About 4 o'clock this morning, the Honorable John Winthrop, Esq., Governor of his Majesty's Colony of Connecticut, departed this life in the 69th year of his age, being born at Ipswich in New England March 14, Anno 1638, whose body is to be interred here on Thursday next the 4th of December."

congregation, entreating them to submit to the dispensation, and offering to them a gratuity of one hundred pounds to enable them to settle another pastor.

On the arrival of the deputation above named, during the last week of December, a conference was first held with Mr. Saltonstall, then the church and town convened, and finally, the consent of all parties being obtained, the Assistants administered the oath of office to the Governor elect on New Year's Day, 1708.

It was at that time a law of the colony, that the Governor should always be chosen out of a list of magistrates nominated by the freemen at the preceding election. This law was repealed by the General Assembly in order to allow the people to vote for Mr. Saltonstall. He was accordingly chosen to office by the general voice of the people, at the election in May, 1708.

Palfrey says: "A clergyman in the chief magistracy was a new thing in New England, but the experiment was in this instance grandly justified by the event."

No greater testimony to his acceptability to the people and his fitness for office can be cited than the fact of his annual reëlection for a period of sixteen years till his death.[1]

Eliot says, (ii. 34) "Of those who followed John Winthrop 2d, William Leete and Gurdon Saltonstall belong to the race of strong and able men." "He was strongly sustained by the clergy through his long term of office. To him mainly was owing the establishment of the Saybrook platform, which tended to unite the Independent churches into a kind of Presbytery."[2]

[1] The proceedings of the Assembly, in changing the manner of electing the chief magistrate from the nomination by the Assembly to a general vote of the people, are recorded on pp. 39, 40, 41 of Colonial Records of Connecticut, 1706-1717.

[2] As Governor, Mr. Saltonstall was perhaps more vigorous in repressing the Rogerine disturbances. Nevertheless, while sitting as chief judge of the Superior Court he used his utmost endeavor by argument and conciliation to persuade them to refrain from molesting the worship of their neighbors. "He gave his word," says John Bolles, "that if we would be quiet, and worship God in our own way according to our consciences, he would punish any of their people that should disturb us in our worship."

Another illustration of his liberality in matters of religion is given by the Rev.

And again: "He was a determined, hot man, but he appears to have been in good control and was a safe governor. He was a scholar, but not a man of weak digestion. He had one of the strongest bodies in the state, and was a man of practical life and sagacity."

Palfrey says, in his " History of New England:" " His hand upon the helm of state proved to be muscular and firm. To some it seemed to be even rough and heavy, but his ability, energy, and various accomplishments were generally allowed, even when his enlightened public spirit failed to secure his just estimation."

It cannot be supposed that during his long term of office he had no enemies; on the contrary, there were many occasions on which prejudice and passion were manifested against him. He found the House of Deputies factious and intractable, and after an experience of ten years in office he resolved to rid himself of the galling burden. He made representation to the Assembly of some "scandalous report very grievous to his Honour," whereupon they made inquiry and reported that "they could not find the least ground for any such reports," and they signified their earnest desire "that his Honour would continue the service of God and his country in the office whereunto he is elected." [1]

When elected for the tenth time, he said to the Assembly, " I have, thank God, this satisfaction in my own mind, that I was removed from a station of public service to which I was (though unworthy) called in the church, unto this that I now

R. A. Hallam, D. D., in his *Annals of St. James, New London*, 1873, who says: "Gurdon Saltonstall courteously entreated Keith and Talbot (members of the Church of England) in their missionary tour, invited them to preach for him, and expressed his good affection for the Church of England."
How truly these relations indicate the inheritance by him as well as by his father and his grandfather of that spirit which was so marked a characteristic of his ancestor, Sir Richard Saltonstall, who, in his letter to Mr. Cotton and Mr. Wilson after his return to England, entreated them to follow the gospel of tolerance and conciliation rather than of "tyranny and persecution."
" I hope you doe not assume to yourselves infallibilitie of judgement when the most learned of the apostles confesseth he knew but in part, and saw but darkely as through a glass." (See letter of Sir Richard Saltonstall, Part 11. 13.)
[1] Colonial Records of Connecticut, 1706–1716.

am, without any the least secret projecting of it in my own breast. It was a real surprise to me." " I can with all assurance say that I endeavored not to go before but to follow (and I hope I did sincerely follow) the conduct of Divine Providence, to which I would be still entirely resigned."

The House then united with the other branch of the Assembly in entreating the Governor " with his wonted diligence and steadiness to proceed in the public business."

He consented finally to withdraw his resignation. " Thenceforward the course of Saltonstall's administration," says Mr. Palfrey, " was tranquil to its close. Its wisdom and vigor moulded the sentiments of a transition period, and no man memorable on the bright roll of Connecticut worthies did more to establish for her that character which was indicated by the name appropriated to her through many generations of " the land of steady habits."

To repeat in this brief and imperfect sketch the details of his service to the colony during his long term of office is unnecessary. Palfrey, Trumbull, Hollister, and Eliot, indeed all the historians of New England, eulogize him in vigorous language; the colonial records show the labors of his office and his unremitting attention to duty. And Quincy says:[1] "In the attributes of public spirit and benevolence he was not surpassed by any of his contemporaries, among whom he attained the highest name as a divine, orator, and statesman."

There is little question that the location of Yale College at New Haven instead of Saybrook was in great measure owing to his influence. In the circumstances attending it his tact and wisdom were conspicuous. In this connection his letter to Mr. Noyes, one of the trustees of the college, is reproduced in heliotype.

At the time of the burning of New London by Arnold, 5 Sep., 1781, the house formerly occupied by Governor Saltonstall was destroyed, as was also that of his son, General Gurdon Saltonstall, on Main Street below the printing-office. These contained numerous valuable papers and letters relat-

[1] *History of Harvard University*, vol. i. p. 420.

Revd & Dear Sr   N Lond. June. 6. 1707

    I have Your kind Letter of ye 3d Instant, by
Your Son, and am much obliged to You for Jt. There was
nothing concluded by ye Court about the Colledge. for my own
part J did not intermeddle, but the Upper House had severall
debates upon the Bills about the Colledge wc came up from
the Lower House, wc were but two. (if there were more they
died where they had their Originall & came not up to Us.)
four of the Gentlemen of ye Assistants yt live upon the Shore,
Vis Mr Christophers, Mr Curtice, Majr Eells, & Capt Fowler,
were absent when ye Matter was put to Vear in ye Upper
House, and yet Jt was not carried in ye Affirmative. Sent
J think ye Majority of that House, will be unwilling to
oppose ye Management of the Trustees. While they tell me
a Majority of ye Lower House, inclined to have the Colledge
built at Saybrook.   J had a good Correspondence
wth Mr Woodbridge, Who, as J came out of town, moved
me to desire a Meeting of the Trustees; J told him J could
not think Jt would be of good Consequence for such a
Motion to begin with Me, but if He would move, J
would give Jt wt favour J might; and offered him
If He would write to take Care of a Lettr to You, Who
would probably discourse with Me about Jt. But He declined
This is all the Account J am able to give You. And for my
own part, J find my Self easyly acquiescing in the Prudence
of the Trustees, and Shall be always so perswaded of Jt, as
not to insert my Self into their Affairs, till J See further
Reason for Jt.   J am Revd Sr Yr most humble Set
I bless God You are recovered from Yr late Indisposition.

                      G. Saltonstall

ing to the family and to the Governor's administration, the
loss of which is deeply to be regretted.

Governor Saltonstall's singular ability and large experience
in the administration of the affairs of the colony brought
him constantly before the public in the measures adopted by
the Council, of which he was the leading member. Many of
his addresses were printed at the public charge. His diligence in the public service was unremitting; the foreign correspondence, and the preparation of new measures for the
government of the colony, were inspired by him, and his
style of expression is recognized in most of the public papers
printed in the " Record."

" In 1709 he declined an appointment of the Assembly to
go as their agent and present to the Queen an address 'pray-
ing for an armament to reduce the French in North America,' who, instigating the Indians, often committed extensive
depredations and barbarous murders on the frontier settlements. The meeting of the governors of the several colonies
in 1711 for planning the expedition against Quebec, which
proved so disastrous, was held at Governor Saltonstall's residence in New London. . . .

" After the peace of Utrecht, in 1713, relieved the colonies
of immediate danger from the French and Indians, new attempts were made to deprive Connecticut of her charter,
because she was thought to be too independent. To avert
the danger required great prudence and decision, as well as
knowledge of the subject. Most of the labor devolved on
the Governor and Council, and principally on the Governor.
The result was successful. But the expenses, with what had
been incurred in the Canada expeditions, could hardly be
met. In this emergency, Saltonstall, to facilitate payments
in England, became personally responsible, and for supporting the credit of the colony abroad received the thanks of
the Legislature. . . .

" He was principally instrumental in introducing into Connecticut the first printing-press, and it was established at New
London in consequence of his being a resident there. . . .

"The interests of Yale College were on various occasions essentially promoted by Saltonstall's countenance and advice, and both he and his wife contributed liberally to its funds. The part he took in enforcing the removal from Saybrook to New Haven, in opposition to Buckingham (H. C. 1690), led to the formation of a powerful party to defeat his election the following year. By advice of the Council he published two speeches which he had made to the Legislature, of which very erroneous accounts had been circulated. His party triumphed."

It remains now to allude to the circumstances attending his sudden death, the best relation being found in the "Boston News Letter" of Oct. 1, 1724, as follows : —

"We hear from New London the very melancholy and surprising news that on the 20th Sept. the truly honorable Gurdon Saltonstall Esq., Governor of the Colony of Connecticut, died very suddenly at his seat there.

"On the 19th he dined well and continued till about 4 P. M., when he seemed something indisposed, and quickly complained of a pain in his head. About six he betook himself to his bed, and illness increasing, he then said, 'See what need we have to be always ready.' At twelve the next day he expired, to the almost unexampled sorrow of all that saw, or since have heard of it, not only through all that government, but the whole land. His most accomplished and virtuous lady survives. He left seven children, three sons and four daughters, and to each of them a plentiful fortune."

The Rev. Eliphalet Adams, who succeeded Mr. Saltonstall in the ministry at New London after his call to the office of Governor, delivered an elegiac discourse which is eloquent with grief and lamentation. Written in the peculiar style of that day, it is undoubtedly a sincere expression of the general sorrow of the people.

The manifestations of grief at his decease were universal. "The blow vibrated through the colony, and a great assemblage of people gathered at his funeral." He was interred with a solemn religious service and imposing military ceremonies, in a tomb which he had prepared in the burial ground in New London after the death of his second wife, Elizabeth Rosewell, who with her infant child are also buried there.   Upon the table stone of this tomb is a hatchment of the family arms, two eagles with wings displayed, and the crest, a pelican out of a ducal coronet vulming her own breast.   The inscription is as follows: —

Here lyeth the body of the Honourable
Gurdon Saltonstall Esquire,
Governor of Connecticut.

(Coat of Arms.)

Who died Sept. the 20th in the 59th year of his age.   1724.

"He was buried on the 22d (September, 1724) with military honors.   'The horse and foot marched in four files; the drums, colors, trumpets, halberts, and hilts of swords covered with black, and twenty cannons firing at half a minute's distance.'   After the body had been placed in the tomb two volleys were discharged from the fort, and then the military companies, first the troop, and afterwards the foot, 'marching in single file, as each respectively came up against the tomb, discharged, and so drew up orderly into a body as before and dismissed.'

"The 'Boston News Letter,' 1 Oct. 1724, speaks of him as 'Just, wise, and indulgent . . . being peculiarly form'd for the Benefit and Delight of Mankind.   He had a wonderful quickness of Tho't, and yet as Strange an attention and closeness, a Bright, Lively, Beautifull Imagination, yet a very correct Judgment, his Excellencies seem'd to meet in the most happy composition, his correct Judgment prevented a wild Luxuriancy in his Fancy, and the beauty and easiness of that softened the Severity of the other.   He had a great compass of Learning, was a profound *Divine*, a great *Judge* in the *Law*, and a consummate *Statesman ;* He made Excellent observations in Natural Philosophy, and had a peculiar Genius and Skill in the Mathematics; Not to mention his lighter Studies in *Philology, History, Geography*, &c. in each of which he excell'd enough to have made any other Man very

Famous; His Person, Mien and Aspect were equally attractive of Love, Esteem and Admiration; The Superiority and Penetration of his great Mind, seem'd to show themselves to our very Senses, in the natural Majesty of his Eye, Look and Deportment, and yet a flowing Benevolence and Kindness seem'd equally visible in the complaisance & easiness of them, that it was scarce possible for a Man that had the opportunity of Conversing with him, to put on ill nature enough, not to Love and Admire him, and especially, if they saw him in the place of an *Oratour* where the agreeableness and even Music of his *Voice*, the strength and perspicuity of his *Reasons*, the beauty and Sprightliness of his *Allusions*, the easy Cohearence, genuine Relation and Connexion in his *Transitions*, the choice of his *Words*, and if it may be so express'd, *Concise fulness* in his *Diction* & *Style*, the Charms in his *Appearance*, *Air* and *Gesture*, commanded the *Eyes*, the *Ears*, the *Soul*, the *Whole Man*, in all that were near him, in such a Strange and Wonderfull manner, that when he has sometimes spoken for *Hours* together there has appeared nothing but *Satisfaction*, *Delight* and *Rapture*, till they have all complain'd, that he *Left off & Robb'd* them of their *Happiness* too soon.   He had, naturally, something of *Warmth* in his *Temper*, but his Wisdom and Vertue gave him the *Ascendant* of it, so perfectly, that he could with the greatest *Firmness* and *Unmoveableness* meet the highest *Provocation* and not only *Forgive* but *heap kindness* upon his Enemies.   He was very much *Fixt*, in the *Establish'd Religion* of *New England*, after a long, strict and critical *Enquiry* into the Principles of it; yet of a most *Catholick Spirit*, full of *Candour* and a sincere *Lover* of all *Good* Men, tho' differing in some things from him.

"' He was as great a Christian as he was a Man, and seem'd to be *Peculiarly* fitted for *Glory* in the next World as he was for *Vsefulness* and the Highest Esteem in this.'

" A similar tribute is contained in the funeral sermon of Eliphalet Adams: ' Who that was Acquainted with him did not Admire his *Consummate Wisdom, profound Learning,*

His *Dexterity in Business* and *Indefatigable Application*, His *Intimate Acquaintance with men and things*, and his *Superior Genius?* And what was more than all this, His *Vnaffected* Piety and *Love to God's House*, His *Exact Life* and *Exemplary Conversation?* In what part of *Learning* did he not *Excel!* He had *mastered* every *Subject* that he *Undertook* and *Nothing* could *Escape his Penetration*; How *Great* did he Appear, whether in the *Court* or *Camp!* He was an *Oracle in the Law*; And no man was better read either in the *Agitated Controversies* or the *Abstruser points of Divinity.* People were wont to *ask Counsel* of him and so they ended the matter.

"'Can we ever forget with what Delight we have seen him at the head of every weighty Affair, in *Courts*, in *Councils*, in *all manner of Conventions*, and we never Despaired of a good Event where he had the Management. Our *Expectations* were still *Outdone*, however they were Enlarged, we stood with a fix'd Attention, with our Ears chain'd to his Lips and Nothing *griev'd us* but that the *Time fail'd*, and so he was under a *Necessity to have done Speaking.*'

"'So *Great & Wise & Good* a man as we have this Day Lost is the *Product of an Age.*'

" Cotton Mather's Essay in commemoration of him says: — ' The Colony of Connecticut was *Exalted*, Yea, all New England was brightness, while we enjoy'd our Saltonstall.'

"' The rare Accomplishments, both Natural and Acquired, of a *Finished Gentleman*, Every where commanded Esteem for him; in regard whereof it might be said of him, *When he stood among the People he was higher than any of the People from his shoulders and upwards.* His *Learning*, His *Wisdom*, His Acute *Penetration*, His *Goodness* and *Candour*, and *Generosity*, were *Ornaments* which *Distinguished* them. Over these there was the *Cover* of an *Agreeable Aspect:* The *Silver Basket* of a comely Body, carrying in it the *Golden Apples* of a well-furnished and well-disposed Soul; And a venerable *Presence* charming with Familiar *Condescensions.* We will not call him a *Star*, but even a *Constellation* of the fulgid Endowments.'

"' And yet, *These* were his *Lesser Excellencies.* Unspotted Piety, Inviolate Integrity, Exemplary Humility, were what yet more potently bespoke for him a place among *the Excellent of the Earth.*

"' But then, After all the *Perfect Work* of Patience which was the Consummation of those *Virtues* in him, that will be *found unto Praise and Honor and Glory at the Appearing of* Jesus Christ. . . . The *Theodosian* Prudence and Calmness, with which he conquered Unmentionable Trials of his *Patience,* was that for which God is to be Singularly *Glorified in him.*'" [1]

The wives of Governor Saltonstall, (1) Jerusha Richards, (2) Elizabeth Rosewell, and (3) Mary Clarke, were in every sense of the word superior women ; distinguished for dignity, grace, and Christian liberality.

The children of the Governor married into the families of Christopher, Ledyard, Miller, Gardiner (of Gardiner's Island), Davis, Brattle, Arnold, Winthrop, and Haynes, all prominent in Connecticut, and identified with her general history.[2]

---

151. MARY SALTONSTALL (VII.), WIFE OF JEREMIAH MILLER

" As an accomplished gentleman and magistrate, Jeremiah Miller was highly esteemed.   He married, soon after his settlement in New London (which was in 1714), Mary, the second daughter of Governor Gurdon Saltonstall, and had a

---

[1] Sibley's *Harvard Graduates,* Class of 1684, vol. iii. pp. 281–284.

[2] " Gurdon Saltonstall bequeathed by will one hundred pounds lawful money to Harvard College ; thus emulating the example of Mary Saltonstall his wife, who the year previous had made a donation of a like sum from her own private estate.

"Mary Saltonstall survived her husband six years, and by her last will bequeathed in 1730 one thousand pounds to the college for educating young men 'of bright parts and good diligence for the service of the Christian Church.'   By the same instrument she made noble and judicious legacies for the advancement of learning and religion, and for charitable purposes."—Quincy's *History of Harvard University,* vol. i. pp. 421, 422.

family of seven children. His wife died in 1749. He contracted a second marriage with Mrs. Ann Winthrop, relict
of John Still Winthrop, and daughter of Governor Joseph
Dudley of Massachusetts. The bride and groom were in all
the dignity of mature age, both verging toward three-score
and ten, and the nuptial ceremony was performed by the
venerable Roger Wolcott, Deputy Governor of the Colony,
on Sunday morning, 30 Sept., 1750."[1]

Of his seven children, three died in infancy; Mary, the
only daughter, died unmarried; and two sons, Gurdon and
Jason, were lost at sea. The surviving son, Jeremiah Miller,
Jr., married, in 1743, Margaret Winthrop.

---

155. CAPTAIN ROSEWELL SALTONSTALL (VII.)

Captain Rosewell Saltonstall, while on a visit to his brother
Gurdon in New London, was seized with a nervous fever the
first day of his arrival, and died twelve days afterwards, 1 Oct.,
1738. He was highly esteemed in New London, being a
man of irreproachable Christian character, and amiable in all
the relations of life. He resided in Branford, on the Rosewell estate, the home of his maternal ancestors. He was
buried with his parents in the tomb of Governor Saltonstall
at New London.

155 A. SIR HENRY ROSEWELL

At Exeter, England, July 1888, Mrs. Frances B. James
read an interesting paper on " Sir Henry Rosewell, a Devon
Worthy; his Ancestry and History," from which much interesting information is derived as to the origin of the name
" Rosewell." " The earliest date we have been able to attach
to this name is 1507–8, when Thomas Rosewell supplicated
for his degree at Oxford." Sir Henry Rosewell was a patron
of the living of Linnington. He was born on the Feast of

---

[1] Caulkins's *History of New London.*

All Saints, 1590, his father being William Rosewell and his mother Anne Walkenden. He was knighted at Theobalds by King James I., 19 Feb., 16$\frac{18}{19}$. He appears to have been married about this time to Mary Drake. There is no record of his children. His mother was buried in Musbury Church 5 Nov., 1643.

When he first took an interest in the movement for the settlement of the colonies in America we have no means of knowing. It is possible he was connected with the Dorchester Company in its early days, 1627–8. After that company ceased to exist, a new company was formed and obtained a grant about 1629 from the Council for New England. Sir Henry Rosewell's name appears first among the grantees. According to the forty-third report of the Deputy Keeper, the confirmation of this grant reads as follows: " Rosewell Sir Henry, Young Sir John, Southcote Thomas, Humphrey John, Endecott John, Whetcombe Simon, and their 20 Associates " (" these gentlemen were residents of Dorchester or its vicinity," including in the last word Dorset, Devon, Somerset, and Kent), " Confirmation to them and their heirs of a grant made to them by the Company of New England with a further grant of incorporation by the name of the Governor and Company of Massachusetts Bay in New England America."

It is not possible to say that he took any prominent part in New England affairs. He lived to the age of sixty-six and died childless, perhaps infirm, and in comparative poverty, owing to American investments and to aiding his Parliamentarian friends. He was buried 3 April, 1656.

The Rosewell estate at Branford, Connecticut, including Lake Saltonstall, came into the possession of Governor Gurdon Saltonstall through his marriage with Elizabeth Rosewell, and he built a mansion there in which he resided, and where his son Rosewell afterwards lived.

Mr. Bond in a footnote to p. 924, " Genealogies and History of Watertown," says: " William Rosewell b. in 1630, m. (by Increase Nowell, Esq.) in Charlestown Nov. 29, 1654, Catherine Russell, dau. of Hon. Richard and Maud Russell, of Charlestown. . . . He moved to Connecticut as early as 1667. He probably first went to Branford, as he was one of the original signers of the 'New Plantation Covenant' of Branford, Jan. 20, 1667; but he must have moved to New Haven very soon afterwards, for on Jan. 13, 1667, the town of New Haven granted him a lot on which he built a house, and 'for some years dwelt in;' was engaged in trade, and owned a bark, trading between New Haven and Barbadoes. He probably returned to Branford in 1671; for on the 9th of Feb., 1671, the town of Branford granted him a tract of land at the outlet of the lake, . . . on condition of his erecting and maintaining a dam there. This dam yet remains. In the same year there was a marriage settlement between Hon. Richard Russell and his daughter Catherine Rosewell of the one part, and Mr. William Rosewell of the other part, settling upon her heirs of this marriage, first male and second female, the farm by the lake, with the negroes (naming them) Albert and his wife, Ruth, and children, Caty, Andrew, and Ruth, and another negro named Peter."

---

158. GENERAL GURDON SALTONSTALL (VII.)

Gurdon Saltonstall, son of Governor Gurdon Saltonstall (149) by his second wife, was born 22 Dec., 1708, the year that his father became Governor of Connecticut, and graduated at Yale College in 1725. Mr. Saltonstall was prominent in all the affairs of New London. When, in 1739, England issued letters of marque and reprisal against Spain, New London, being much exposed and entirely undefended, the inhabitants became alarmed and petitioned the Governor for the immediate fortification of the town. The apathetic reply of the Governor provoked a second petition, and Messrs. Gurdon Saltonstall, Jeremiah Miller, and three others were named as a committee to personally urge action upon the Governor. In the year 1740, war having been declared by England against Spain, Gurdon Saltonstall was promoted to the rank of colonel of the militia.   In 1744–5 he superintended the raising of troops for the expedition against Cape Breton.

In all the measures of the town relating to the Revolution he took a prominent part.   In October, 1767, he was first named on a committee of fifteen to consider the Boston resolution to abstain from the use of certain articles of merchandise, and in 1770 he was sent with William Hillhouse, Nathaniel Shaw, Jr., and William Manwaring to represent New London in a grand convention of the colony held at New Haven.   He was Chairman of the Committee of Correspondence for 1776; in 1777 Moderator; in October, 1779, Deputy to the State Convention at Hartford in company with John Latimer.

The military operations around Boston consequent upon the battle of Lexington withdrew from Connecticut all available forces.   New enlistments were made to supply their places.   In New London, Colonel Saltonstall remained with seventy men newly enlisted under his command, and, amid many difficulties arising from want of unanimity, lack of means and material, he prosecuted the work of defense with energy and to the satisfaction of his superiors.   The constant appearance of the enemy's ships off the harbor of New London kept the inhabitants in constant alarm.

On a reorganization of the forces, Colonel Saltonstall, then commanding the third regiment, was appointed brigadier-general[1] (10 Sep., 1776), and placed in command of nine regiments from the eastern counties, with orders to serve at New York, viz.: The 3d Regt., Lt.-Col. John Ely; 7th Regt., Maj. Sylvanus Graves; 11th Regt., Col. Ebenezer Williams; 20th Regt., Maj. Zabdiel Rogers; 5th Regt., Lt.-Col. Experience Storrs; 12th Regt., Col. Obadiah Hosford; 21st Regt., Col. John Douglass; 8th Regt., Lt.-Col. Oliver Smith; 25th Regt., Col. H. Champion.   Brigade Major, Winthrop Saltonstall (son of General Gurdon).   General Sal-

[1] *Record of Service of Connecticut Men:* 1, In the War of the Revolution; 2, War of 1812; 3, Mexican War, by Henry P. Johnson, A. M., Hartford, 1889.

tonstall proceeded with his brigade to New York and took post in Westchester County. He was then sixty-eight years of age.

In the burning of New London by Arnold, a considerable number of old family homesteads were consumed, — the most valuable being those of General Gurdon Saltonstall and of his father the Governor.

At the close of the war the State of Connecticut was divided into two collection districts, — New London and New Haven. The first collector appointed for New London was General Gurdon Saltonstall. He died at the house of his son-in-law, Thomas Mumford, in Norwich, 19 Sep., 1785, at the age of seventy-seven.[1]

---

165. REBECCA SALTONSTALL (VIII.), WIFE OF DAVID MUMFORD

Rebecca, second child and eldest dau. of General Gurdon and Rebecca (Winthrop) Saltonstall, m. 1 June, 1758, David Mumford of New London, second son of the fourth Thomas Mumford, b. 10 March, 1731. Their children were : —

1. David, b. 20 Dec., 1759; d. 21 Feb., 1823.
2. Rebecca, b. Aug., 1761 ; m. Robert Allyn.
3. Gurdon Saltonstall, b. 29 Jan., 1764.
4. Abigail Cheesborough, b. 18 April, 1767 ; m. —— Phillips. Child : —
   Ann Phillips, m. David Lee, whose dau. Mary Esther, b. 1838 or 1840, m. 1st, in Sep., 1864, Prince Frederick of Schleswig Holstein Sonderburgh Augustenburg; m. 2d, Alfred, Count von Waldersee, Chief of the Emperor's Staff. She is a person of great influence in Germany.
5. William Cheesboro, b. 5 March, 1769.
6. Thomas, b. 13 July, 1770; m. at Litchfield, Conn., 20 Jan., 1795, Mary Sheldon Smith, b. 29 Oct., 1773.

[1] See Caulkins's *History of New London.*

He removed after his marriage to Cayuga, where he
d. Dec., 1831. Children : —
1a. William Woolsey, b. 13 Nov., 1795; grad. Yale
   Coll. 1815; m. Angelina Sarah Jenkins of Hudson,
   N. Y., b. 1807, d. 25 March, 1836. He d. 9 Jan.,
   1848. Children : —
   1b. William Thomas, b. 21 Jan., 1829; m. Cornelia
      Shearman ; d. 10 April, 1856, *s. p.*
   2b. Mary Smith, b. 27 Sep., 1830; d. 23 Nov., 1833.
   3b. Sarah Scoville, b. 27 Sep., 1830; d. 5 March,
      1834.
   4b. George Elihu, b. 20 Nov., 1831; grad. Hamilton
      College 1852; m. 18 Sep., 1860, Julia Emma
      Hills, b. 7 July, 1840. She d. 27 May, 1882.
      He died 2 Feb., 1892. Children : —
      1c. William Woolsey of Rochester, N. Y., b. 24
         March, 1862.
      2c. James Gregory, M. D., of Boston, b. 2 Dec.,
         1863.
      3c. George Saltonstall of Boston, b. 18 Aug.,
         1866, m. Isabella, dau. of George C. Lee.
      4c. Norman Winthrop of Florida, b. 30 Oct.,
         1868.
      5c. Julian, b. 3 Feb., 1871; d. 3 Feb., 1874.
      6c. Philip Gurdon of Rochester, N. Y., b. 30
         Sep., 1874.
   5b. Angelina Jenkins, b. 30 Aug., 1833.
   6b. Elizabeth Scoville, b. 1 Nov., 1835; d. 16 May,
      1836.
2a. Helen Frances, b. 17 Aug., 1797; d. 6 Dec., 1877.
3a. Henry Huntington, b. 20 Jan., 1800; d. 15 April,
   1810.
4a. Elihu Hubbard Smith, b. 1 April, 1802; d. 17
   March, 1844.
5a. George Huntington, b. 27 Nov., 1803; d. 5 April,
   1805.
6a. George Huntington, b. 21 July, 1805; d. 30 Sep.,

1871. He was the father of Mrs. Louis C. Washburne, now of Rochester, N. Y.

7a. Mary Pierce, b. 8 Feb., 1809 ; d. 20 Feb., 1863.

8a. Henrietta Saltonstall, b. 21 Dec., 1811 ; d. 11 Nov., 1889.

7. John, b. 11 Feb., 1772.

8. Ann, b. 3 Oct., 1773; m. John T. Durgee.

9. Silas Dean, b. 20 May, 1777.

---

167. WINTHROP SALTONSTALL (VIII.)

Winthrop Saltonstall, son of General Gurdon (158), always resided in New London, and took an active and influential part in its affairs. In 1767 he was one of the Committee of Fifteen. He was in active service in the militia, and held the commission of brigade major when the troops were ordered to New York, just before the close of the war. After the war he was appointed Register of the Court of Admiralty.

167 A. WILLIAM AND JOSEPH WANTON

In " No. 3, Rhode Island Historical Tracts, History of the Wanton Family of Newport, Rhode Island, by John Russell Bartlett," we find a very full account of William and Joseph Wanton, whose names appear as connected by marriage with the Saltonstall family of Connecticut. From this history we have copied the following interesting particulars : —

" Among the citizens of Rhode Island who have rendered distinguished service to the State since its foundation, none are more prominent than the Wanton family. For a century their names appear among those who were prominent in social, political, and commercial life. For several generations they were the leading merchants in the colony. They were active in support of religion; and in all works for the interest of the town where they resided, as well as for the colony

at large, they were always found among the leaders.   During
the war between Great Britain and France, when two of
them filled the office of governor, they rendered distinguished
service which was acknowledged by their sovereign.   Four
bearing the name were at different times elected governor:
William Wanton, elected in 1732, served two years; John
Wanton, elected in 1734, served seven years; Gideon Wanton, elected in 1745 and 1747, served two years; Joseph
Wanton, elected in 1769, served till November, 1775.
Another, Joseph, Jr., held the office of deputy governor.
Portraits of William, John, and Joseph are preserved in the
Redwood Library at Newport, and copies from the same have
been placed in the State House in Providence."

The following particulars of their personal history before
they entered public life will be found interesting: " In consequence of religious differences in the family, some of the
members being connected with the Episcopal Church and
others with the Quakers, William and John removed to Newport, where they established themselves as shipbuilders. The
former was soon found to be a man of more than ordinary
capacity.   He rose in public esteem and became very efficient
in the colonial government " (page 24).   Among their ex-
ploits was the capture of a " piratical ship of three hundred
tons, which had greatly annoyed the inhabitants of Newport.
This took place when William was but twenty-four and John
twenty-two years of age."   " Again, in 1697, just before the
peace of Ryswick, . . . a French armed ship had taken
several prizes in the Bay. . . . William and John repaired
to Boston, where each fitted out a vessel, . . . put to sea,
and in a few days fell in with the French ship and captured
her. . . . This prize was very valuable, as she had the choicest
spoils from the prizes she had taken, and the Wantons were
greatly enriched, besides rendering a valuable service to the
colony."   " In 1702 they went to London, and were received
at court among the naval heroes who had added lustre to
the British flag.   Their portraits were painted by the court
artist."

Queen Anne granted them an addition to their family coat-of-arms, which was considered a great honor, and with her own royal hands presented each with two pieces of plate, a silver punch-bowl and salver, with these words in Latin engraved upon them: —

> Omnipotente numine magestro
> Volat hic Hercules ocyens Vento
> Multo cum sanguine capuintur
> Vincenti poculum dabitur Wantoni.

Which may be freely translated thus : —

> Swift as the wind the intrepid warrior flies,
> Under the smiles of all-approving Heaven,
> The trembling captive feels his power and dies —
> To conquering Wanton let the bowl be given.

This bowl was stolen at an election festival when Joseph Wanton was elected Governor of Rhode Island and Providence Plantations.

"They now entered the arena of politics. William, who is styled major, was in 1705 elected a Deputy to the General Assembly and chosen Speaker. The following year he was chosen an Assistant.

"In 1709 William and John Wanton took an active part against the French in Canada."

"In the boundary dispute we find Colonel William Wanton, as he is now styled, one of the commissioners sent to that colony."

"From 1705, when he first entered public life as a Deputy to the General Assembly, William Wanton continued to serve the colony as Deputy or as an Assistant until 1732, when he was elected Governor. He was reëlected the following year, and died in December of that year."

"All accounts state that William Wanton was not only an enterprising merchant, but a most 'polished gentleman of easy, polite, and engaging manners, very hospitable, and fond of entertaining his friends.'"

168. COMMODORE DUDLEY SALTONSTALL (VIII.)

In early life Dudley Saltonstall made numerous voyages in mercantile pursuits, and gained the reputation of being a courageous and skilful commander. In the Revolutionary War he attained the rank of commodore, and had command of the American fleet in the Massachusetts expedition against Castine, at the mouth of the Penobscot, in 1779, an enterprise which proved the most unfortunate in her military history. The haste with which the expedition was organized, the insufficient equipment of the militia, and the inexperience of those who commanded them, created at the outset differences of opinion between the leaders of the land and naval forces, produced fatal delays, and increased demoralization.

" Directions were given forthwith by the Board of War to engage or employ such armed vessels, state or national, as could be procured and prepared in six days.

" The command of the land forces was given to Solomon Lovell of Weymouth." " He was by profession an agriculturist, and in the militia an officer of high repute," " but he had not been accustomed to the command of an expedition in actual service." " The expedition was put in motion by Massachusetts," " though with the knowledge of Congress." " Although 1,200 men were ordered, we had less than 1,000, about the number of the enemy." " They were undisciplined troops, having been paraded together only once." " They were, however, brave and spirited men ; " " and had circumstances justified an attack, they would, without doubt, have done their duty manfully."[1]

" Such was their zeal and confidence of success, that it is said the General Court neither consulted any experienced military character, nor desired the assistance of any Continental troops on this important enterprise, thus taking on themselves the undivided responsibility, and reserving for their own heads all the laurels to be derived from the antici-

[1] Williamson's *History of Maine*, p. 470. Williamson erroneously calls the Commodore Richard.

pated conquest." "This combined force sailed about the
20 July."[1] The troops started on the 20th and arrived on
the 25th July.

"Saltonstall was in favor of attacking as soon as they arrived, but General Solomon Lovell, commander of the militia,
was unwilling."[2]

An attack was made on the 28th, in which 100 men out of
400 were lost, "the marines suffering most, as they forced
their way up the precipice here 200 feet high, and extremely
difficult of access."[3]

The evidence is very conflicting as to where the blame lay
for the delay in renewing the attack. Those writers who
had been attached to the land forces, or who, in the heat of
the discussion which ensued on the failure of the enterprise,
espoused their side of the argument, naturally give strong
coloring to their accounts of it against the Commodore;[4]
while on the other hand there is strong testimony to show
that, while the Commodore was anxious to renew the attack,
he found no acquiescence on the part of Generals Lovell and
Wadsworth. Perhaps the strongest proof of this is in a journal which was found on board the Hunter, a Continental
ship of eighteen guns, one of the fleet, which was evidently
written by some one from day to day as events progressed,
and bears every mark of truth.[5] It reads as follows: —

"Friday, Aug. 6. — A signal from the Commodore was displayed for all the Captains of the fleet to come on board and
consult about attacking the British shipping and fort. The
result was that if the General would attack the fort . . . a
number of the largest ships should go into the harbor and
attack the shipping. The plan was sent to the General for
his approbation."

"Saturday, 7th. — The above plan was not conceded by
the General, supposing that as his army consisted chiefly

[1] Thacher's *Journal*, p. 203.
[2] Appleton's *Am. Biography*, vol. v. p. 380, with authorities cited.
[3] Williamson's *History of Maine*, p. 473.
[4] See Thacher's *Journal;* Williamson's *History of Maine.*
[5] *Historical Magazine*, vol. viii. p. 51.

of Militia, and that they were undisciplined, he should be defeated in the attempt. Therefore the conclusion was to continue the siege till intelligence could be obtained from Boston respecting reinforcements."

" Wednesday, 11th. — The General, not being ready for the attack, thought proper to advance out upon a plain to manœuvre his men; . . . a detached party of 250 proceeded to the small battery near the S. E. point to excite the British troops to attack them from their citadel. After they had paraded themselves in the battery, about 55 regular troops sallied from the citadel, and, advancing with resolution, put the whole party to flight without discharging a gun. They pursued them to the main body, and then, discharging a volley, drove the whole 750 into the fort in the greatest confusion imaginable, the officers damning their soldiers, and the soldiers their officers, for cowardice, many losing their implements of war. The Captains of our ships were invited to see this grand manœuvre of the Militia troops, the detached British party exulting with loud huzzas."

From the details presented by Thacher's Journal, by Williamson's " History of Maine," and by Winsor's " Narrative and Critical History of America," there is abundant evidence to show that the expedition was conceived and organized by the General Court, " without consulting any experienced military character," and without desiring the assistance of any Continental troops; that they appointed to command their army a man who had not been accustomed to the command of an expedition in actual service; and that the troops were insufficient in number, and wholly undisciplined.

The disastrous issue of the expedition was then attributable to the unfortunate dissensions of the commanders, to the insufficiency of the force,[1] and to the fatal delay which permitted the approach of the English fleet, led by Sir George Collier in the Rainbow of 44 guns, the largest American vessel being the Warren of 32 guns. To have given battle under such circumstances would have resulted in the certain

---

[1] Williamson's *History of Maine*, p. 473.

capture of the American fleet. The Commodore, therefore, had no other course than to escape up the river, destroying his ships, but saving his men.

J. Fenimore Cooper, in his "History of the Navy of the United States," in reviewing the situation as presented on the arrival of the British fleet says: "It could not surely have been thought that privateers armed with light guns were able to resist two-deckers, and the fact that the English had such a fleet on our coast was generally known. The Warren, the largest among the Americans, was a common frigate of 32 guns, and had a main deck battery of 12-pounders. Whatever might have been attempted by a regular force was put out of the question by the insubordination of the privateersmen, each vessel seeking her own safety as her captain saw best."

The failure of the expedition caused so much criticism that the Legislature of Massachusetts at its next session, September 9, appointed "a Committee or Court of Inquiry" of nine, principally Massachusetts militia officers and civilians, to examine into the causes of the failure and to make their report. After two sessions the court decided that "the principal reason for their failure was the want of proper spirit and energy on the part of the Commodore;" "that General Lovell throughout the expedition and retreat acted with proper courage and spirit, and had he been furnished with all the men ordered for the service, or been properly supported by Commodore Saltonstall, he would probably have reduced the enemy." Thus the State officers were completely exonerated, and the whole blame for failure was thrown on the Commodore, who was "adjudged incompetent ever after to hold a commission in the service of the State."

Fortunately there is ample evidence to show that this was not the opinion of all his contemporaries. In a letter written by Eben. Hazard, six months after the failure of the expedition, he says : —

" In that report (Report of Committee of both Houses) the principal blame is laid upon the Commodore. I have no doubt that he was very culpable ; but from the face of the report it appears to me that, as he was a Continental officer, his bulk would keep the smaller fry out of sight, and thereby the credit of the State would be saved, and a plea furnished for saddling the 'Continent' with the expense. But were I member of Congress I should, when that matter came upon the carpet, ask some such questions as the following, from which, perhaps, some light might be thrown upon it: —

"Was General Gates consulted at all about the expedition? He was then the Continental officer commanding in this department and was at Providence, not a day's ride from Boston. If the Continent were to bear the expense, it was certainly proper to consult at least the principal Continental officer in the neighborhood, especially when it could be so easily and expeditiously done.

"Was there not a proposal in one of the Houses compos-ing the General Court for calling in aid some Continental troops, which was rejected with a remark similar to this, 'If but ten Continental soldiers are concerned, the Continent will take the honor'?

"What occasioned the deficiency of nearly one third of the men ordered upon that service?

"Upon whom was that shameful neglect chargeable? What number of shells or bombs was sent with the howitzer which the Board of War was directed to send to the Penobscot?

"If there were none, upon whom was that neglect charge-able, and what punishment has been inflicted for it? . . .

"Why was not General Gates applied to for assistance be-fore it was too late to hope that his troops could be of any service?

"If it was owing to want of information from Penobscot, why did not General Lovell send the information sooner?

"Did not Colonel Revere return to Boston without orders and without men? What censure has he received for this?"[1]

The questions proposed by Mr. Hazard disclosed a know-ledge of the details as to the formation and conduct of the

[1] *Mass. Hist. Soc. Proceedings*, vol. iv. p. 129; Appleton's *Cyclo. Am. Biogra-phy*, vol. v. p. 380.

expedition which he could gather from the dissatisfaction of the community with the whole affair, and their suspicion that it was intended to charge its cost to the Continent. The composition of the court was suited to this intention, and the verdict was so worded as to emphasize it.

We may well suppose that Saltonstall smarted under such flagrant injustice. Identified with the navy from its earliest organization, steadily promoted from the Alfred, 24 guns, to the Trumbull, 28, and the Warren, 32, it may reasonably be supposed that his ability and experience should have been considered, if not deferred to, by militia officers having little if any experience; but this was not the case. He appears to have been treated shamefully and cruelly sacrificed. Those of his kindred and friends acquainted with his character and the value of his services urged him to address Congress, and he may have done so by letter, though he never made application in person.

" Among the first naval captains appointed to the regular Continental Navy by the resolutions of Dec., 1775, was Dudley Saltonstall of New London. In the first arrangement of naval officers he is named the leading captain, being second in command to Commodore Ezek. Hopkins, and in command of the Alfred. The expedition to New Providence under Hopkins brought about a new arrangement of the Continental Navy by which Captain Saltonstall became fourth on the list, and was changed from the Alfred to the Trumbull, a 28-gun frigate, which in April, 1777, captured, after a sharp action, two armed transports filled with valuable stores. Captain Saltonstall was then transferred to a larger frigate, the Warren, 32 guns, which with two other Continental vessels were detailed to take part in the Penobscot expedition, concerning ' which he might have been liable to censure, but the failure of the expedition was more the result of the publicity given to it than any other cause, and this was not his fault.' His enterprise, seamanship, and courage were undoubted, and he was worthy of a better reward than that given by the Continental Congress." [1]

[1] *New London Co. Hist. Soc.* Part II. vol. i. p. 47.

Saltonstall was not the man to bear patiently the stigma which had been so unjustly placed upon him, and the brigantine Minerva, which he commanded, was, at his earnest request, converted into a cruiser or privateer by her owner, Adam Babcock, who wrote him as follows : —

" It is perfectly agreeable to me that you should command the Brigt. as cruiser rather than as merchantman, and chiefly that you may regain the character with the world which you have been most cruelly and unjustly robbed of in a manner as new and unusual as it was barbarous and tyrannical. You never lost it with me, and this I believe you never doubted."

This was the letter that sent the Minerva to sea, and it was during the cruise which followed that she captured the Hannah, a British ship with a cargo valued at £80,000. The vessels were equal in armament, and the victory was won only after a stubborn contest.

---

169. ANN SALTONSTALL (VIII.), WIFE OF THOMAS MUMFORD

Thomas Mumford, b. in Groton 10 Sep., 1728; m. 7 Dec., 1752, at Shelter Island, N. Y., Catherine Havens. She d. 2 Dec., 1778, leaving issue, and in 1780 he m. Ann, the sixth child of General Gurdon Saltonstall. No issue. He was one of the eleven who organized the expedition against Ticonderoga generally known as the Ethan Allen expedition. His house at New London was singled out and burned by Arnold with that of General Saltonstall. After that he lived in Norwich till his death in 1799. General Saltonstall died at his house 19 Sep., 1785.

Thomas Mumford and his brother David (Part II. 165) were directly descended from (1) Thomas and Rebecca (Sherman) Mumford, (2) Thomas Mumford of Kingston, R. I., (3) Thomas and Hannah (Remington) Mumford of South Kingston, R. I., and (4) Thomas and Abigail Cheesborough of Groton and New London, Conn. The two brothers were actively engaged together in the affairs of the Revolutionary period.

173a. MARTHA SALTONSTALL (VIII.)

Martha Saltonstall m. 8 Oct., 1748, David Manwaring, first of New London, afterwards of New York. Children : —
1. William, b. 12 Nov., 1767; d. May, 1768.
2. Rebecca, b. 27 Dec., 1768; m. 20 Jan., 1793, Elisha Coit.
3. Hannah, b. 29 Nov., 1770; d. 19 July, 1771.
4. David, b. 13 May, 1772 ; m. Lucy Colfax; d. July, 1811.
5. Martha, b. 15 May, 1774; d. 24 Nov., 1788.
6. Gurdon, b. 10 Nov., 1776; m. Ann Adams; d. 7 Jan., 1838.
7. Lucy, b. 19 Dec., 1778; m. David Greene Hubbard, who d. 1825.
8. Susannah, b. 23 Sep., 1783; m. 20 April, 1805, Gurdon Buck, b. 30 Dec., 1777. She d. 13 April, 1839.

---

174. HENRIETTA SALTONSTALL (VIII.)

Henrietta Saltonstall m. 28 Feb., 1772, John Still Miller. Children : —
1. Jeremiah.
2. Ann, d. in infancy.
3. Ann, d. young.
4. John Still, b. 4 Sep., 1779; m. Dec., 1824, Anna D. Coit. Children: —
   1a. J. S. W. Miller, b. 13 Oct., 1825.
   2a. Ann Dudley S., b. 1 May, 1827; d. 21 Aug., 1828.
   3a. Gurdon W., b. 16 Feb., 1829.
   4a. Ralph H., b. 1 Sep., 1830.
   5a. Russell Hubbard, b. 26 June, 1833; d. Aug., 1838.
   6a. Mary Coit.

5. William, b. 12 Nov., 1780; m. 20 Oct., 1805, Sarah
    Taber; d. 27 Oct., 1823. Children : —
    1a. William J., b. 20 Aug., 1809; m. 20 June, 1838,
        Catherine D. Taylor.
    2a. Sarah R., m. 1834, Samuel T. Hubbard.
    3a. Frances H., b. 3 Aug., 1818; d. 10 Sep., 1825.
    4a. Henrietta S., b. 9 June, 1807; m. 15 Oct., 1828,
        John Brinkerhoff, M. D., of New York.
6. Gurdon, b. 18 May, 1782; m. Ann Maria Taber.
7. Henrietta, b. 24 July, 1784; d. unmarried.
8. Dudley, b. 17 June, 1786; d. 26 Oct., 1786.
9. Dudley, b. 6 Aug., 1787; d. 10 Nov., 1787.
10. Frances, b. 22 Oct., 1788; d. unmarried.
11. Elizabeth, b. 18 June, 1789; d. unmarried.
12. Richard, b. 11 Oct., 1792; bur. 21 Aug., 1797.
13. Lucy, b. 27 Oct., 1794; m. Lieut. John Movers, U.
    S. N.

---

175. CAPTAIN GILBERT SALTONSTALL (VIII.)

Captain Gilbert Saltonstall was connected with the marine
service on the Trumbull, which sailed on her first cruise in
April, 1780. She took and sent in several prizes of small
value, and on the 2d of June, off Bermuda, she fell in with
the English ship Watt, letter of marque, 34 guns, mostly 12-
pounders, and having a crew of 250 men, commanded by
Captain Colehart. The Trumbull is supposed to have carried 28 guns, 24 twelve and four six pounders, but some
accounts say she was pierced for 32 and carried 30 guns, —
24 twelve, and six six pounders.

The account of the bloody action which followed, and
which lasted more than two and a half hours at close quarters
and without intermission, in which the Watt is said to have
lost 92 men in killed and wounded, and the Trumbull 39,
is graphically described in two letters from the captain to
his father, General Gurdon Saltonstall. These letters were
written from Boston, June 14th and 19th. He says: " It is

beyond my power to give an adequate idea of the carnage, slaughter, havoc, and destruction that ensued. Let your imagination do its best, it will fall short. We were literally cut all to pieces, not a shroud, stay, brace, bowling, or any other of our rigging standing; our main-topmast shot away, our fore, main, mizzen, and jigger masts going by the board; some of our quarter-deck guns disabled; through our ensign 62 shot, our mizzen 157, mainsail 560, foresail 180, and other sails in proportion; not a yard in the ship but received one or more shot; six shot through her quarter above the quarter-deck, four in the waist. Our quarter, stern, and netting full of langrage, grape, and musket ball.

"After two and a half hours' action she hauled her wind, her pumps going. We edged away, so that it may fairly be called a drawn battle.

"As you will observe my name among the wounded, you will doubtless be anxious. I have eleven different wounds from my shoulder to my hip; some with buck-shot, others with the splinters of the quarter-deck gun. I had one shot through the brim of my hat, but was not disabled as to quit the quarter-deck till after the engagement."

---

176. SARAH SALTONSTALL (VII.)

Sarah Saltonstall m. 3 Dec., 1775, Daniel Buck of Wethersfield, Conn. Daniel Buck was directly descended from (1) Josiah and Ann (Deming) Buck, (2) David and Elizabeth (Hubbert) Buck, (3) Emanuel and Mary Buck of Wethersfield. The children of Sarah and Daniel Buck were:—

1. Anna, b. and d. 1776.
2. Gurdon, b. 30 Dec., 1777; m. 20 April, 1805, Susannah Manwaring of New York; d. 4 Aug., 1852. Children:—
    1a. David, b. 29 Jan., 1806; d. 15 Aug., 1875, at Marblehead.
    2a. Gurdon, b. 4 May, 1807; m. 27 July, 1836, Hen-

rietta, dau. of Albert Henry Wolf of Geneva, Switzerland; d. 6 March, 1877, in New York. Children: —

1b. Amelia Henrietta, b. 11 Feb., 1838; m. Alfred North, M. D.
2b. Susan Manwaring, b. 1 Nov., 1839.
3b. Louisa Monsell, b. and d. 1841.
4b. Albert Henry, b. 20 Oct., 1842; m. Laura Abbott (dau. of Rev. J. S. C. Abbott of New Haven). A prominent physician of New York city. They had 2 children.
5b. Alfred Linsley, b. 1842; d. 1848.
6b. Gurdon Saltonstall, b. 23 Oct., 1848.
7b. Francis Dudley, b. 11 Oct., 1850; m. 1st, Clara Tillon, 2d, Anna Tillon.

3a. Charles Dudley, b. 29 Nov., 1808; m. 18 Sep., 1844, Sophronia Smith of Wilbraham, Mass. Children: —

1b. Charles Gurdon, b. 13 April, 1847.
2b. Grace Winthrop, b. 20 July, 1851.
3b. Margaret Smith, b. 29 April, 1857.
4b. William, d. 30 Sep., 1870, at Orange, N. J.

4a. Daniel Winthrop, b. 27 Nov., 1810; d. 4 March, 1832, at St. Croix, W. I.

5a. Sarah, b. 28 Dec., 1812; m. Jona. D. Steele (his second wife); d. Dec., 1855. He d. 25 Aug., 1872. Children: —

1b. William Dayton, b. 1851.
2b. James Alexander, b. 15 July, 1853.

6a. Edward, b. 6 Oct., 1814; m. 6 June, 1841, Elizabeth G. Hubbard; d. July, 1876. Children: —

1b. Helen Alice.
2b. Infant.
3b. Walter, b. 29 Sep., 1847.

7a. Elizabeth, b. 16 Nov., 1816; m. 3 June, 1835, John Auchincloss of New York. He d. 26 June, 1876. They had 9 children: —

1b. Henry Buck, b. June, 1836; m. Mary Cabell of Charlotte, Va. They had 7 children.
2b. Sarah Ann, b. July, 1838; m. 1859, James Coates of Paisley, Scotland. She d. 1887, at Providence, R. I.
3b. John Stuart, b. 1840.
4b. William Stuart, b. 1842, m. Martha Tuttle, dau. of W. C. Kent of Philadelphia. They had 3 children.
5b. Elizabeth Ellen, b. 1844.
6b. Edgar Sterling, m. 21 May, 1872, Maria La Grange, dau. of Samuel and Maria E. Sloan. They had 7 children.
7b. Fred H. Lawton, d. in Yokohama.
8b. John Winthrop, m. Joanna Howe, dau. of C. H. and Caroline H. Russell. They had 4 children.
9b. Hugh Dudley, b. 1858.
8a. Rebecca Coit, b. 6 Nov., 1818; d. 18 July, 1870, at Rye Beach, N. H.
9a. George, b. 14 Aug., 1821; d. 1824, in New York.
10a. Henry, b. 6 Nov., 1824; d. 3 Sep., 1891, in New York.

3. Daniel, b. 27 Oct., 1779; m. 14 Oct., 1805, Julia, dau. of Stephen Mix Mitchell of Wethersfield. She d. 9 Oct., 1807, *s. p.* He m. 2d, Elizabeth, dau. of Ezekiel P. Belden of Wethersfield, 30 Jan., 1812. She d. 4 March, 1887, aged 103 years, – months, and 24 days. Children: —

1a. Daniel, m. 4 June, 1839, Mary E. Imlay, dau. of W. H. Imlay. She d. 17 Nov., 1862. They had 5 children; Dan. Winthrop, William Imlay, Frederick Clarence, Charles Ezekiel, Mary Elizabeth.
2a. Ezekiel.
3a. Charles.
4a. Julia.
5a. John.
6a. Susan.

4. Charles, b. 21 March, 1782; m. Catherine Bradford of New York. He d. 5 June, 1858.
5. Winthrop, b. 9 Dec., 1784; d. 19 Aug., 1862, at Wethersfield; m. 29 Jan., 1812, Eunice H. Parsons of Amherst, Mass. No children. She d. 5 Aug., 1812. He m. 2d, 28 Dec., 1814, Eunice, dau. of Dr. Abner Moseley of Wethersfield. Children : —
1a. Martha Ann, b. 26 Nov., 1815; d. unmarried.
2a. Winthrop, b. 6 Dec., 1816; m. 24 Dec., 1845, Charlotte, dau. of Sylvester Woodhouse of Wethersfield. Children : —
  1b. Edward Winthrop, b. 28 Feb., 1847; m. 12 Sep., 1876, Abbie B. Osborn of Wethersfield. Children : —
    1c. Winthrop, b. 21 Sep., 1878.
    2c. Edward Osborn, b. 25 June, 1883.
    3c. A daughter, b. 2 July, 1888.
  2b. Louis Dudley, b. 13 Aug., 1850; m. 10 Feb., 1881, Laura, dau. of Samuel O. Church of Hartford, Conn.; d. 19 March, 1887. Children : Charlotte, Mary, Louise Dudley.
3a. Eunice, b. 31 Dec., 1819; d. unmarried.
4a. Maria, b. 30 Jan., 1821 ; m. 5 Feb., 1856, Edmund G. Howe of Hartford, who d. April, 1872, *s. p.*
5a. Robert, b. 8 March, 1823; m. 5 Aug., 1860, Helen Frances, dau. of Elisha C. Jones of St. Albans, Vt.; d. Aug., 1881. Child: Robert J., b. 1865; m. Mary Marcy of Watertown, N. Y.
6a. Rosewell Riley, b. 1 Oct., 1826; m. 8 Nov., 1866, Maria C., dau. of Dr. Josiah Barnes of Buffalo, N. Y. Children : —
  1b. Harriet Moseley, b. 16 Aug., 1867.
  2b. Winthrop Seymour, b. 3 May, 1870; d. 24 May, 1878.
  3b. George Sturges, b. 18 Feb., 1875.
7a. Kate Moseley, b. 1 Feb., 1833; m. 6 Nov., 1866,

John Buckingham of Chicago. He d. 21 Aug., 1881. Children: —
1b. Henry Winthrop.
2b. Arthur Hale.
3b. Clifford Hale.
8a. Henry, b. 6 Dec., 1834; m. 30 Nov., 1875, Theresa, dau. of George Robinson of Hartford. Children: —
1b. Harry Robinson.
2b. John Saltonstall.
3b. Charles Howe.
6. Ann, b. 12 Oct., 1786; d. 6 Feb., 1788, at Wethersfield, Conn.
7. Dudley, b. 25 June, 1789; m. 25 Sep., 1827, Hetty G., dau. of John Hempstead of Hartford; d. 12 June, 1834. Children: —
1a. George, b. 16 Sep., 1830; m. Lucy Farrer, dau. of Rev. Rich. Hall of New Ipswich, N. H. She d. 16 July, 1870. Children: —
1b. Horace Hall.
2b. Mary Eliza.
3b. Lucy Farrer.
4b. Mary Eliza.
5b. George Dudley.
6b. William Winthrop.
7b. Hetty Saltonstall.
He m. 2d, 5 April, 1877, Josephine L. Hitchcock of Southington, Conn. Child: Grace Hamilton, b. 1880.
2a. Mary, b. 1832; d. 1833.
3a. Dudley, b. June, 1834; m. 3 Oct., 1865, Lizzie Van Wagner of Burlington, Vt. Children: Edward Terry, Dudley Saltonstall, Madeline. He m. 2d, Sep., 1837, Martha Adams of Portsmouth, who d. 1864. Children: Dudley, James.

179. MARY WANTON SALTONSTALL (IX.)

Mary Wanton Saltonstall m. 29 Nov., 1789, Dr. Thomas Coit of New London. Children:—

1. Anna W.
2. Mary Gardiner.
3. Hannah Saltonstall.
4. Augusta Dudley.
5. Martha.
6. Thomas Winthrop, b. 28 June, 1803; m. Eleanor, dau. of Simeon Forrester, an old merchant of Salem, Mass. (who m. Rachel, dau. of Daniel Hawthorne, an aunt of Nathaniel Hawthorne), and widow of Thomas Carlile. By her second marriage she became the grandmother of the children of Gurdon S. Coit (No. 8, below), brother of Thomas W. She d. 21 June, 1885. Children:—
   1a. Winthrop Saltonstall, b. 1829; d. 1878.
   2a. Charles Forrester, b. June, 1830; d. June, 1886.
   3a. Thomas Gurdon, b. 1835; d. unmarried.
7. Elizabeth Richards, m. Edward Coit of Norwich, b. 1806; d. 1837. Children:—
   1a. Edward, b. 1835; d. 1835.
   2a. Edward, b. 1837; d. 1837.
8. Gurdon Saltonstall, m. Eleanor F., dau. of Eleanor Forrester and Thomas Carlile. Children:—
   1a. Gurdon S., b. 4 Feb., 1839; m. 14 Dec., 1874, Mary Benedict Treadway.
   2a. Thomas, b. 11 April, 1840; d. in China, unmarried.
   3a. Forrester, b. 14 Oct., 1841; d. 1 March, 1883, in China, unmarried.
   4a. Eleanor Forrester, m. Fred. J. Peck.
   5a. William Wanton, b. 1845; d. 1846.
   6a. Mary Saltonstall, b. 28 Aug., 1847; m. 1870, Daniel R. Banks.
   7a. Augusta Dudley, m. John Pierce.

8a. Simeon Forrester, b. 1851.
9a. Caroline Calhoun.

T. S. Collier, Esq., secretary of the New London County Historical Society, has furnished interesting memoranda concerning Dr. Thos. Coit, the father of Thomas Coit who m. Mary Wanton Saltonstall. "He was born in 1725, and died in 1811. He was an able, useful, and assiduous practitioner. Few physicians of that day stood higher in public esteem." The second Dr. Thomas Coit was the oldest son of the former physician of that name, and entered into practice as the companion of his father. His professional career extended over a period of forty years."

181. DR. WINTHROP SALTONSTALL (IX.)

Winthrop Saltonstall, after graduating at Yale College, studied medicine at Columbia College, New York, and visited Bengal for further medical information and experience. Afterwards he went to Port of Spain, Island of Trinidad, W. I., and there commenced practice as physician and surgeon. After being in practice for some years, he formed a business connection with a Dr. Clark. During a visitation of the yellow fever he was attacked, and after a short and painful illness died on the 27th June, 1802. He was 27 years of age. "We shall not attempt a portraiture of his character. . . . Of his professional attainments he has left a record, not only in the English but in the French and German languages, that will transmit his name and genius to distant posterity so long as the elements of chemistry shall be held in estimation. His inaugural dissertation,[1] published in New York in the year 1797, will be considered as one of the brightest and most literary as well as useful productions on the subject. He was the only surviving son of Winthrop Saltonstall, Esq. The family mourn the loss of this second son and

[1] Saltonstall–Winthrop. An Inaugural Dissertation on the Chemical and Medical History of Septon Azote or Nitrogene, New York, 1796, 8vo.

brother, and whose life has been lost in the West Indies, in the vigor of youth and in the enjoyment of the most flattering prospects." [1]

His profile likeness and various mementos are in the possession of F. G. Saltonstall of New York.

---

190. ANN SALTONSTALL (IX.)

Ann Saltonstall m. Rev. Charles Seabury.   Children: —

1. Samuel, b. 9 June, 1801; m. 17 May, 1829, Lydia Huntington Bill, who d. 16 April, 1834.   He d. 10 Oct., 1872.   Children: —

   1a. Anne S., b. 14 April, 1830; m. 13 May, 1852, Rev. Wm. Walton, D. D., who d. 15 May, 1853. Child: Anne, d. aged 5 years.

   2a. Lydia, b. 28 Nov., 1833; m. 18 April, 1855, Samuel P. Bell.   Children: Frances Griffin, Mary Huntington, Charles S., Alice, Lydia H.

   He m. 2d, 17 Nov., 1835, Hannah Amelia Jones, who d. 18 Sep., 1852.   Children: —

   3a. William Jones, b. 25 Jan., 1837, m. Alice, dau. of Thos. M. and Mary Susan (Saltonstall) Beare. Children: Susan Saltonstall, Samuel, Lydia, Muriel Gurdon, William Marston.

   4a. Kezia, b. 30 Dec., 1842; m. 22 April, 1862, James Weeks.   Children: William Carnes, William Seabury, Amelia Seabury, Robert Doughty, James, Lewis.

   5a. Mary, b. 1 Jan., 1845; m. Rev. H. A. Parker.   Children: William Ainsworth, Gurdon Saltonstall, Stanley Brampton, Henry Seabury, Reginald.

   6a. Ella Amelia, b. 3 Aug., 1847; m. Rev. Charles W. Ward, who d. 1872.   Child: Charles Seabury.

   He m. 3d, Mary Anna, dau. of Samuel Jones and Catherine Schuyler, who survived him.   Child: —

---

[1] *New London Gazette.*

J. G. Saltonstall

7a. Catherina Regina, b. 1858.
2. Charles Saltonstall, b. 10 Dec., 1802; m. 1827, Ruth
   Hawkins Mount. Children:—
   1a. Charles Edward, living 1888, unmarried.
   2a. Thomas Shepard, d. 1880, U. S. of Colombia.
   3a. Julia Ann, d. 1857.
   4a. William, d. young.
   5a. Maria.
   6a. Ruth Frances, d. 1880, unmarried.
   7a. Samuel, Lieut. U. S. Navy.
3. William, b. 30 March, 1805; d. unmarried.
4. Edward, b. 14 May, 1807; d. unmarried.
5. Richard Francis, b. 21 July, 1809; m. 18 June, 1836,
   Catherine Eliza Russell. Children:—
   1a. Lydia Maria.
   2a. Charles.
   3a. Samuel.
   4a. Richard Francis.
   5a. Mary Amelia, "Sister Fidelia," lives in **New**
       York.
   6a. Jeannette Russell.
   7a. Catherine Eliza.
   8a. Frances Saltonstall.
6. Mary Elizabeth, d. in infancy.

---

196. MARY H. SALTONSTALL (X.)

Mary H. Saltonstall, m. 21 July, 1812, Rev. Daniel Huntington. Children:—
1. Anne Moore, m. Alfred Hebard.
2. Hannah, m. Franklin Chappell. Children:—
   1a. Frank Huntington, m. 17 June, 1873, C. Gertrude
       Bishop. Children: Minnie H., b. 28 Aug., 1874;
       Robert B., b. 2 Aug., 1876; Donald, b. 30 Nov.,
       1877; Harold, b. 27 Sep., 1879; Marion, b. 5 Feb.,
       1882; Lawrence A., b. 16 July, 1883; Franklin
       H., b. 25 Sep., 1885.

2a. William Saltonstall, m. 21 Nov., 1869, Isabel Norton Culver. Children: Annie H., b. 24 Jan., 1872; Edward, b. 29 March, 1874; William S., b. 9 May, 1877; Isabel S., b. 26 Aug., 1880.

3a. Alfred Hebard, m. 12 May, 1849, Adelaide C. Shepard. Children: Frank, b. 12 Feb., 1846; Geo. S., b. 2 Jan., 1877; Philip A., b. 28 Sep., 1878, d. 15 Jan., 1882; Henry Clarence, b. 27 April, 1880; Ruth Huntington, b. 11 June, 1883; Edith M., b. 21 May, 1884; Thomas, b. 13 April, 1885; Theodore H.

Mrs. Hannah S. Chappell, b. 26 Aug., 1816, the mother of Frank H., William S., and Alfred H., is now living (1895) in New London, Conn., as are her sons and grandchildren.

---

197. WILLIAM WANTON SALTONSTALL (X.)

" Since the year 1837, from the early days of Chicago, has been seen in our streets one of moderate stature, but of manly bearing and courteous address, unpretending and retiring in manners, yet genial, warm, and kindly of nature, who won without claiming notice, and who, the better he was known, was all the more esteemed and loved. Should any one have sought on our thoroughfares the finest and best model of a gentleman of the 'old school,' the most finished specimen of a polished manhood, far might one look before finding a truer realization of the ideal than in him.

" The old residents of Chicago will recognize, doubtless, in the above description, a just portraiture of the estimable man whose name heads this notice.

" The original of the picture so well known has at length passed away. Born January 19, 1793, at New London, Connecticut, he was a worthy descendant of that distinguished Sir Richard Saltonstall memorable in New England history, and of Governor Gurdon Saltonstall of Connecticut; besides tracing his lineage and deriving one of his names from Gov-

ernor Joseph Wanton of Rhode Island, whose daughter was
his paternal grandmother.

" Mr. Saltonstall came in its early days to Chicago, where
he has since lived for a period of a quarter of a century, shar-
ing in the stirring scenes and events of our young and prosperous city.   Unambitious of political distinction, he has pursued the tranquil career of an upright and faithful private
citizen, everywhere esteemed, trusted, and honored as a man
of probity, intelligence, and manly courtesy.   Near twelve
years ago he received the honorable appointment, from the
President of the United States, of Assignee in Bankruptcy, a
post which he continued to hold until his decease.

" The event of his death occurred on the 18th instant, after
a short illness borne with calm and Christian equanimity, at
the age of sixty-nine years and two months, — his last days
cheered by the loving care and watchfulness of those he has
left to bear and preserve among us his honored name.

" By not a few will the form of our departed fellow-citizen
be missed from the scenes which once and so long knew him.
In the hearts of many will his memory be durable and kindly
cherished." [1]

[1] *Chicago Tribune,* Friday, 21 March, 1862.

INDEX

A

In this division will be found only the names of persons bearing the surname Saltonstall. The number which follows each name is that given to the individual in the Genealogy, while those at the end of the line indicate the pages of the Genealogy where the name appears. Items of interest in Part II. are grouped under the names to which they belong.

B

In this division are given the names of all persons except those bearing the surname Saltonstall. Individuals intermarrying with the family of Saltonstall are shown by the appropriate Genealogy number in brackets, following the name. For references to other than personal matters, see division C.

Abbot, Benjamin, 167.
  George, 14.
  Laura, 236.
  J. S. C., 136.
Adams, Abigail, 135.
  Ann, 233.
  Arthur, 135.
  Arthur, 136.
  Benjamin, 134.
  Charles Francis, 122, 135.
  Charles Francis (Jr.), 135.
  Edward F., 25.
  Elizabeth Ogden, 136.
  Fanny, 135.
  George Caspar, 135.
  Henry, 136.
  Helen, 134.
  Henry Brooks, 136.
  John, 136.
  John Quincy, 135.
  Louisa Catherine, 135.
  Louise Catherine, 135.
  Martha, 239.
  Mary, 135.
  Mary, 136.
  P. C. Brooks, 136.
Agassiz, Louis, 30.
Aiken, —— (199), 43.
Alexander, Francis, 130.
Allers, Dr. Henry, 44.
Allyn, Robert, 221.
Andrews, Mary, 40.
Andros, Sir Edmund, 153.
Appleton, Daniel F., 29.
  Francis, 31.
  Georgiana C. (124), 31.
  Sir Isaac, 100 n.
  Ruth, 29.
  Samuel, 100 n.
  William, 100 n.
Armine, Elizabeth (10), 5.
  Hugh, 5.
Arnold, Lucretia (157), 34.
Ashburton, Lord, 158.
Ashton, Samuel, 51.
Atherton, Lieutenant, 91.
Athurst, Sir H., 154.
Atkyn, Robert, 143.
Atwater, Jeremiah (172), 37.
Auchincloss, Edgar Sterling, 237.
  Elizabeth Ellen, 237.

Auchincloss, Fred H. Lawton, 237.
  Henry Buck, 237.
  Hugh Dudley, 237.
  John, 236.
  John Stuart, 237.
  John Winthrop, 237.
  Sarah Ann, 237.
  William Stuart, 237.
Austin, James T., 169.

Babcock, Adam, 231.
  Frances (168), 36.
  Harriet (175), 38.
  Joshua (Dr.), 36.
Bache, Jane Lowndes, 28.
Badger, Moses (Rev.), (106), 213.
Baker, Henry (37), 12.
Baldwin, Samuel, 127.
Banks, Daniel R., 240.
Baring, George, 158.
  Mary, 158.
Barnes, Josiah, 238.
  Maria C., 238.
Barrett, Dacres (79), 18.
  Edward, 98.
  Elizabeth, 98, 100.
Bas, Elizabeth (49), 15.
Bateman, John (21), 9.
Beare, Alice, 242.
  Alice Van Wyck, 44.
  Charlotte, 43.
  Francis, 44.
  Isabel, 43.
  James Johnston, 44.
  Jane Johnston, 44.
  Louisa de Laguel, 44.
  Mary Susan (Saltonstall), 242.
  Thomas M., 242.
  Thomas Marston (200), 43.
  Thomas Marston, 43.
Beaumont, Edward, 5.
Belden, Elizabeth, 237.
  Ezekiel P., 237.
Bell, Alice, 242.
  Charles S., 242.
  Frances Griffin, 242.
  Lydia H., 242.
  Mary Huntington, 242.
  Samuel P., 242.
Benner, Ida M., 24.
Benson, Frank W., 30.

C

This division includes names of places, estates, etc.; also references to all matters, other than personal, which are not to be found in divisions A and B.